HOW TO ~~SURVIVE~~ *THRIVE* ON A TROPICAL DESERTED ISLAND

A Primer for the Shipwrecked Sailor
Or
Living off the Land in Paradise

by
Mike Riley
Art by Karen Riley

Published and Printed
by Mike Riley
Aboard the *Beau Soleil* while sailing the Seven Sea

ISBN 978-0-9828247-4-0

sailingbooks@rocketmail.com

Dedication

This book is dedicated to my wife, Karen Riley, who lovingly and willingly ate every weird fruit and plant I pulled off of trees and found laying on the ground on islands around the world, all the while drawing pictures of them with grace and style and laughter.

TABLE OF CONTENTS

Preface

One of the most enduring daydreams of adventurous souls worldwide is living in the lap of luxury on an abandoned tropical island with a bevy of beautiful sirens and/or hunky young men. In the dream, delicious food is grown on short trees, big fish are dying to bite your hook, there is always a cache of rum, and all your playmates think you are a wonderful singer.

Then reality gets its innings, you remember that its a crowded world where deserted islands are always owned by rich men with rifles, mean dogs and barbed wire, that you were never that good at climbing trees, that you average $50 of fishing gear for each pound of fish you catch, and that you really are a terrible singer. You think about insect bites, imagine how difficult it is to build a grass shack, how hard it is to make one of those coconut leaf hats, how boring it would be to live without the internet and how much you hate to miss a meal. The daydream fades away and you get back to your boring old life with a sigh. But it doesn't have to be so.

On hundreds of islands worldwide, all the young people have moved to the big cities to make a new life for themselves and the older people have gone to the great big isle in the sky. No one lives there anymore. No one. There are a myriad of islands waiting for you in the Pacific and Indian tropical oceans. Many still have plantations with fruit trees and grass shacks and docks by the bay. They haven't been fished for so long, the fish are tame, and believe me, there are no people. The islands are waiting just for you! All it takes is a boat and the will to reach for the dream.

Well, not quite. You need the knowledge of how to live on your own, on a deserted island. This book, a result of visiting hundreds of islands over a forty year span of oceanic cruising and learning from their then remaining inhabitants, and the many uninhabited islands where I experimented and developed my own style with the knowledge gained during 2½ circumnavigations, is the book I hope you never need, co-titled; 'How to Survive after a Shipwreck', and for those of us who are lucky sailors and still floating,

'How to Thrive on a Deserted Island.' It is really true. You can live like Robinson Crusoe and Friday in the utmost happiness with three square meals a day and lots of time to swing in your hammock wearing a coconut leaf hat you made yourself. And just in case your island didn't come with a cache of rum, within discover how to brew your own. The singing, well if no one else is there, you are a great singer by default. If Friday was shipwrecked with you, I hope you took singing lessons or if not, she really, really loves you!

Introduction

This book is written in three general parts, Things to Eat, Things to Make and Things to Brew. Just for fun and just in case, I included directions for Polynesian navigation, canoe carving, starting a fire with two sticks and, of course, how to weave a coconut frond hat. Feel free to read the entire book from one end to the other, but I also encourage you to use the book much like a shell book, open it at an interesting page or search for the plant or animal or skill you need information about. Once you are familiar with the layout, each section is independent of the others and can be read on its own with a healthy usage of the index.

Here in one volume is all the information you might need to not only survive but to thrive on a deserted tropical isle. Carry it with you when walking on the beach. Peruse it's pages when finding a new species, stuff it in your man-over board bag, study it when dreaming of far away islands just waiting for you without any of civilization's self inflicted problems. Use the book as a guide to a new, romantic, exciting, adventurous life! There is an adventure waiting out there. One that you will always remember. Being shipwrecked or marooned or even if you just fell overboard is a great big adventure. If you are not alone on a deserted island, enjoy it.

Friday made Robinson Crusoe's story a thousand times more interesting.

After all, is that your girl stretched out topless on the beach? Is that you bursting from the water, teeth white in a delightful smile, a lobster in each hand? Or no, maybe that is you, ashore by the beautiful grass shack swinging in the hammock while your girl Friday cooks by the fire with flowers in her hair, shells around her waist. Or, is it her naked under the waterfall, washing with soap you made yourself. Is it? Let's find out.

The Arrival

You won't have much when you arrive on the island. Maybe your boat sank at sea and you swam ashore. Maybe you had a life raft and it stayed afloat with all your gear, all your survival equipment. Chances are the raft ripped its bottom out crossing the reef and all your gear is lost. Maybe you chose to visit a tropical paradise just to see if you have the Right Stuff, and by choice you arrived with nothing but what brains and brawn God gave you. Any which way you arrived, for the purpose of this book, I am assuming you have almost nothing but the rags on your back, if any. No radios, no guns, no food, no water, no tools – except in the interest of keeping you from dying a boring death; as you crawl ashore, stuck in the sand, like Excalibur, is a machete. This is your only gift. This is the key to the kingdom, left perhaps by the last local to leave the island, to you, the new caretaker. Don't look for any other gifts. Everything else you are going to make, catch, grow, harvest, invent, or create.

It is a daunting experience arriving in a strange new world. Are there monsters? Head hunters? Cannibals? Sharks? Crocodiles? Vampire bats? I'll let you in on a secret. Your imagination can create far worse terrors than reality can ever come up with. That is the key to Hollywood's success. My secret is I pretend that I am spear fishing. I love to spear fish. On the reef, I believe I am the ultimate predator. Any shark that wanders by my reef when I am there soon realizes it is prey. I am master. At least in my own brain.

But that is what it is all about. You are who you think you are. If you feel you are a scaredy cat, you are, if you feel afraid, you will be. If you think you are the master of creation, you will act like it. On deserted islands, I put my spear fishing hat on and become the master of the island, the ultimate predator of the isle. Just as the sharks sense my self induced eye of the eagle, so I imagine, will anyone or anything else on the island. Sure, if I came face to face with a blow gun carrying pigmy head hunter, my delusion would come crashing down on top of my soon to be shrunken head. But failing that I am not being pursued by non-existent demons while I am trying to survive.

Before I continue farther, if you are not really good at sticking your finger down your throat, please stay within the parameters of this book. Don't go experimenting with interesting looking plants, seeing if they are as tasty as they are pretty. Dogs like to eat new plants. But they are also very good at throwing them up if the plants make their tummies hurt. Unless you are a good up-chucker, don't be inventive.

This is not a physiological book, but a practical treatise. The above is the last psycho-babble you will hear from me. I only included it as your first few hours on a deserted island can be frightening, needlessly. Nature, raw and hungry, is really easy going in the tropics.

So, without further delay, are you hungry? Thirsty? You should be. After all you just paddled, swam, floated for days to get to the island. Let's find out what there is to eat and drink.

The Fruits

There is nothing like fresh ripe fruit that fall right off the tree and into your hands when you are hungry. Now that you have been washed up onto your island, you are going to be ready for something to drink and something to eat. Traditionally, coconuts are the first thing you are supposed to eat and drink but this is not always wise. It is tough to open a coconut at the best of times, and having just survived the sea when it was having a bad hair day, you won't be at your best. It is better to walk into the shade of the trees along the shore and eat some fruit. It is just hanging there, waiting for you, and then when you have some strength back, climb your coconut tree like a regular beachcomber and drink your fill.

Fruits are full of water, sugar and vitamins and in even a short walk around the island you might well discover an ancient well. That is wiser than chopping a finger off while trying to open a coconut while still dizzy from too much salt.

To my way of thinking, nuts and some vegetables are fruits. Fruits to a beachcomber are things that grow on trees and are sweet. Hey, that's easy. Take cashews, for example. Sure, they are a nut and are not sweet, but the cashew fruit that the nut grows from, is both sweet, nourishing, can be eaten right from the tree and is filled with a quenching nectar that is wonderful on a hot day. Is a cashew a fruit? You bet it is!

We will get to the palms and the fruits that they bear. Coconut palms especially, are crucial to the survival of shipwrecked, castaway, beachcombing sailors. But rest up, hydrate up, and relax before whacking away with your brand new to you, machete.

Sea Grapes

Sea Grapes are just what they sound like. Grapes that grow along the sea shore. They grow in bunches, just like grapes. They turn purple when they are ripe, green when they aren't, just like some grapes, and they have that indescribable tannic grape taste that keeps you coming back for more.

When I was a boy in Hawaii, we knew sea grapes as autograph trees. When we wrote our names on its leaves, the tree wouldn't erase our scribbling till eventually the leaf died naturally. We saw the berry like fruit the tree bore, but our mothers told us, "Don't eat that. Here, have a Twinkie instead."

It wasn't until Malta, of all places, that I first tasted Sea Grapes. In the Mediterranean, Sea Grapes are used to prevent coastal erosion on beaches. They love salt air and spray and like to grow just barely above the high water mark. In Malta, during the summer cruising season, they sell fresh bread at two o'clock in the morning when it is cool enough to bake. It was useless to go in the morning, the bread would be sold out. I lined up with the other men who were finishing partying and had just remembered their wives told them to pick up some breakfast on the way home. (You just have to love the Med!)

All the guys were lined up by the beach waiting as patiently as Maltese men could and eating these weird looking fruits off autograph trees along the beach. I was young at the time and wife was expecting my first child, so when offered, naturally I grabbed a double handful of grapes.

They were great. Granted, we had spent the last five hours drinking, but really, they were great. They had that tangy, half sour, half sweet flavor of high quality grapes with the salty taste of the sea. Plus, they somehow sobered us up enough to avoid dropping the bread in the drink as we back clambered aboard in dawn's early light.

Sea Plums

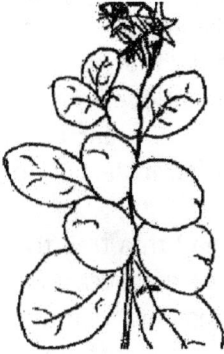

Sea plums are rather tasteless fast food, but they have three great advantages. They love to live right above the surf line, they make great jelly, and three, when you swim ashore after floating around for a few days, after your boat sank, and you are dying for a drink of water, eat a sea plum, they may be tasteless but they burst open when bitten with a gush of slightly sugary water.

In Polynesia they are considered survival food. You wouldn't want to eat it normally, but if you are drying for a bit of sugar water, there is no lack of them. I like to grab a couple as I explore islands, just to have something to nibble on. Sure, I could open a coconut, but that involves work and if I am not that hungry, or am feeling lazy, or if my hammock is right next to a sea plum bush and by swinging it just so I can grab a handful, what is so wrong with that?

Sea plums live everywhere along the sea between 40°N and 40°S. It is a small bush, rarely exceeding ten feet in height. The plums start out green and are ready to eat when they turn a dark red to purple color. They aren't hard to find. They grow to ping pong size. Try 'em out!

Mountain Apple

I used to climb up the ridges of ancient, now verdant volcanoes in Hawaii with the local climbing club that met once a week. It was a great experience but I never seemed to carry enough water. It was hot, thirsty climbing. Not a problem.

Silver, an experienced Hawaiian, never carried any water. He ate mountain apples instead. Bursting with flavor and moistness, they grew wild along the slopes, just waiting for a thirsty sailor or climber.

Also known as water apple, Java apple or Semarang, the redder the fruit, the tastier it is. Not only is it red like an apple, it has the same crispness as we bit into them. They had a slight acrid flavor on the first bite, but take a second and you will fall in love with the mountain apple. If you can't wait for the fruit to ripen, eat them when they are still green. Just cut them in half and sprinkle a bit of salt on 'em. Yum!

Worldwide in the tropics, it is a tallish (60 feet) thin tree that grows both in the valleys and the ridges as well as the occasional volunteer just inland along the coasts. In season, it is best identified by the ripe fruit that has fallen to the ground. It is tough being a sailor in the forests, keeping one eye for fruit high in the trees and one eye for fallen fruit along the ground. But wait, that's what sailors do best, one eye on the sails, one eye on the horizon, watching for shipping!

Mountain apples are known in Hawaii for their smoothing affect they have on rough, red and blotchy skin. Either press out the juice or better apply the mashed peeled fruit right on to your skin and then wash off after it has dried. Not only does it feel good, it makes you look younger. (Hey, guys. You are going to get a lot more action out of Friday if you look sexier. Especially if she is the one applying the Mountain apple's mask. And what, exactly, are you going to do with your spare time without Monday Night Football?) The mountain apple season only lasts a few months but those months will be among the happiest on your deserted island.

Chocolate

I love snacks. I really do. If I had my way, I would eat snacks all day long. That is tough to do on a deserted island, right? Wrong! We have lots of snacks.   Deserted islands are full of snacks, in fact, we have chocolate!   Yay!

Chocolate is made from the fruit of the Cocoa tree.   The cocoa pod grows right out of the trunk.   It looks like something from the movie, 'The Invasion of the Body Snatchers'!   But fear not.   We are going to get them (not them us) and we will soon be having our fill of wonderful, creamy chocolate!

Cocoa trees grow in the shade and in well watered, mossy areas.   When you walk through the island, keep your collecting eye out.   They normally are a low non-descript bush, non-descript if you ignore the pods growing out of their sides.   When the pods turn yellow, they are ready.   Twist them off the tree and crack the top off the pod with the back end of your machete.   Inside, tightly packed, are whitish fruit sections each with a bean inside.   Eat the pulp on the outside of the bean.   It is delicious.   The sweeter the pulp, the sweeter the chocolate will be.   Gather all your beans and let them ferment for three days in the shade for better taste, or for healthier dark chocolate proceed directly to the drying stage.   100% chocolate, unfermented is very effective against high blood pressure.   The beans have to dry for ten to fifteen days, have to be protected against rain and dew and have to be turned now and then to aid uniform drying.   Carry them around with you, build an umbrella over them for the night, keep an eye out for them, sleep with them.   Hey, we are talking about chocolate, here!

OK, the beans are all dry, they will feel oily, and have turned dark.   It is time to roast them.   Get a nice hot fire and move the big logs away.   (See the fire section.   Hint, look in the index.)   Cover the coals completely with a thin layer of sand.   Lay your cocoa beans on top of the sand for about an hour turning them all the time.   You will know when they are done as the bean will enlarge and pop open its protective membrane.   As soon as it is completely popped,   like popcorn,
take them out of the sand and let them cool completely.   The oil inside is very hot.   Don't pop one in your mouth till it has cooled completely.

On a windy day rub the beans between your hands while standing and drop them into a basket below, over and over again.   The shards of the bitter membrane will fly off downwind.   When all the shards are gone, you are almost ready. Pound the beans between two rocks (or your pounder, you guessed it, the index!) until the biggest pieces, the nibs, are as big as a grain of rice. Pick up some. Eat 'em. Good, huh! And you made it yourself!

If you want a chocolate bar, you will have to grind the nibs until they are paste. It is weird, but once the nibs are ground they aren't as sweet. This is because grinding releases the bitterness of the bean. Keep grinding until a liquid is released that flows to the top of the paste. Mix in some sugar, either from cane or toddy or sugar palm. It is ok, no, it is recommended to taste as you mix in the sugar to the mixture till it is just right. Be careful you don't taste it all up! Once mixed, pour it into some kind of mold, coconut shell, clam shell, or just pour it onto a banana leaf. Be warned, every insect in the world is going to try to get at your chocolate as soon as you add the sugar. Don't do this next to your sleeping hut. They will set up residence and wait till you make some more! Chocolate was originally considered a miracle medicine as just a little bite could bring a sick person back from near death. Let's hope you don't have to find out if it still works!

Cashew Nut

Cashew nuts are the best and most dangerous nut in the world. Chances are if you are shipwrecked on an abandoned island, there are cashew trees there, somewhere. They survive very well indeed without man's help(?). They like harsh conditions, love sand, and don't mind salt air. Insects won't go near the nut, with good reason. There are two shells on the nut, between them is an incredibly dangerous chemical

that scientists are still trying to understand. All you need to know is when you pick the fruit, (the fruit part is just above the nut and is also good to eat, as long as you are not allergic), it is best to test the fruit's juice first on a less important portion of your skin, before you get it anywhere near your mouth, face and especially eyes.

   The nut itself, is not dangerous at first. Pick it, (It is born green in color then when it is ripe it will turn red) dry it for a day in the shade and then, before it is totally dry, this is the tricky part, you have to roast it over a weak fire. When heated, the first of two shells will burst releasing an extremely toxic gas. Don't be downwind at this juncture. Even if the fire starts to burn down your whole island, don't get in the smoke. It eats your skin, your lungs, your eyes, the lining of your nose and other more important parts! Don't get in the smoke!

   If the fire is too hot, if the nuts are too dry, the whole nut will evaporate into lethal smoke. Keep the fire mild. After the nuts are roasted, (while I hope you went off to the windward side of the island for a few hours), crack the inner shell between some rocks and then roast them again! No worries, this time all the poisons are gone. The second firing is just to loosen the inner membrane beneath the second shell. (Are you starting to realize why this tree is so successful against insects and, if the truth be known, humans?) Finally, there is the cashew nut, your cashew nut. At this time it is still raw. I know, I know, you have cooked the hell out of it, but believe it! Raw cashews are really great, but if you want that down home experience spread a thin layer of sand over your coals and roast the nuts a third time!

   The cashew fruit, which tastes just like cashew nuts makes a great juice, eat it like an apple (No poisons), stomp on it to release the juice and ferment it for an awesome aperitif for Friday. (Index, Right?)

Mangosteen

The Mangosteen is absolutely the queen of the tropical fruits. It is mind blowing in flavor, in texture, in tidiness, in appearance, in everything. It doesn't travel well, so you will never see it in your local grocery store, but if you are looking for a island to be shipwrecked on, make sure the island has mangosteens on it first. You will never want to go home.

The Mangosteen is about the size of a very small orange with a hard purple or red rind, when ripe. Inside are four segments of pure white incredible glory. Unfortunately, now that I have you all hot and bothered, they normally only grow on high islands, far from the salt air. However, in the last century, they have been spreading from island to island until now, they are scattered throughout the Caribbean, the Indian, and most of the high islands of the Pacific. If you are on an atoll, sorry, it would take a miracle.

Star Apple

I have never tasted a star apple until I was in my 60's. I don't know why. Never had the luck. Everywhere I went, people say, "You should have been here last month, we were throwing them away." It comes in three colors, purple, red and green and that the core looks like a star when cut. It is quite good. It pales nest to a Mangosteen but so does every other fruit in the world. The tree rarely grows above 30 feet with long branches which are easy to bend to pick the fruit. It is ripe when a beautiful aroma seeps out of the stem side. Don't eat the rind. It is yucky to use a beachcombing term.

Sea Almonds

One of the things I miss most living on island paradises are snacks. True if we have prepared properly we have lots of popcorn, nuts and Twinkies, but still, variety is the spice of life. Besides, if we are shipwrecked, the last thing we will be looking for as we abandon the boat is popcorn. But fear not, our island has come to our rescue with a delightful, tasty and plentiful almond. This plant grows along the shore just above the high water line on the beaches. The nut is green as it grows and when it falls to the ground. As the fallen fruit turns brown it is time for us to harvest it. Cut the bark off the nut to reveal the inner shell. Cut this in half with your trusty machete and pry out the large almond. The bark, like that of the coconut, allows the sea almond to undertake considerable sea voyages. In fact the sea almond is now spread world wide in the tropics. It shares with your grocery store almond the tremendous health benefits of protection from heart attacks and high blood pressure. Not that we have a lot of stress on islands. (Except for roasting cashews!)

One of the great pleasures of almonds is making almond milk. This wonderful and delicious beverage is made by chopping up our sea almonds and covering them all with three times the water, leave it in the shade, maybe by the waterfall, if you have one, where it is cool. Cover your container with whatever you have unless you want to share with the insect kingdom. Do not disturb the bowl (or whatever you are using for a bowl, half a coconut shell?), and in three days remove the top layer of nuts and underneath will be a most pleasant milk. Really! It even tastes like milk, with an almond undertone. Delicious with coconut cereal or with mangos as a dessert!

It was on Roatan, in the Bay islands of Honduras, where I first experienced Sea Almonds. I had heard that they were edible for years, but never tried them. There, the wildlife ate the outer covering leaving just the inner shell. The beaches were lined with them! In the grocery stores California almonds cost a fortune. On the beach, they were free, taste better and each tree has thousands. Shipwrecked sailors rule!

Passion fruit and Guava

The big difference between passion fruit and guava is that you eat the seeds in passion fruit and throw away the guava seeds. The seeds of the passion fruit, not only are tasty but are also the home of the passion part of the name. (The sex part does work if you have been without vitamins for a while. But, then, so do avocados.) Passion fruit sometimes has old, wrinkled, even moldy skin. This is normal. The fruit inside is still good. (OK, now I get it. "Look young thing, even us old moldy, wrinkly people are sweet and good and full of passion, inside. Give me a try!")

Guavas, which have much the same taste (but not nearly as good a press agent) have inedible seeds. Cut them in half, throw away the seeds, and eat the flesh much like you do while eating a papaya. The seeds can be strained to get more juice out of them, or you can suck on them and then spit them out. The seeds won't kill you if you eat them, but don't bite. Yuck!

Guavas grow everywhere. In fact they are very hard to kill. They will grow right on the beach, high in the mountains, in swamps, on the edge of arid grass lands. You can cut down a guava tree and within two years it will re-grow and bear fruit. To transplant, cut little one inch sections of a root and throw 'em in a hole. That's it.

Passion fruit flowers contain reproductive parts of both sexes in separate blossoms on the same tree, which is unusual enough by itself, but the entire blossom rates as one of the most beautiful in the world. Unfortunately it is so fragile that it doesn't travel well. Hey, lucky you, there you are on your abandoned island, enjoying your own private flower show! Passion trees are hard to transplant and dislike the salt air. Look for them inland and the higher the better.

Mango

The mango has oft been called the fruit of the gods, with good reason. The best varieties are the second most delicious fruits in the tropics, if not the world. Not every mango tree is a good one no matter how full of fruit they may be. In fact the taste of some might be best described as kerosene that has been left out too long in the sun to rot. Forget those. We will ignore them for the time being.

The trouble is that all mangos are much the same shape and when they are green, the same color. They do come in different sizes, the largest topping out at 6 pounds. However, when they ripen, their color gives an indication of the taste. The more rainbow colored they are the better the flavor. The more the colors of the rainbow they have, the more delicious. It is like they are calling to us. "Eat me!" When pressed lightly, a ripe fruit will give slightly and a exotic scent will be emanate from the stem end. The better the smell, the better the taste.

Many people are highly allergic to the skin of the mango. This is not uncommon in tropical fruit. They don't want anyone or anything to eat them, till the seed has reached its full maturity. If you are an unfortunate, get Friday to peel them for you. Chances are, you can eat the fruit without harm. Never touch your fingers to the mango's skin and then your fingers to your mouth or eyes. Never, especially with green mangos. Trust me, I know! If you are allergic to poison ivy, watch out, you might also be allergic to mango skins.

Green mangos are eaten by the local populace, but don't be fooled. They have eaten them from birth. Watch out! You can peel them and dice them up under fresh water and use the green fruit for chutneys. Chutneys are a great way to preserve fruit for the off season. Sometimes when it is nasty out, it is nice just to sit in your grass shack and eat chutney on dried breadfruit. Really!

The large central seed of the mango can be roasted and then ground into a powder to store for use in breads and puddings if you are really, really, desperately hungry!

Papaya

The Papaya is rated the king of tropical fruits if only because it grows in abundance almost everywhere, it bears fruit for eleven months of the year and if you look around carefully, you can find a papaya plant that bears a fruit that is reddish inside. As the Hawaiians say, "Break the jaw, it so good." Cut it in half, scoop out the seeds and squeeze the juice of a lime on it and you will be eating like a king. Some say the papaya has potent medical potential, read the Natural Medicines chapter for more information. Papayas also lend themselves exceptionally well to drying. (Cut 'em into cigar like sticks and dry in the shade.) The plant can be found anywhere on any island in the tropics, but it is especially prevalent in the mountain valleys, streams and flat low lands. It doesn't overly like the salt air so search inland a bit. Papayas grow on every tropical island, even atolls, look for 'em.

The green, unripe papaya can be cooked like a potato or squash, peel it, remove the seeds and boil it, or cook it wrapped in leaves in an underground pit heated by fire warmed lava rocks. The young leaves can be eaten after boiling, but change the water several times while cooking like you would while cooking taro. (They have a nice tang to them, if you like that kind of thing.) The papaya grows out of the trunk or stem of the plant much like cacao. It makes it easy to pick as the lower fruit always ripens first. Pick the fruit just before it is ripe or the flying foxes and birds will eat it for you. The green fruit ripens easily in the shade of your cook house. If the tree is too high to gather the fruit, and you have plenty plants, cut the tree down about six feet from the ground. The plant will branch out and grow outwards like an apple tree.

Be careful not to get the sap in your eyes, it can cause intense pain and even temporary blindness. The green fruit can be used as a meat tenderizer and is full of vitamins. Get into the habit of throwing a piece of green papaya into the pot when cooking. In

24

some trees, the fruits are not overly sweet when ripe. In this case score longitudinal lines down the green fruit after you pick it, just penetrating the skin. This will release the excess sap that is making your fruit, blah. When you do this the papaya will start to look very yucky (to use a technical term) as it ripens. Not to worry. It will be great inside. (I always tell my wife, Karen, the same thing, I may be yucky on the outside, but I have a good heart, inside. I don't think she believes me!)

If you find more fruit than you can eat, peel and slice the papaya and set it out in the shade to dry. Cover it with coconut gauze (Do I have to keep saying index?) to keep the bugs off it. It will dry in two or three days. Cover it at night. It makes a nutritious great tasting snack when it comes time to climb around searching for the proper rocks for the umu you will use to cook food during a luau, or to stock up your canoe on a voyage of exploration.

Pineapple

I love pineapples. I really do. I didn't used to. It was just too much work to remove all the eyes and skin and core and everything. Then I tried a pineapple that was ripened on the plant, in the field and tended to everyday. Wow! In Fiji, I learned that the eyes grow in a spiral and can be cut out all in one piece with an artistic twirl of your machete. I started to love the pineapple.

But let's not get ahead of ourselves. You have been watching your pineapple plants. (I know everyone says they like the sun but they are wrong. Pineapples like shade with only a couple hours of sun a day. Look in the shade to find wild pineapples. Shade with water near by.) OK. Your pineapple is ready to pick. You know it is because you can easily pull a leaf out of the top of the pineapple topnotch. Grab the fruit and twist it off the mother plant. Cut off the crown (for want of a better word) growing out of the top of the plant. Include about a half an inch of pineapple in the cut. Peel away the lower pieces of husk off the crown until little roots are exposed. (Aren't they cute? Just like real roots, but so small!) Bury the crown, roots down, at least eighteen inches away from the mother. If the mother plant doesn't recover and start a new baby within six months or so, dig her up, cut everything off the main root and bury her root again in a different place.

Listen, who really knows how long we are going to be on this island. We have to start living with nature sooner or later instead of just going around raping the natural world, taking but not replanting. Start being a gardener, not a plant rapist, that is, if you want to keep eating in the style you so recently have become accustomed.

Ok, we have our pineapple with the top cut off. Slice off the bottom, then quarter it lengthwise right through the length of the core. Are you with me there, Survivor? We now have four boats. (Come on, use your imagination. That's what it is there for.) With the tip of your machete or your obsidian knife separate the hull of the boat from the crew (the flesh) and then separate the mast (the core) from the men. (Their eyes will be left in the boat! It is kinder if they don't have to watch as we eat them.) Don't cut the very ends or your mast will fall down. Slice through the men, (they are huddling together wondering what is going on and where the hell the captain is) and there you are, a pineapple boat. To eat, just push one of the men out from under the mast and devour. Does eating too much pineapple make you write like Homer? (Sometimes, I just crack myself up!)

Or to be more traditional. Skin the pineapple, cut off the bottom, observe the eyes. They grow in a spiral. Follow the spiral with the blade of your machete up and then down and pop out the eyes. Slice the fruit horizontally and then reassemble (like it was never cut) to be artistic! Friday will have new respect for you! She will see you in a new light. She will think you understand her. It is ok to let her (or him) think that. Really! And then let him/her prepare the next pineapple!

Bananas

Tropical islands teem with life on land and above and below the sea, but few things are as delicious and as useful as the banana plant. This plant gives us the queen (how many queens can one island have?) of all the fruits. We all know the Dole and Chiquita brand of bananas but once on the island, you will discover that bananas come in dazzling array of sizes, shapes and tastes.

The plantain is one of the mainstays of tropical island life. At first, the shipwrecked sailor might shy away from the plantain. This banana plant bears a huge stalk of very large fruit which will disappoint you when you first peel and eat a yellow one. This is a cooking banana. When first picked it is very starchy and can be baked on a hot rock in its own skin, steamed in a umu or fried much like a potato. Eaten raw it is little better than a raw potato. Everyday, after it is picked, it changes its taste as the starches are turned into sugar until, when the peel has turned black (rotten looking black), it is a very sweet fruit. At this stage, I like to sprinkle cane sugar on top of it (hey, I have a sweet tooth, all right!) as it is frying on my rock by the side of the fire and then I pour a little arrack on top of it and ignite it in a glorious flambé. Not to worry, we will get around to making our own sugar and alcoholic drinks. What is life without temptation?

There are many types of eating bananas on our island. The most common is the small Lady Fingers or the Apple banana. This plant grows prolifically all over most islands. It is a small tree so the fruit is easy to reach. But don't just cut the banana stalk off and leave the tree. All banana plants will only bear fruit once in their life. Don't leave the plant standing after you harvest the bananas. It will not die and it will steal water and sun from its babies growing up beside it. Don't just cut the plant and just leave it there. Inside the top of the banana plant is a heart, much like the heart of a coconut tree. It can also make a salad, but instead of millionaire's salad, we can call it skinny poor man's salad, mostly because it is a very thin heart (about the width of a cigar).

Bananas grow by shoots or 'pups' that grow out of the 'mother' root system or the mother stalk after it is cut cleanly with a machete. Who knows how long you might be on the island? Think about growing food for tomorrow. If more than one pup grows out of the mother's root system, none will grow a complete stalk of bananas. So dig up and transplant other pups when they are one to two feet tall. If you don't have time to transplant, chop down the other pups when you pick the fruit leaving just the largest healthiest one. When you are ready to harvest a stalk of bananas, first slice off the flower, the red purple thing that grows out of the bottom of the stalk. This will 'finish' off the bananas, give them that extra sweetness and creaminess that is the banana's trademark. But not too soon.

The bananas are born inside each leaf of the flower. As each petal falls, another hand of bananas appears for awhile. Each banana plant is bisexual. It starts out in life as a female, grows its bananas, then turns into a male! The petals keep falling from the flower, but now pollen is released instead of another hand of bananas! Generally, a good rule of thumb is when the flower is two to three feet below the last hand of bananas, cut off the flower. Don't throw away the flower. It is delicious as a vegetable. Cook it up by the side of the fire, discard the outer leaves, and there you go, a side dish from the bounty of nature. For some reason, every flower seems to taste different to me, but generally expect artichoke-green beans flavor. Inside of each 'leaf' of the heart resides another set of possible bananas or male stamens. These are the part you eat. I don't mind the inside of the 'leaves' also eaten like an artichoke. If it is not cooked enough it is very bitter also plantain flowers tend to be bitter, but a nice bitter.

The tastiest of all the bananas is the red banana. When ripe its peel is red. Talk about a 'Here I am, eat me!' sign. This fruit is half as wide as it is long and has a creamy texture that rivals an avocado. The medium tall red banana plant grows in the shade in the foothills of taller islands, far from the sea but not so high up the mountain to restrict the water supply. All bananas like to grow on a slope where they are not sitting in water, but still have a good supply of it. So when looking for bananas on your island, search the hills first for the best eating. Notice which plants that are growing baby bananas so that you can return in the future when they are ripe. If you wait too long, you will discover all your fruit eaten by insects and flying foxes. (Flying foxes are fruit eating bats.) Bananas will ripen after they are cut from the plant, but wait, you knew that! Everyone who has bought beautiful looking bananas at the grocery store and found two days later a black thing surrounded by fruit flies, knows that. After you pick your bananas on your island, the same thing will happen. They will all ripen at once. A stalk has as much as a hundred bananas in it, all ripening at once. Be prepared to eat nothing but bananas for days, and loving it!

In the event you can't eat all your bananas, no matter how hard you have tried, the best thing to do is to dry them for a time when you just need a snack, a pick-me-up, in the middle of a thunderstorm when the world is coming to an end outside of your grass shack, but inside you are nice and cozy but hungry. That is the time for dried fruit. To dry, bruise the banana while still in its skin, then cut into long thin slices. Dry in the shade, covered with coconut gauze as all insects love drying fruit, especially bananas.

If you still have so many eating bananas that they are rotting all around you, mash up one that has turned almost black. Don't be squeamish. After you have a nice puree apply it to your face as a mask. Bananas have nothing inside of them that will do you harm. Don't worry. After the mask is good and dried, wash it off in the waterfall with a beehive ginger blossom as soap. Your skin will thank you for it! Bananas are high in vitamin A which your skin loves. Try it, I did! (Come on, guys, the girls held me down and smeared it all over me! But it was worth it in the end!)

One of the pleasures of living on your own deserted island, is the almost unlimited fruit that is available for your consumption. Enjoy your bananas, when you are rescued and back in civilization, as much as you might hate it now, you are going to miss your little slice of paradise filled with every tropical fruit under heaven.

Breadfruit

Breadfruit made its mark on history with the ill-fated voyage of the Bounty under the command of Captain Bligh. Caribbean slave owners needed another source of food as European plants couldn't stand the onslaught of hungry tropical insects. So the British Admiralty sent Bligh who had been a sailing master under Captain Cook to Tahiti to gather and transport young breadfruit trees to Jamaica. All went well until it was time to leave the paradise of Polynesia and return to cold and harsh Cape Horn. Bligh, like many of the British captains of the time, was a harsh dictator. The mutiny made him famous, that and the fact that he made a 2000 mile sea voyage in an open boat and then court martialed his helmsman for speaking without permission when he called Bligh's attention to a reef dead ahead. Eventually breadfruit did make it to the West Indies where after all this trouble the slaves wouldn't eat it, preferring bananas and plantains. However breadfruit can now be found world wide in the tropics, including your island, I'm sure, as the wonderful breadfruit is one of our most useful of fruits.

Its most interesting aspect is that, like many fruits, it changes its taste as it matures. Picked green it is a vegetable-like food with the consistency of potatoes; very ripe, it is a sweet pudding; in between it is a mixture of the two. Strangely, it never tastes or looks like bread except, perhaps, when it is sliced thin when uncooked, rinsed in salt water, dried for two days, and then toasted on a rock in the fire. It is a big fruit about the size of a small bowling ball and one can feed a lot of people or just yourself for several days. The fruit starts with spur like growths all over its outer rind. As it matures these spurs become less pronounced and when fully ripe and sweet, the rind is smooth with just the outline of little pentagons all over the surface. The tree is tall, reaching 100 feet when mature and its branches are rather fragile making climbing a risky business at best. Not a problem when the fruit are an easy reach from the ground but when the one you want is out of reach, it is time to make a picking pole.

Picking poles can be made out of any wood, but bamboo is traditional. A 'u' shaped piece of driftwood is lashed to the top of the pole. A firm pull with a twist is all that is needed, plus the skills of an outfielder. Did you ever wonder why so many great baseball players are Puerto Rican? Perhaps, it is because they spent their youth catching breadfruit, mangos, papayas, etc. And throwing rocks to get them down!

There is a seed or seeds in the fruit. Mostly you will find only the variety with one large central seed, luckily as this is the best tasting breadfruit. Normally the breadfruit is cooked in the embers of the fire for an hour or two, turning it this way and that with a stick, until it is well blackened. Peeled it, cut the seed out and enjoy. The seed can be roasted and eaten with salt as an appetizer and is a great source of niacin. Niacin is the vitamin that helps keep the damn bugs away. The sap, boiled with coconut milk makes a excellent caulk for canoes and an all purpose glue. And last but not least, the flower makes a great tinder when thoroughly dried for starting fires.

Coco-bread Pudding

Take a mature breadfruit (the rind gives easily when pushed) and cut out the top, like carving a pumpkin for Halloween. If you are lucky when you lift off the top the central seed will come with it, if not dig out the seed and fill the space where the seed was with fresh eating coconut that has been grated but not squeezed. Add a cup of coconut milk from another coconut. Replace the top and set the breadfruit standing upright on the coals of a fire and cook for several hours until well blackened. Unbelievable.

Breadfruit Chips

Take a breadfruit whose spurs are just starting to loose their edge and peel. Remove the seed, quarter, and slice sideways into thin chips, thinner the better. Soak in salt water for 15 minutes to remove any sap, place in the sun till mostly dry, then fry until they just start turning golden brown. Spice up with whatever and enjoy. Awesome!

Avocado

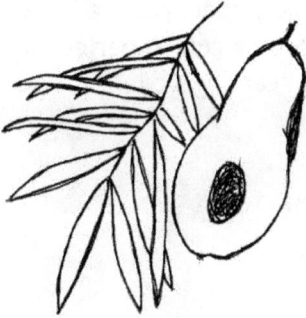

The avocado is the emperor of the fruits. Not only is the taste superb but it is very good for you. It protects against high blood pressure, heart disease, stroke and prostate cancer. In season, the trees are very prolific, often one tree can bear hundreds of fruit. One of my fondest memories was when I was a fisherman in Hawaii. I sat in my little boat tending my nets, eating avocado after avocado. They were so good, I just couldn't stop myself. For some reason they don't make you fat and fill you up quickly, even a guy in his early 20's.

Modern man has existed only a few thousand years, but our genetic ancestors, Cro-Magnon and Neanderthal survived for hundreds of thousands of years. They survived mostly from the practice of eating whatever was available at the time. If blackberries were in season, they ate nothing but blackberries for weeks at a time. If apples or pears came into fruit, that was all that they ate. Many authorities believe that humans are genetically predisposed to eat in this way and that eating just one food product at a time is the true way to better health. Whether it is or it isn't, when avocados come into season on your deserted island, don't shy away from feasting exclusively on their creamy fruit. It is one of the few fruits that can be called a complete food as it contains measurable amounts of protein as well as loads of vitamins.

It is difficult to survive in the tropics without a full head of hair. It not only cools the head, it keeps the sun away from the brain.   For those who would like a little extra hair growth, there is nothing better than mashing an avocado into your scalp and massaging.   Because avocados are rich in vitamins A, D and E, all necessary for hair growth and because avocado oil easily penetrates the scalp, you may cure your bald spot while on your deserted island.

The best way to eat a avocado is to cut it in half, vertically, pry out the seed, and dig in with your spoon. You don't have a spoon? Of course you do! The next drinking coconut you open, cut the husk a few inches from the stem side with a sideswiping cut. A perfect, if crude spoon will jump off the husk. With a little carving, voila!

Dragon Fruit

OK, I bet you never saw this one! Ha, I got you. Dragon Fruit is a vine like cactus that grows either along the ground or up trees. It doesn't overly like salt air so look for it on the edges of forests or upon the mountains. The reason you don't recognize it, is it is a night blooming cactus, and like all night bloomers, it is very fragrant and elusive.   The flowers have no spines and can be eaten right after picking; you know, like for a midnight snack. Don't be upset by the many tiny little black seeds, they are mostly hollow and very, very sweet. If they do bother you, dice up the flowers and place them in a joint of bamboo filled with water. Let them soak until morning and then discard the flowers and drink the juice. When you return to civilization, orange juice in the morning will just not be quite the same.

While you are wandering around in the middle of the night, stumbling over trees and rocks, keep an eye out for other night bloomers, especially for a tropical variety of night blooming jasmine called tiare. In Tahiti they add this flower to coconut oil to make an incredibly beautiful body oil. The girls there either bathe with this oil, or after bathing in a waterfall, rub beehive ginger and tiare flowers all over their hair. The effect is unbelievable. It goes a long way to explain the mystic and romance of the South Pacific. Men use tiare oil also. It is believed that it is a repellant for sharks and they rub it all over their bodies before going diving. I tried it once, but then I have never had a problem with sharks, so I can't say. I did have a considerable female audience while rubbing it on, though!

So there you go, Friday. Not only to you have a reason to go walking around in the middle of the night, but you come back smelling incredible plus holding the best wake up morning juice in the world. Isn't being shipwrecked a wonderful thing?

Starfruit

Starfruit are on my all time list of great tropical fruits. When I was a boy in Hawaii I could usually be found after school, high up in the nearest starfruit tree with the other junior malcontents moaning our fate of having to wear shoes while going to school. We were hard to understand as our mouths were always full of the wonderful flavor of ripe starfruit. They form a five sided star when looked at on end.

The starfruit shares with the apple a delightful crunch when bitten into, an aftertaste of honey and a beautiful star shape which when cut up sideways improves any salad. It is a tree which can grow to sixty feet but usually is around the twenty foot level. The fruit start out green and as the ripen they become yellow. When they reach the golden stage, eat them right then as they will be rotten tomorrow. The starfruit does contain small apple seed like seeds. The seeds are edible but not particularly tasty.

When crushed at the peak of their performance, they yield a wonderful sweet juice that ferments well. It can be distilled into a gin like alcohol but it is a waste. Star fruit wine is totally awesome!

Star fruit trees come in two species. One is sour, one is sweet. There is no way to tell by looking which is which. Grab hold of a fruit and get to tasting. The sour starfruit makes the best vinegar in the world. Make a wine out of the fruit and then cover the wine with some porous coconut matting and leave it untouched for a few months. It will get really gross, what with bacteria and fungi and alien looking creatures growing on the surface. No worries. It is just doing its thing. After three months scoop all the aliens up and use them for fertilizer and filter and decant the liquid through some kapok. Use this vinegar in the morning as a mouthwash, go ahead and swallow it afterwards, it is good for you. The aliens in the ground, hell, they invaded us, they got what was coming to them!

Tamarind

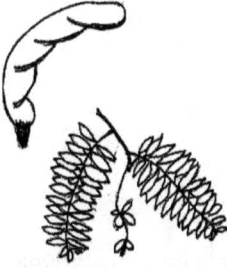

Tamarind is the local island candy bar of all the Pacific and Indian Islands. Want to find all the local kids after school? Hint: they will be climbing and enjoying the nearest tamarind tree. It is closely related to the tree called St. John's Bread or Carob. Any of which can be grounded up into a flour for making bread. All three are in a strange way a substitute for chocolate. If the truth be known, all of us are addicted, at least emotionally, to chocolate. The carob tree unfortunately grows in North Africa along the sides of the Sahara which kind of puts us out in the cold on an island in the middle of the ocean. However, we still have the Tamarind which may not be as chocolaty as carob or St. John's bread but is still great.

Personally, eating tamarind right from the tree is a once a year, if that, event. But Friday loves it when I make my special tamarind donuts for breakfast. And that puts me in a good mood for the rest of the day.

The best way to grind up the tamarind after you split open the dried pods and remove the seeds, is to mix them with coconut milk and a bit of coconut oil and grind them into a paste. It makes the stickiness much easier to handle. Don't worry if the paste isn't uniform, it will still taste great. Add your choice of flour, peanut, cassava, or sago. Mix well and add a bit of coconut yeast. Coconut yeast is made by opening the top of a brown eating nut, adding a glug of toddy, putting the top back on the coconut loosely and waiting a couple of hours.

Add the yeast to the donut mix, knead, and set it out in the sun. After a couple of hours pound the bread down, form into patties (you can put holes in the middle if you are anal retentive) let it rise again and drop them one by one into a coconut shell of more or less hot oil. As long as the shell is by the edge of the coals and the oil doesn't run out and doesn't spill into the fire, the coconut shell won't burn. If you cut your coconut shell just right (see bowls and plate section) you can put the top back on after the oil is cool and save the whole kit and caboodle for next time.

Sapodilla

Sapodilla are a delicious relatively unknown fruit. The tree is tall, up to a hundred feet, with glossy, evergreen, leaves that are pointed at both ends. The flowers are like tiny bells of various colors. The fruit, when immature, seems inedible. Be patient and you will have a wonderful taste treat.

The sapodilla fruit looks ever so much like it is covered in brown sand. The flesh can be brown or more often reddish brown. You will know when one is ripe as it becomes soft and pliable and develops a sweet scent much like a pear. Normally slice the fruit open, remove the collection of seeds in the center and spoon out the nectar like fruit. The seeds have a hook on one end and must not be eaten. The hook impales itself on the sides of the throat while swallowing and is very difficult to dislodge afterwards. However, the seeds are easy to see and easy to remove from the fruit. There are normally, three to twelve seeds per fruit. Sapodilla taste kind of like a combination of pineapple, mango, papaya and vanilla and with the texture of ice cream.

The tree likes to grow in old coral, marly areas. It isn't fond of salt air so look inland for your tree. If you like, pick the fruit while still hard after it has reached at least a diameter of three inches and leave in the shade away from bugs for five to nine days. Sapodilla are high in vitamin C, calcium and phosphorus.

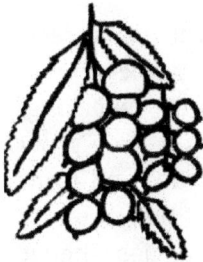

Macadamia nuts

Macadamias are the best nut in the world, really! If you have a macadamia tree on your island you are very lucky. They grow in shady areas at sea level and in full sun up in the mountains. They hate salt air and will not grow where they get even a little salt. The nuts are often hidden by the leaves, so the tree may have nuts, but you just aren't looking hard enough!

Macadamias shells are very, very hard. Trying to open them is enough to put you off nuts for life. It is very difficult to tell when the nut is ripe, so just picking them up when they fall to the ground is a lot easier. The outer shell isn't too hard to remove. Once it is off, sun dry the inner shell (the hard one) for a week or so in the hope it will become brittle, just to give yourself a fighting chance. I have tried every different way to open them, the only thing that really worked was a betel nut guillotine. This tool is sharper than any razor and closed inside of a race. Sorry to say, you aren't going to find one on your island. Time to go back to caveman style. Smash 'em between two rocks! Watch out for your fingers! If you are practicing on your boat, vise grips work wonderfully!

Macadamias contain twenty two percent Omega-7 which is the newest (well kind of) stay young and healthy drug. Wouldn't it be something if you came back from being a castaway and you looked years younger? "New health kick, live by yourself on a deserted island for a year, if you don't starve to death you will look years younger!" I should have been an ad writer!

The oil in Macadamias also makes your skin more cushiony, if that is a word. So, if you really get the knack for opening the nuts, you can have beautiful skin to go with your busted fingers!

Jack Fruit

Jack fruit can be huge. You could feed yourself and Friday for a couple of weeks on one Jack Fruit. They get up to three feet long, weighing over a hundred pounds. They grow both from the tree trunk (like cacao) and from branches like normal fruit. When you find a tree, don't be put off by the smell. (All plants in the tropics have antisocial tendencies when it comes to being devoured!) On the tree they smell like rotten onions, yuck, but once you cut them open, they smell like a mixture of papaya, pineapple and banana. Before the fruit is ripe, it has no odor. Cut it up then and cook it as a vegetable. The only bad part is it has a sticky sap that will get all over your machete unless you cover the knife with coconut oil. Isn't your island wonderful with all these types of food it is supplying to you? Isn't island life great?

The insides are filled with seeds up to one inch long. Don't freak! The seeds are good. As you cut up your jack fruit to use in a stew or roasted up in the fire, pick out the seeds, dry them for a day or two. You don't have to get carried away. After they are a bit harder, roast them on hot rocks in the coals of your fire or boil them in water or for a real treat, in coconut milk with a squeeze of lime or mountain apple. I hope you like Christmas as they taste just like chestnuts.

Jack fruit are a mainstay in the preparation of curries in Southern Asia. One of the reasons that curries are so hot is the jack fruits are so big you have to make a huge pot to fit it all in. The curry leaf, or whatever they are using for their curry, prevents any germs from growing in the dish. That is a problem for us. There is no way we could eat the whole thing before we get sick of it. (I mean, the same thing over and over for weeks at a time when the island is loaded with good things to eat?) So save the jack fruit for feasts and luaus when you are cooking in the umu. Go ahead and cook the whole thing 'as is'. Later, you can pull the seeds out and lick your fingers!

Durian

No one voluntarily eats a durian for the first time. You will have to force yourself. But once you do, you will be devoted to them for life. The durian has the worse smell of any fruit in the world. The best description of the smell is of a pair of socks worn by an ogre for a couple of years straight. Ogres, by the way, never bathe, ever. I know that from my nephew who apparently is knowledgeable about such things. But durians taste great. As bad as the smell is, the taste is a hundred times better. Ambrosia for angels if you like cream cheese mixed with onions! But really good custard like cream cheese!

They are easy to find in the wild in the Indian Ocean, if only by the smell and the characteristic spines all over the husk. Sometimes they can be found in the western Pacific and Caribbean, but you really have to look for them. It is a low tree with leaves that are oblong. The tree looks just like an elm. The fruit has five internal compartments with embedded seeds. Eat the pulp, try not to smell as you enjoy it, keep the chestnut size seeds and roast them on a hot rock turning every few minutes. Durians are favorites of animals and birds, so you are not likely to find many. If you do, grab one and eat it up, just so you can tell the story after you are rescued and they put you on national TV. (They are only going to want to know about sharks, weird things you had to eat and, of course, all the UFO's you saw!

Ice cream bean

There comes a time for every castaway when he/she starts to dream about food, hamburgers, steaks, hot dogs, you know, all the civilized food, but mostly about ice cream. It makes for a great daydream. You can sit on a beach and dream about every flavor of ice cream you have ever eaten. But, when this happens to you, remember to stop dreaming and start eating. There are ice cream plants on most of the larger islands in the tropics. Really! I am not joking!

The ice cream bean grows on a tree that reaches twenty feet when full grown. It likes to live on hill sides, well watered and isn't overly concerned with salt air from the ocean. Its pod, holding maybe fifty beans, is a meter long and tastes just like your favorite ice cream, as long as it is vanilla. You open the pod by twisting it and then pull out the beautiful white covered beans. Don't eat the bean, just suck the sweet, juicy white pulp off of it. Actually, you can eat the bean but it doesn't taste of ice cream and after the delicious pulp, everything else pales in comparison.

When first opened the pulp tastes like a cross between cotton candy and ice cream, but within twenty minutes exposed to the air, the flavor is pure vanilla ice cream. Soon after the flavor fades and after an hour, might as well go back to your daydreams. But at least for that hour, you can sit under an ice cream tree and dwell in paradise!

Loofa

The loofa sponge is one of the delights of the tropics. I bet you are used to going to the store to buy your sponges, all lined up on shelves. But, not on your deserted island. There you pick 'em off of the tree! It is kind of a money tree, in fact your island if full of money trees. You don't have to pay, so look at all the money that you are not spending!

The luffa is a type of squash, it looks like a squash, it tastes like a squash, it almost is a squash. The big difference is that when it is green and young, you eat it. When it gets old and brown you break it open and inside is a sponge! When you do, the sponge part is full of pulp and seeds. By all means keep the seeds. Dry them and then roast them to eat while pretending to watch the ball game. (You know, like on the beach at sunset.) They taste like peanuts. Throw the pulp away, unless you are like really hungry! It isn't my favorite part, by a long shot. Once the insides are clean, just wash the loofa in water, fresh or salt, and set out to dry. Do you know how much a natural loofa costs in the civilized world? Isn't surviving fun and rewarding?

If your loofa is really green and young, just cut the whole thing up and boil it in coconut milk. Mmm good, as they say. By all means, stew up the yellow flowers and young leaves. Don't eat the leaves raw. Don't eat the vine part. Did I tell you that the loofa is a vine? Squashes grow on vines. There, now you know. Like a watermelon. (Just to add to your confusion!) (Don't worry, Friday will understand!)

Loofas are exceptional good at surviving in the wild. Some plants (and some people) are, you know. Look for them in old fields, or close to old houses where some land was cleared once, giving them a chance to get started.

Lime Trees

On the seventh day when God was resting, he really wasn't. All the hard work was finished. You know, he invented the devil, grade school, sleet and hail, George W. Bush, all the hard stuff. But on that last day he invented the lime tree. Boy, he made up for a lot of mischief when he made limes! Think of it. Something that is good for you that you can put inside alcohol so you could pretend to improve your health while drinking!

But we don't have to save limes for our arrack and toddy. No sir! The best way to use limes is to cook seafood. The hassle with seafood is you can't just leave it laying around for a couple of days till you are hungry enough to eat it. Do that and you will discover why God invented refrigerators on the first day. The trick is if you aren't hungry, leave that fish in God's refrigerator, the sea. But if you caught it anyway, clean it up real nice, chop it up into little bite size pieces, and cover it with lime juice. The flesh will turn white as the acid in the lime juice chemically cooks the fish. Later when you get hungry, or just want some thing delicious, add coconut milk and make ceviche.

Lime trees really like limestone and, naturally, do really well on abandoned tropical islands made by lime producing reefs. If your lime tree is in sand and is having a light fruit year, put some pounded up dead (it has to be really dead, like white and all) coral or sea shells around the roots. The roots of a lime tree go out as far as its branches

reach. The really bad killers of lime trees are the insects. Wewe's, leaf cutter ants, will devour lime trees. Then, as soon as they grow back some new leaves, the ants will come back and eat those, too. Every effort has to be made to destroy Wewe nests. It is easy to do. Follow the little buggers back to their nests by the leaves they drop as road markers. Get a stick (by this time I hope you always have a stick in your hands) and stick it directly down the hole. (Their hole looks like an elephant's trunk stuck out of the ground!) The queen will grab it quickly. Pull her out and boil her in water. Tastes like scrambled eggs!

Defend your lime trees. They are also a terrific medicine. (Check out the Natural Medicines section.) Besides, Friday is going to expect a lime wedge in her nightly cocktail if you want her to be happy!

And trust me, you do want her to be happy!

Pommelo

Pommelo is a wonderful grapefruit. Not only is it juicer, sweeter and more favorable than a Florida grapefruit, it grows naturally right by the sea, right by your grass shack so you can wake up in the morning, reach out the window and pick breakfast. It that living or what? In the Pacific it is called a Tahitian Grapefruit even though it originated in Malaysia and Thailand. That is because there are so many Pommelo trees there in the Societies.

The peel is very thick compared to a Florida fruit but is very loosely attached to the fruit like a tangerine, easy to peel. The health uses of the tree are many, but I haven't tried any, so I haven't included it in the medical section. I just eat them up! But having said that, it is reported that:

Decoctions of the leaves, flowers and rind are sedatives for epilepsy, chorea, and convulsive coughing. It can also be spread on swellings and ulcers. The seeds are good against coughs, dyspepsia and lumbago, The gum that exudes from dying trees is collected and used as a cough remedy in Brazil. If you believe all of the above I have a great bridge in New York that I can sell to you cheaply. Real cheaply. But you never know, it could be true!

Litchi

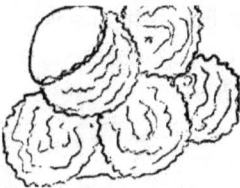

Litchi or lychee originated in China but had spread through out the South Pacific, Hawaii, South Asia and Florida by the 1900's. The tree always has very bright blue green leaves and often can be spotted some distance away by the color alone.

The fruit is ripe when it is strawberry red and about one inch in diameter. Break open the thin skin and suck the flesh off the large seed. It is very sweet.

Rambutan

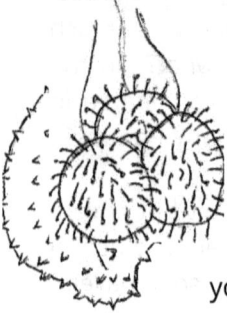

Rambutan are almost identical to Litchi in every respect except appearance. Rambutan are more delicate than Litchi and are only rarely canned. Lucky you if you have some of these trees on your island!

Soursop

Soursop together with custard apples, sweet sop, sugar apples and durian form the Guanabana type of trees. They are spread throughout the world, one fruit or the other dominating its own area. Soursop dominate the new world tropics from the Caribbean to Fiji. Again like cocoa they grow out of the trunk or the branches remaining green in color its entire life.

Soursops are normally processed into ice creams but can be eaten raw. The fruit is covered with small knobby spines which easily break off when the fruit is ripe. Unripe Soursops can be eaten as a vegetable after cooking. Soursops contain up to 200 half inch seeds which you don't eat. Bummer, huh?

Sweetsop

Much like its big brother the Soursop, the seeds of the sweetsop, also called the sugar apple, are very dangerous to get anywhere near the eyes especially when ground up. The ground up seeds are an effective insecticide.

Sweetsops ripen when green while sugar apples are orange to yellow when ripe. Alligator apples, much the same in shape, but with fewer bumps in the skin, are not edible raw. They are dark brown when ripe.

Miracle plant

Grown mostly in the Pacific islands this red fruit when eaten (don't eat the seed) make other sourer fruit taste very sweet for about twenty minutes. Imagine eating a pineapple that tastes sweeter than pure sugar. Or a lime that suddenly becomes an addictively sweet fruit that you can eat like a pear! I had one of these as a boy and it blew my mind. They are fairly rare, but still, if you find one on your island, you may not want to be rescued, or if you are, you better hire a lawyer first thing as every candy maker in the world is going to want to talk to you about GPS coordinates.

The Palms of Paradise

No one realizes how important palm trees are to survival in the tropics until you are shanghaied and left on an abandoned island. Without palm trees your life is going to become one of desperate choices, none of them good. The tropics and palm trees belong together. If it wasn't for the romance of swaying palm trees and lovely wahines, the Mutiny of the Bounty would have been but another footnote in the annals of history.

There are many types of palm trees. Sure, the coconut palm is most likely to dominate any tropical island, but other palms, similar but different might be hiding amongst them. All of them can assist a castaway's survival. Here are some highlights.

The Coconut Palm

We could survive on a tropical island without coconut trees but it would not be much fun. The coconut palm gives food, drink, shelter, clothing, and is the most romantic of the tropical plants. From the castaway resting under a palm to a tropical maiden walking down a beach with a coconut leaf hat, this famous plant has enthralled us and bewitched us with its promise of edens in the far off South Seas. And it was not by any means, a false promise.

While there are hundreds of varieties of coconut trees, there are only four main types of coconuts; the copra nut, the eating nut, the UU and the drinking nut. Each have their own uses on our island and we need to be able to tell one from the other.

Copra Nut

The copra nut was the cash crop back when our island was inhabited. In the beginning of the last century, coconut oil was, with whale oil, the most desired oil for machinery, for lighting, and as it still is now, for beauty products and also for cooking in the third world. Over 90% of the coconut trees on the average island are copra nut trees. Copra nuts are elongated, triangular in cross section, develop a 'waist' and develop brown streaks in their husks very early in their life cycle. Copra nuts could be considered the least valuable of the four types for surviving on our island, except for two exceptions. The tree makes the very best toddy, an alcoholic drink (we will most definitely explore this later!) and it supplies us with the best lighting and cooking oil. To remove the meat from the copra nut a knife or thin lever is inserted between the meat and the shell after the nut is cracked in half by using the back edge of the machete. (Husking the nut gets its own chapter!) The meat is then dried in the sun and after most of the moisture has evaporated, is squeezed between two logs to remove the oil. Because the coconut oil is saturated it doesn't oxidize and can be stored easily. The oil gathered by pressing can be filtered through a layer of kapok held in a coconut leaf basket for a purer, tastier oil. Alternately the copra can be boiled in water and as the oil raises to the surface it can be skimmed off, if you have a pot large enough. Gourmets say that this oil is not as tasty.

UU Nuts

Every coconut consists of coconut meat surrounded by a shell which in turn is surrounded by the protective husk. On one end of the shell are three 'eyes', the end where the nut was attached to the tree. When the nut falls to the ground and starts to become a new tree the meat inside of the shell starts to sprout and turns into a fibrous mass. The roots come out of two of the 'eyes' and the trunk of the new tree comes out of the third, growing at first from the fibrous mass as its energy source. In Polynesian culture the coconut tree is considered to grow through four stages in its life cycle; this

stage is called the 'uu' stage. The 'uu' is at its best when it has a root system growing down and about a two or three foot stalk growing up but is not yet firmly attached to the ground. By grabbing the stalk the nut can be lifted off the ground. To get at the 'uu', crack open the nut with one giant blow of your machete and detach the fibrous mass inside. The shell and husk are weak by this stage. The 'uu' by itself is rather plain tasting, its only remarkable qualities are its total lack of a coconut taste and the tremendous amount of vitamins the sprout contains. It can be added to any dish to good effect but almost everyone's favorite use is to make 'uu' burgers. If you have been beachcombing, shipwrecked or anchored in the lagoon long enough, these 'burgers' will taste better than McDonalds!

Recipe Uu Burgers

Collect one nut for each person, they are everywhere, it isn't hard. Remove the core and squish the sprouts all together, adding any flour and a bit of flavoring, curry leaf, lime, peppers, whatever. (Check out the spice section) Considerable water will flow out of the sprout as you squish it, don't throw it away! It is loaded with vitamins. Mix everything together, adding flour until you can form them into patties and fry it up into hamburgers. Trust me, you will want seconds.

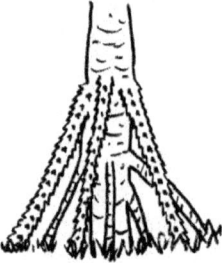

Eating Nut

The eating variety of the coconut is the most useful. While you can eat the coconut meat of the copra nut, it is pale, dry, and tasteless compared to the eating nut. The eating nut is more of what we would expect what a coconut should look like. It is rounder, slightly less triangular and stays greener longer. The meat is moister and has more milk while the copra nut has more oil.

Please try to avoid, after the nut is husked, using the sharp edge of the machete to open the nut. I speak from experience! The meat of an eating nut is removed by scraping. This is done with a special built tool, available at most hardware stores in the smaller islands of the Pacific or more properly made up by yourselves and stashed in your 'shipwrecked' goody bag. In worse case scenarios, the meat can be removed like a copra nut and then shredded with a grater or chopped with your machete. However, most islands were occupied at some time in the distant past and important plants were cultivated. One of these was the Walking Palm. The legs of the Walking Palm have very sharp short thorns on them, almost designed to shred coconut and squeeze the milk out. Repeat adding hot water to the shredded coconut and squeezing out the milk several times and eventually you will end up with several bowls of coconut milk and a cheese cloth filled with the desiccated coconut, like you buy in a grocery store. The coconut can be added to any baking project, cookies, cakes, candy. Yes, I did say candy! The first rinse is the richest, it is from this liquid that we will make our coconut cream and coconut butter. Yes, I did say butter! The second rinse is less creamy but still tasty.

Coconut Candy

Nothing is as nice as candy when the island is going to pieces, the rainy season is in full bloom, the roof leaks, every bug in creation has invaded your thatch roof to try to keep dry, and Friday isn't talking to you. Back in the world it is so easy to drive down to the supermarket and pick up a dozen candy bars and a couple of flowers just to be sure. But that isn't going to happen on a deserted island. But all isn't lost; we can make our own candy, coconut candy. Here is how to make two different types, coconut bars and coconut fudge.

Coconut bars start with a mature eating coconut that you have shredded, hopefully you have made your coconut shredder by now, it makes it so much easier. Remove the milk as usual, keep the water from the coconut when you open it and mix the water with the milkless coconut. Add some ground up cinnamon. Add an equal amount of sugar liquid and cook it just short of boiling until it turns brown and starts to solidify. Watch it closely. With a stick, sample it every few minutes until it gets to the 'crack' stage. The candy mixture will ball up on the end of your stick at this stage and when you pull your stick from the mixture, the candy will start to become hard. Remove from the coals and pour into little bars on top of a clean rock. Don't sample it! It is very, very hot! It will give you third degree burns inside of your mouth. After an hour for cooling, start the party and enjoy.

Coconut fudge isn't real fudge but is the closest word to describe this delicacy. Start with the spoon meat from a drinking coconut. Cut it into little one inch squares and cover it with liquid sugar for a couple hours. Remember to cover your container, bugs will like your sugar water just as much as you. Warm up some flat lava rocks in the main fire. When the rocks are good and hot, move the fire a few feet away, brush off the rocks with a couple pandanas leaves. Spoon out the little squares of spoon meat and lay on the rocks. Pour some of the left over sugar water over the squares and sprinkle some cinnamon on top with a little of your sugar granules. When the rocks cool off, prepare your mouth for a delight forgotten by our packaged, preserved world.

Heart of Palm

The best part of the coconut tree to eat is the heart of palm. This is the lettuce-celery like substance that grows just below the crown of the palm in the center of the plant. It can be eaten as is, right out of the tree or more traditionally, made into Millionaire's Salad. It is so named as you have to be one to afford to cut down a coconut palm to get at it. On our island, the long gone inhabitants grew fields of coconuts palms close together for the purpose of cutting them down long before they reached the coconut bearing stage and eating their salad, plus building with their fronds and using the brown burlap clothlike gauze around the base as a fire starter or sewn together as a mosquito net. This stuff will light wet or dry. If you look around the Island, I'm sure you will find one of these fields of palms or you can also start your own. Just line up any Uu's you have left over in a grid pattern in a sunny area with a meter between each other, and forget them. Come back next year if you are still on the island, if not, then you have aided the survival of any explorers that follow in your footsteps.

If you are out exploring and need a snack, tug at the middle leaf of a young (less that four feet tall) coconut tree. The leaf will pull out exposing a delicious celery like core. Don't worry, the tree will grow another, you won't kill the tree. Coconuts are very hearty.

If you are on the island during the hurricane season, an adult coconut tree may fall down. Be sure to harvest the heart from the crown of the tree before it dies.

(*Warning!* The root of the coconut contains narcotic properties and should never be chewed especially after it has been shredded and dried in the sun on top of black lava rocks for a week, being sure to protect it from the rain. Especially don't do this if you are all alone on the island and are feeling lonely. Trust me. Really!)

Drinking Nut

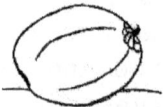

The coconut we all love is the drinking nut. This isn't the one they sell you on the beach at resorts with a little umbrella, a straw and enough alcohol to dissolve whatever resistance you still have to safeguarding your children's inheritance. That is an eating nut they are giving you.

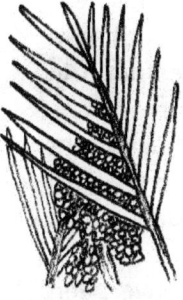

A drinking nut is a thing of wonder. It looks much like an eating nut but has little meat inside (an eating nut does go through a spoon meat stage with little meat inside also, but that doesn't make it a drinking nut. It does taste close to the same, but in comparison it pales). Usually, drinking nuts are slightly paler in color to down right yellow or light orange. But the real difference is in the drinking. Open the nut up by slicing the husk off the pointy end (the end away from the part that was attached to the tree). The husk carves away very easily, not at all like the eating nut.. When the shell is exposed, open it up with a whack with the back of your machete while holding the nut right side up. After a few nuts you will get better at this. The trick is not to loose any of the elixir inside. (Or your fingers!)

The drinking nut water explodes inside of your mouth with an avalanche of bubbles and zesty wonder that revives and revitalizes. If you can't identify which tree is a drinking nut, then it is time for a taste test. Try every likely tree on your island. Believe me you will know when you sip your first drinking nut. And you thought you missed your coca cola. After you are rescued, you will really miss your drinking nuts!

Spoon Meat

Spoon meat is the just barely solid coconut that resides inside the shell of a young coconut or drinking nut. The Polynesians fed their babies and aged this meat as it almost dissolves in your mouth and is ever so easy to swallow. For us survivors, it is an interesting change but hardly worth the effort of opening the nut. It can be used in candy making and puddings.

Date PALM

If you are following along in your encyclopedia, I imagine you are getting very huffy about now. I don't blame you. It says right in there in World Book that date palms grow in the desert in Northern Africa. That doesn't sound like a deserted island, does it? But I have news for you. The real world rarely resembles the one found in encyclopedias.

In Hawaii, just outside the Honolulu Zoo are a magnificent stand of date palms. How we loved to pick those when we were kids! Because of their success in Hawaii, so many decades ago, date palms were sent to islands all over the Pacific and Indian Oceans. In the Caribbean I have tasted fantastic date palms. And you have been buying them from stores all these years?

On most islands in the tropics, date palms can be found. They don't mind salt air in moderation, and they don't mind cold conditions found up in the mountains. Keep your eye peeled. A good date palm will keep you and Friday well fed for months, to say nothing if you are stocking up your canoe with dried food for fishing trips or explorations. Unripe, the dates are very bitter. Wait till they are yellow, then go for it! Dry them out in the sun if you must, two weeks for best drying results. Cover them during rains.

The dates you eat from the store are really rotten dates. They are picked and left out in the sun to dry where they develop that sticky, gooey taste. The ripe date is a thing of delight. Refreshing, crisp and bursting with flavor. Think of grapes instead of raisins. Just to think, you had to get shipwrecked to find out what crummy food they are selling us in grocery stores!

Waree Palms

Waree Palms are not nice. They do not believe in a kinder, gentler world. Their trunks are riddled with long, black, sharp spikes, and they hurt. Believe me, they really hurt. Any sensible sailor would steer clear of such nasty plants if it wasn't that they have delicious nuts. When young they are full of water, but as they age they taste like baby coconuts. There isn't much of a husk so open them up with a swift blow with the back of the machete when the nut is on a rock. There isn't much meat compared to a coconut but you don't have to climb the tree or husk the nut as you eat them when they fall to your feet.

Just like the coconut palm, the heart of the Waree Palm is delicious. Cut the palm off right at the part where the fronds are separating. Cut away the outer layers of the plant. The heart is pure white and can be eaten as soon as you can get your greedy little hands on it. You could bring some back for Friday, but was she out there risking getting stabbed by nasty spikes?

Keep on the lookout for shoots when opening the plant. These are brand new branches, just being born and are very, VERY, good. Eat them right up or chop them up to add to your salad.

The spikes make great needles for all your island sewing projects. They are ever so sharp and last forever. Use another spike to make the eye in the end of your new needle. Careful about pricking your fingers. They are so sharp they will go right through your finger!

Jippi Jappa

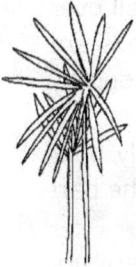

This plant is of the palm family. They have a long stem climbing straight up with the palm shaped like an umbrella. It grows in rainy valleys and often in little nooks in the shade of larger trees most anywhere on abandoned islands. You can eat the shoot. It looks like the stem of a palm frond coming out of the middle of the plant. The tender white heart of the shoot is delicious if small. Not really worth while collecting for dinner, but really great for a snack as you are out exploring your island. Just grab it down towards the base of the plant and it will pull right out easily. Not to worry, it doesn't hurt the plant. It will grow a new leaf in a couple of weeks, just in time for your next explore! The shoot tastes a little like a mixture of cabbage, artichoke and celery with the crunch of carrots. Not bad, and you didn't have to pack it and carry it all the way back to your camp. Isn't exploring Fun?

Sago Palm

Just when you thought it was safe to go back in the water, someone tells you of yet another disaster just waiting to happen. I didn't think it would be me, but in the interests of better warned than dead, I have to tell you there are two Sago Palms, one deadly poisonous and the other as great a food source as you could ever find.

You would think they could come up with some original names when they are out botanizing, wouldn't you? Especially with poisonous plants? Luckily for us the two plants don't look like each other at all.

The little Sago is a cycad. All cycads are more or less poisonous. The Sago is deadly. It is used as a house plant all over the world and is responsible for many dogs dying. The seeds are especially poisonous. (Hint. Don't forget this if you are invaded by wild savages who are after Friday's virginity!)

The other Sago Palm is found in rainy valleys usually near waterfalls. Almost all the parts of the plants are edible, but the part not to
miss is the pith inside the trunk. Chop down the tree, (there are usually hundreds). Full grown they reach thirty feet with a trunk about five inches thick. Split the trunk and scoop out the sago. A full grown tree will feed a man for a year. Cut it down just before it flowers as once it starts to fruit, it will eat itself to death. The palm only flowers once and then dies. Prepare the sago, pound the whitish inner pith and then kneed it in water. Strain the liquid through a few layers of coconut mesh or kapok, into containers. The sago will sink to the bottom of the container. Squeeze off the excess water and use it as you would wheat flour. It is about as nutritious as rice. The upper part of the trunk doesn't contain any sago but don't forget the delicious heart and shoots of new branches.

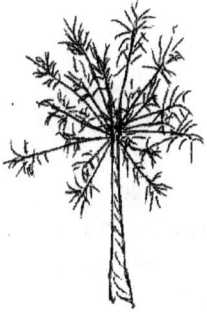

Palmetto Palm

Palmettos are a very hearty species found on islands and the sea coasts of continents from 30°N to 30°s. The old Hawaiians told everyone that the Palmetto was a survival food for them, that in times of want they could eat the hard seeds, if your teeth were tough enough. In reality, the heart of the Palmetto is the largest and most delicious of any palm. As usual, it is found just a foot or two under the beginning of the branches and working its way up the trunk.

The bad part of harvesting a Palmetto heart is you have to kill the tree to do so. Best to do so just for feasts and holidays, much as the wily Hawaiians did. The last thing they wanted the white man to do was rape all of their trees! Best to take a smaller tree. Not only are they not reproducing yet, but they are easier to cut down and for their size, their hearts are bigger.

Imagine if you will a cabbage but a cabbage with the crispness of baby carrots, the creaminess of an avocado, the whiteness of fresh cauliflower and you begin to get a feel of a Palmetto heart. In truth, it is indescribable but totally delicious.

A brief note on machete chopping. A machete is not an ax. Don't be like Paul Bunyan and make huge chops, attempting to cut down the palm in one mighty blow. Be instead like a bee. Make lots of little chops, accurately, just in the right spot, one after the other, like a machine gun, rapidly fast. Not only will you be less tired, your machete will have less chance of damage and the whole job will take a fraction of the time. I was taught this by a four foot tall Thai girl in Chagos. Us men were each taking turns being Paul Bunyan and making little progress. After fifteen minutes, she pushed us aside in exasperation, and chopped the tree down in less than a minute. We people of the "first world" think we know so much, Ha! We know so little of what counts. Like how to feed yourself without a grocery store.

Peach Palm

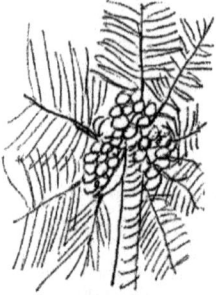

Yes, they do taste like peaches! No, you can't pick them off the palm tree and eat them up, you have to boil them in salt water for three hours first. A lot of work? Oh, yeah, and a lot of firewood, but it is worth it. I tried boiling them in fresh water instead, but as usual, following the directions, works.

The thing is because they don't ripen on the tree, all the birds and bugs don't get to eat them first. You get first pick. Locate your favorite tree and pick a stalk. Don't worry about the others. They will still be there when you get hungry for them again, because the fruit have no natural enemies, except, of course, hungry beachcombers!

Leaves, Stems and Flowers

Edible vegetables grow all over the world. The kind of vegetables you are used to, the kind that are sold at your local grocery store, do not commonly exist on islands in the tropics. They have no defenses against veritable armies of tropical insects. That doesn't mean that you are going to starve, far from it. But it does mean that you are going to have to learn to eat new types of veggies. Don't end up being shipwrecked and then dying from starvation because of lack of knowledge of the edible world of the topics. Explore islands when you get the chance. Identify edible plants. Eat some when you feel adventurous. Be like Robertson Crusoe. Be like Friday. Create a world for yourself, by yourself. People would pay good money for a chance like this. An island of your own!

Bamboo

Bamboo is a really big, tall grass. And as such, like all grasses, you can eat their seeds just like rice. Of course, nothing is ever that easy on a deserted island. By now, you have realized that. You can also eat the young shoots, make containers, blow guns, musical instruments, cooking pots, medicines, rafts, fishing poles, walking sticks, and make paper. Bamboo can grow almost anywhere, but it prefers a partially shady, well watered, non salty area. If you can find bamboo on your island, your life will be much easier.

It takes twenty to a hundred years for bamboo to produce seeds, and they do so only once in their lives, so when you harvest some, don't waste them. Like all grasses, they create a fluffy growth on the top of the plant where the new seeds are incased in husk. Pound the husk and then pour the seeds from one container to a mat on the ground while standing in the wind to separate the husks from the seed. You now have brown bamboo rice. To get to the seeds you have to cut down the bamboo. Think ahead of what you can use the bamboo for, before you start hacking away. Once cut the bamboo will start to become harder and more brittle. The small new shoots are a delicacy in oriental cooking. Strip the outer, sometimes hairy, covering and boil (in a bamboo pot, naturally!) in water for twenty minutes. Raw shoots are very bitter.

One interesting idea is to make a didgeridoo. This is the Australian Aboriginal giant flute. Burn out the intervening bamboo joints with long ignited sticks and use breadfruit sap mixed with coconut milk to build up a lip guard. The didgeridoo is difficult to master but what else are you going to do during the long nights when you can't sleep, and are wondering who won the Oscars?

Lashing three or more bamboos together forms a useable bow. A bow and arrow can be very useful; shooting fruit off trees, lines over tree limbs, fish swimming on fringing reefs, fruit bats off trees. (If you are shipwrecked in the Western Indian or Southwestern Pacific. Fruit bats are giant fruit eating bats. They sleep during the day, and are fairly easy to catch if you are a good tree climber and can forget all the vampire movies you ever have seen. They taste like chicken. They do!)

Paper can be made by mashing new bamboo leaves in water, adding sulfur (yellow mineral high up the volcano found in little patches) to dissolve the pulp, (if you aren't on an island with a volcano, extinct or active, forget about paper, make tapa.) adding ground coral to stop the ink from spreading all through the paper. Build a woven mat out of the finest, thinnest leaves you can, then dip the mat into the dissolved pulp, let dry, then dip again until you are happy with the result. Ink obtained from octopus' ink glands, (See Octopus chapter) and, voila, you have the makings of a log book, a movie play, or a best seller. (What else are you going to do during the long days when you can't sleep?) Feathers make great pens. Cut the tip of the feather ever so slightly, opening just the smallest possible hole into the hollow core of the quill and still forming a point. Luckily there are lots of feathers to practice on!

Making a raft out of bamboo can be very useful if the fringing reef on your island is overrun by spiny sea urchins, making walking on it a risky business at best. Cut the fattest bamboos you can find and lash them to cross pieces with sisal or any other roping material.

(See rope chapter) When sailing your raft the cross pieces are in the water. Don't try to paddle. Pole yourself along the reef. If you want to go in deeper water, check out the canoe chapter.

Bamboo makes a great cooking pot. As long as there is water inside the joint of the bamboo section, the wood will not burn. It is perfect for those castaways that hate doing dishes. After the cooking is done, throw the pot into the fire. One bamboo plant will supply you with a month's worth of pots! Check out the cooking methods chapter.

When making a grass shack, consider making the lower walls out of thin sections of baby bamboo. It could look very oriental and if you wanted to make a sand garden to rake when the stress becomes too much, there are no lack of raw materials

Sea Rocket

Sea Rocket is a small plant that grows along the sea shore just above the high water line that resembles arugula lettuce. It is related to the mustard family, is a scurvy grass and adds tremendously to a great tasting salad. Pick the leaves when the plant is young. Once the plant has gone to seed, the leaves turn bitter and unpleasant.

For a great experience, pop some sea rocket into your mouth as you beachcomb and your eyes will pop with its peppery savory flavor and its I-have-to-have-another desirability. It is an amazing pick-me-up during a long harvest hunting afternoon and will turn a ho hum dinner into a magnificent feast.

Sea rocket grows just about everywhere. Keep your eyes open and enjoy it quickly. It turns to seed after a few weeks of growth. The new seeds will sprout after a month.

Okra

Okra is a fruit. I know they tell you it is a vegetable but it grows like a fruit and gets sweet like a fruit and has seeds inside like a fruit. Your okra isn't sweet? That is because it is eaten when it is still a baby. Unripe, it is a great vegetable (or whatever). It grows wild on almost every island in the tropics. It doesn't like the salt, so look deep inside the island. The shape of the fruits is a dead give away. However if you are having trouble finding yours, it grows to about six feet, leaves are palmate (as they say, which means it looks like a marijuana leaf!) with an odd number of leaflets, the flowers are white or yellow with a purple spot at the base of each petal.

Eat 'em like asparagus (boil them for eight minutes) when it is still unripe, cut them up to make a stew, or after it is stewed make a nice salad with the cut up pieces. Sounds weird, doesn't it? But it is really good. Throw in the regular stuff, too, heart of palm, wild tomatos, wild garlic, bit of ginger. Or just fry it up with your breadfruit and plantains. When the okra are golden they are done.

When the okra ripen, remove the many seeds, crush them and make a coffee substitute. It ain't all that bad. Depends how long you have been on that damn island! Ripe okra can be eaten raw, but are better mixed with other fruit to make a great salad. They taste great with cinnamon vinaigrette.

In the 'real' world, okra are used as a thickener for stews and especially gumbos. We can do that, too. But as always it comes down to having a big enough pot. If I ever get shipwrecked, I will ignore the GPS, the VHF, the EPIRB, and grab the GBP (great big pot!) I mean really! It doesn't need batteries, doesn't break when you need it most, doesn't need updates to keep working, and will last your life time. What more can we ask?

Pigeon Peas

Pigeon Peas are one of the most successful plants of the tropics but you never hear of them. It's because they look like every other plant. There is nothing distinctive about them. Not like a coconut tree. You see a coconut tree and you know what it is. But given all of that, you can survive nicely on pigeon peas.

The pigeon pea originated in India where it is the base for dhal. From there it spread all over the tropics. I can almost guarantee that every island in the tropics larger that an acre has at least one pigeon pea plant on it. The plants are proficient seeders so it is easy to gather enough in a minute to feed yourself. Pick the pods when green to have peas. There are about four or five peas in each pod. Or, wait and pick them when they are dry to use as a bean, or to grind into flour, or sprout them for extra nutrition.

Like alfalfa, pigeon peas are nitrogen fixers. Everytime you harvest the peas, prune the branches, or chop down the tree it releases nitrogen into the soil. They will grow everywhere. Good soil or bad, wet or dry, salt air or cold! When you do trim the branches, separate the wood for special cooking fires. Pigeon pea wood burns very hot and makes good charcoal. If you want to grow the trees closer to your shack, grow them from the seed. Germination takes three weeks and they go through a semi hibernation for three months after they are a few feet high. Don't worry, after that they will take off!

Carob Tree

The time will come when you are living so high on the hog that you start to get fat. Time to go on a diet. And what is the first thing to get cut from our diet? Chocolate. Its true! There are a few islands around where carob trees live. They like arid conditions high up on the volcanos where there is plenty of sun and wind and the living is hard. Because they are so unusual, don't worry about searching for them. You will notice them and say, "What the heck!"

They are prepared like so many other seeds. Dried to preserve them and pulverizing the already sticky seeds to cook with. Rather than trying to make a chocolate substitute with them, throw them in your breads, your soups, your grains. Anything to give a little extra jazz to a already ho-hum day. Am I saying that anyone could get tired of paradise? Well, maybe not. But the island you end up on may not be as paradisiacal (is that a word?) as the ones I plan on being shipwrecked on!

Perhaps your best option is to pull up to a deserted island and pretend to be shipwrecked. Practice making your hat. Try to make a shelter. Find food to eat. Make a fire. Brew some arrack. These are all worthy skills. If it becomes too much, if the shelter leaks, the hat becomes a Frisbee, the food unfindable, the fire mutinies, the arrack impotent, then you can always go back to the boat for a few days of rest and relaxation.

Agave

Agave is a cactus like succulent. You might know it more commonly as a century plant. It only flowers once in its life and then dies. It might be found on your island. It grows on deserted islands where few other plants can grow. Look for it on the lee side of the island protected from the sea air by a rock or two.

If you find a plant that is flowering, cut the tall, massive flower stalk off by the base of the plant and drink the refreshing water like liquid the flows from the cut end. Then boil the flowers and buds for a good thirty minutes before eating. The rest of the plant is not edible.

The tips of the leaves have very sharp spines that are useful for sewing and the leaves can be pounded between two rocks releasing a sap which is a natural (if slightly non-effective) soap. Afterwards separate the fibrous strands of the leaves and soak them in salt water for a day. The strands are very long and weaved together make an effective sisal like rope. Some people are allergic to the sap of the leaves. Proceed with care at first. Tequila is made from the sap in the base of the mature plant, after it flowers. Cut off the leaves, roots and flower stem and boil to remove the 'meil'. Distill after fermenting with cassava yeast. Check out the brewing section.

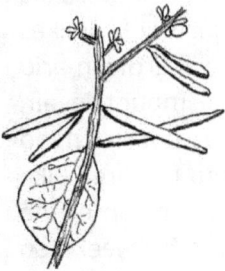

Mung Beans

Sprouts are one of my favorite food groups. When you eat a sprout it is like eating a fish only better. You know the fish is dead

64

by the time it gets into your mouth but that sprout is still alive. We eat them alive! It doesn't get any better than that! Anyway, mung beans are really hard to kill. If they ever managed to get onto your island in the past, they are still there, somewhere. You just have to find them. You can also eat them fresh, you can cook them for just five minutes, or you can sprout them by soaking them in water for two hours, changing the water, soaking them for another two hours and then letting them drip dry. If you give them a brief soaking twice a day and then letting them drip dry they will continue to grow until they are four inches long. At this point they start to become woody and loose their delightful crunch.

Full of vitamins, minerals and trace elements (so important on tropical atolls that have been isolated from the 'world') Mung bean sprouts are an important part of healthy living for a beachcomber.

Sugar cane

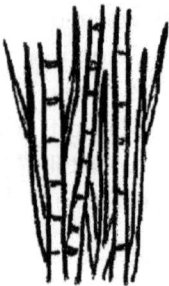

OK, it's true, sugar is bad for you. Everyone says so, I guess it must be. I don't know why I like it so much. Am I a bad person, deep inside? Is liking bad things a failing of the human psyche? I didn't know this was a philosophy book! I do know that I would have a easier time on a deserted island if I had access to sugar. Maybe you would too?

Sugar is easy to come by. Sugar cane is a weed, it will grow anywhere. It is almost impossible to eradicate it. It will be on your island somewhere, just look. It likes flat land but will grow on slopes, it likes water but will grow in arid conditions, doesn't mind salt air, doesn't mind cool mountain air, doesn't mind stones and rocks, hey, it is a weed, it doesn't mind anything. Once you find it, don't forget. Wait for it to mature. (like any weed, when it gets pale brown or golden tassels on top of the stalk containing the seed, it is ripe.) It will stay mature for weeks, so just cut what you can handle for the day. Cut it about six inches from the ground with a diagonal cut and you will have a new sugar cane plant in three to four months.

To get at the sugar, it is best to cut your stalk into two or three foot sections. Peel the outside of the stalk until it starts feeling moist, then pound the cane with your pounder. (see tools section) Squeeze the sugar out of the bagasse, the husk, and pound the next section. Filter the liquid and you have pure sugar. Dry the liquid in the sun in a coconut shell cup, stirring everyday, and in a week you will have first stage sugar. Of course, if you need energy during all this, pop an inch of peeled cane in your mouth, chew happily, and spit out the bagasse after you have swallowed all the juice. What could be easier?

If you want white sugar, soak it in strands of Hibiscus branches! Really! Check out the Hibiscus page. Isn't the natural world wonderful?

Cattails

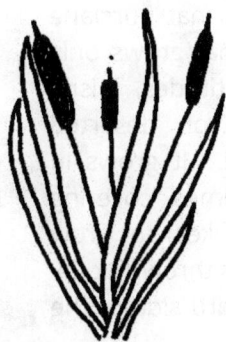

Yes, it is true, you can eat cattails. And yes, they are in the tropics. In fact, they are just about everywhere, They are a very invasive species. It is our duty to eat them up, so lets get started.

As you would imagine they are always near fresh water, often right on the shore of a creek or pond. Dig them up and eat the roots. They can be eaten raw but are better (they are never what you might call haute cuisine) roasted or baked. Either way chew them up to get all the starch (starch is good, it is the only part of Wonder Bread that is edible, if it is edible) and then spit out the fiber. The flowering spikes, the part before where the tail grows, are Ok for salads, don't eat them when they turn into a tail. Sounds yucky, right? So why am I telling you about them?

Cattail pollen is equal to bee pollen in minerals, protein and energy and is easier to harvest. First, cattails don't try to sting you and second, they aren't hiding in a hole in a tree. It is way easy to get a lot of pollen. Wait until the cattails are ready, (the pollen is ready to come off in the wind) and just draw the cattail through your hand then shake your hand off in a basket or bowl. If there is one cattail there will be thousands, plus you aren't harming anything. Well, I guess you are slowing down the future cattail generations, but Mother Earth will thank you! You can eat the pollen by the spoonful but it is messy. Better to put it in salads, in your soup, in your bread. In just about anything. Talk about a quick pick-me-up-er. You will be hopping around the island after dining on some cattail pollen!

Cattails also were used by American Indians for medicines, for thatching roofs and for bedding. Be inventive. When your rescuers come, just say, 'Ugh.'

Purslane

There is a belief that purslane is a sub-tropical plant that grows only at higher latitudes and altitudes. It isn't true. Purslane grows on deserted atolls around the world. It grows in great profusion sometimes covering acres of ground. It likes to grow behind small coral ridges thrown up by storms just above the high water mark on the windward side of the island.

Purslane grows close to the ground, seldom exceeding an inch in height. The stems often have a red tinge. Usually purslane covers large areas, preferring full sunlight to the shade cast by coconut trees.

As the plant grows larger it becomes bitter so pinch off the smaller leaves and add to your salads and stews, or just pop them into your mouth as you explore your island. The stems are edible but

I prefer them cooked rather than raw. Either way we cannot ignore any plant that adds to our vitamin intake.

Tropical Lima Beans

Lima beans were native to Central America but since Columbus have spread throughout the tropics due to their tolerance, almost liking, to salt water and spray. The vines can grow to ten feet or less on most tropical atolls and up to a hundred feet long on most high islands.

The flower looks almost like a small snap dragon, pale blue to purple and the bean pod which follows the flower within a couple of weeks starts out as pale green. Leave the pod alone. It is not edible until the pod turns yellowish brown and the shape of the seeds can be seen clearly pushing against the pod. The pods are camouflaged very effectively. Lift the leaves with a stick to discover them.

Don't eat them right from the pod, like most beans and peas. Dry them (unless the pod is very brown) for a week and them boil them for five minutes, twenty minutes if they have been drying for longer than a month. Like most things they go well cooked in coconut milk and curry leaf.

Prickly Pear

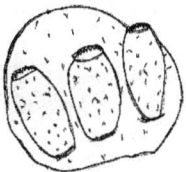

Prickly Pear is the fruit of a cactus plant. The fruit is edible if you don't mind the spines. The big ones are Ok, but there are also little hair like spines that detach from the mother plant and penetrate into your skin with ease. Normally, instead of a de-spine effort, it is better to peel the fruit, carefully.

They are native to the Americas, but were transplanted world wide in the 1600 by explorers, where the plants, having no predators or parasites took over many islands as well as significant portions of Africa and Australia. So don't feel bad about eating Prickly Pears, you are doing Mother Earth a favor.

The small new leaves are edible also, after they are peeled. There are prickly-less species. Lucky you if your island has one of these! In Mexico, Prickly Pears are eaten after a hard night of drinking, something we should remember! They are boiled and fried and are very nice with eggs, and also make nice jam.

Roots and Vegetables

It is fine to gather fruits in season and flowers and leaves when they are available, but when people really need to eat, they need root vegetables.   Root vegetables can be picked ahead of time to be eaten on a rainy day or a trip of exploration in your canoe. Yes, I know that you are on your island living a life of freedom, spending everyday doing whatever you feel like; but survival often depends on thinking and planning ahead. Bummer, huh? All root plants in the tropics have exotic defense systems, often very effective against humans.   Please don't go around eating roots till you have determined how to disarm the alarms!

Cassava

It isn't that the climate on your deserted island isn't good for potatoes and oats and carrots and celery and broccoli (It isn't really good, but they should grow after a fashion), it is that all the insects on the island are always on the lookout for a new taste treat. You know, looking for a new restaurant to bring their future Miss Feelers. What does succeed, plant wise, is the tried and true crops that have been on the island forever and every insect, bird, rat and whatever is bored with and would only eat if they are starving or have a death wish. Cassava is one of those plants. It is the most important root crop in the tropics rivaled only by the kumara (the best sweet potato you have ever eaten). It is the third most important crop world wide. (Behind rice and corn.) So just because you have never eaten or cooked with cassava, doesn't mean you shouldn't. If fact, unless you want to starve after being shipwrecked, you better get used to identifying, harvesting and cooking it now.

The most important thing to learn, is cassava plants and roots contain cyanide. Ok, I can hear you now. Go to a deserted island and get poisoned to death, great, that is just peachy keen. And I paid money for this book? Whoa! Wait a sec! The cyanide is what keeps the pests from eating the plant. To get rid of the cyanide is the trick to cooking with it. Oh, you have cooked with it before without side effects? No upset tummy or migraine the next day? Some cassava plants have more cyanide than others, we have to assume that the plants that are still surviving on our deserted island are loaded with poison or they wouldn't have survived.

The first thing not to do, is to peel the cassava. Boil the whole root in bamboo or whatever container you have found. Boil it for ten minutes at a full rolling boil, cool it and then dump the water down that annoying ant hill just by your grass shack. Now comes the hard part.

What you have to do is not let the outside of the peel touch the cassava inside. With your machete or obsidian knife, barely score the skin around both ends and one middle. With one movement pull the two parts of the skin apart and dump the cassava onto a banana leaf, then go and wash your hands. Does this sound like too much work? Do you want a loaf of bread or don't you? Now, boil it again for an hour. Throw away the water. Bread? Did he say bread?

After your hands are washed, squeeze the cassava between your hands and save the juice that comes out of the root. Don't worry, the cyanide is all gone now. Now you have a choice. Save and dry the cassava for use another day, or proceed directly to bread making. If you wish to dry the starch, form thin patties and lay out in the sun. It will take two or three days. To make bread after the cassava is dry, pound the patties into powder, add fresh water and proceed as below.

Cassava bread is easy as it comes with its own yeast. The water you squeezed out and saved, (not the ones you poured down the ant hill) is loaded with natural yeasts. Take your squeezed cassava and knead it well discarding any hard bits, add a touch of water, a bit of palm toddy (Toddy is the stuff straight from the plant. It is kind of like maple syrup. Arrack is the alcoholic drink made from toddy), a pinch of salt, a glug of coconut oil and a half a coconut shell of your saved yeast water and knead well. Set it aside and let it rise like wheat bread. Wheat flour is the only grain that forms large amounts of gluten, the stuff that makes bread taste like bread. Gluten also allows wheat bread to absorb 200 times its weight in water. Nothing else is going to taste just like wheat bread. Sorry to disappoint. All other grains have their own distinct bread flavor. Cassava bread has great taste of its own. On your first try, you might think it is a cracker, it is so flat. It will rise, but only if you really knead it half to death. (And what else have you to do?) (And what, exactly, is wrong with crackers?)

Let your cassava bread sit out in the sun for an hour, at least, rising before you cook it. When it is as high as it will ever be, (which isn't much) wrap it in leaves (what else?), move the fire over (see fire chapter) place the bread in the middle of the coals and bury it and the coals in sand. Give it a good hour. I promise that if you have been on the island for a long time, you will love every bite!

If you want to make crackers, proceed as in bread, but make thin sheets the size of your largest rock. Put the rock in the middle of the coals and when it is nice and hot, lay on the cassava sheet. Don't turn it over, instead sprinkle the top with salt, red pepper and with your imagination. Serve with whatever or just eat them for snacks.

French Fries

Lets face it, without French Fries no paradise is worth living in. Really! Without French Fries we might as well forget the house and hat and just build a canoe to sail away to another island that does have the proper cuisine. I mean some things are just not done! The good news is almost every once inhabited island I have ever been on has a stand of cassava somewhere. You just have to find it.

For French Fries (some things are always capitalized. Like major food groups.) after you boil the cyanide out of the root and open the peel, don't boil it again. Instead, cut it into fries like sections and dump them into a pot of water. When all the cassava is cut up (you aren't just going to make a few are you? A feast is a feast! It is time to gorge!) Take them out of the hot water and dry them on a flat rock or banana leaf in the sun. When they are mostly dry, but still a little moist, one handful at a time drop them into hot coconut oil. (Have you read the coconut section? Have you made your own oil?)

If the fries don't bubble and bob up and down, one of two things are wrong. Either your oil isn't hot enough or you put too many fries in at the same time. The hard part about French Fries is getting them out of the oil. We are not going to dump the oil! After you have made the oil by hand, you definitely are not going to waste it! I guarantee it! We have to get the fries out with sticks.

It really helps if you ate at oriental restaurants as a kid. Yes, we are going to use chopsticks to remove the fries, but really long ones. You really don't want to get burned on an abandoned island, far, far from medical care. (If you do, run, don't walk, into the ocean and stay there. Oil burns are so bad because they burn down through all seven layers of your skin and keep burning. You have to cool off the oil; you have to cool off all those layers of your skin. Stay in the water for at least fifteen minutes. Really! I know the French Fries are just sitting there and your oil is boiling over. It doesn't matter. Stay in the water.

Ok, the French Fries are laying there on a banana leaf platter, all salted with sea salt that you dried yourself, Friday is looking at you with hero worship in her eyes and she is letting her hair down. It doesn't get much better than this!

Taro and Yams

Taro is one of the staples of island life. If ever you get really hungry, the taro is always there waiting for you. As it contains about three percent sugar, it is more like a sweet potato than an Irish potato. It is the root of the plant with the leaf that looks like an elephant's ear. Taro is the plant with the leaf that goes down, elephant ear is the plant where the leaf goes up, and is not edible. Do not eat raw taro leaves as they will cause a serious inflammation of the throat and mouth from the poison, calcium oxalate. If you boil the taro, exchange the water at least once. If roasted there is no problem. In either case don't eat the skin. To make it less dangerous, and since the skin is poisonous, scrub the taro in the surf on the beach. (It won't hurt your skin.) Use the sand to scrub the surface of the root. Eventually the fibrous part of the skin will be removed and then the whole root can be eaten.

Taro, like yams, like well watered, rich soils. That is about all they have in common. Pre-Captain Cook island communities in the Pacific usually picked one root crop or the other for their daily meals. Yams will keep for months if they are kept dry, but they are a annual crop and require a great deal of labor. Taro on the other hand, grow and can be harvested year round. Just dig up the corns, cut off the plant and stick the stalk back into the ground. In three months you will have more taro. No work, no labor. Which should we harvest? Is this a trick question?

Islands with tight communities, kept their people in control by basing their food source on yams which required lots of team work. Other island chiefs who let their people do what they wished, based their food source on taro which could be harvested year round.

What does this mean to us? If Friday is starting to take long walks by herself and is gazing at the horizon much longer than is normal, tell her we need to eat more yams. If Friday is uptight, is constantly cleaning up the camp, and is getting on your nerves, tell her it is time to eat more Taro!

Taro can be pounded, after being roasted in the fire for a couple of hours, and left in a sealed (as best as possible) container for two days to ferment. This gives the taro an interesting flavor, sour but savory at the same time. What you are doing is making poi! Those Polynesians had it right. If you want your kids to eat their vegetables, ferment them first! Just kidding!

Kumara

Kumara are the best tasting sweet potatos in the world. I know that is a hell of a statement but it is the total truth. Really. They are so good, they blow away the competition so far, that there isn't even a second place. They are found all over the South Pacific, on every island, no matter how small. With luck, you will find them in the Indian Ocean islands and the Marshalls and Carolines. Close relatives, sweet potatos are found everywhere. They are the second most important root crop in the tropics coming a close second to the cassava. Like the cassava, kumara plants contain a deadly poison. In kumara's case this is solanine, a neurotoxin related to belladonna. The symptoms include vomiting, convulsions and death. Again, like cassava, this poison prevents the plant from being eaten by the myriad of insects living in tropical isles. Never eat the plant of the kumara, just the root. Kumara root skin can be eaten after roasting but not raw. Place the root in the coals at the side of a fire. If the fire is very hot, wrap the root in leaves first. Ti leaves are best but any can be used. After an hour, pull the kumara out, tear it open and eat the most fantastic feast in the world. Don't season with butter, salt, pepper. Don't put anything on the kumara. It would be redundant. It is incredible just the way it is. The insides come in many colors, each variety has its proponents. Myself, I think dark orange kumara are the very best. Kumara look just like any other sweet potato but just take one bite and you will know the difference.

Again, if you find a kumara in the wild don't dig it up and eat everything you see. Live with nature and be sure to start some new plants. Kumara don't have eyes and can't be grown by cutting up pieces of the root. Always leave one root connected to a stalk when harvesting. For transplanting, bury the whole root. (One kumara might have fifty to seventy roots.) Yams are also found on islands worldwide. They are tasteless in comparison and have one root, at the bottom of the single plant. Kumara grow like pumpkins or watermelon, sending vines all over the ground, but then bury their roots underground. Kumara contains large amounts of beta-carotene which humans digest and turn into vitamin A. They, like carrots, bestow great night vision.

It was the existence of the kumara in Polynesia as well as Peru that drove Thor Heyerdahl to make his famous voyage on Kon Tiki. He felt that it was only logical that early Americans would carry root crops on voyages of discovery. How else, he reasoned, did the Peruvians and the Polynesians cultivate the kumara but no one else in the world? How could it be brought east about and not leave a trace in the many civilizations it must have passed through. To this day no one has been able to explain this mystery although so many called Thor a publicly seeker and charlatan. In reality, Europeans felt that how could an "inferior" race cross the huge mysterious Pacific when Europeans had such a hard time crossing the Atlantic.

In Fiji, kumara reach their cultivation peak. Each island has its own variety which they think is better than all the others. If you are cruising thru, try them all. If you are shipwrecked on an abandoned island, find the kumara beds on your first week on the island. Then when you buckle down to make your canoe, grass shack and hammock, you will have plenty to eat.

Ti

Ti plants supplied the grass skirts that so enthralled the crew of the Bounty, enough so they mutinied rather than leave paradise. But the ti plant supplies much more for the shipwrecked sailor. Not only is it a food, (boil the roots and young leaves before eating); a type of aluminum foil, (wrap food in the leaves before cooking in the fire or umu); a sterile dressing for wounds, (use the top leaf but only if it is still furled, you know, like a fern); as hosiery, (cut the leaves to form liners for your shoes especially if you have a blister); as rope, (cut the leaves into strips and weave into ropes); but also as rainwear and emergency tents. When building tents or even houses, many times locals use more than one type of thatch. Because Ti has such a hearty leaf, it is often included in grass shack construction as an inner layer.

Mashed up Ti roots make a particularly powerful alcoholic beverage. The plant stores its energy in the roots in the form of sugar instead of starch like a normal root. This eliminates one step in the brewing process. Chop up the roots and boil for an hour to, hopefully, kill any bacteria, then throw in some yeast and wait for a couple of weeks or until it stops bubbling. Allow it to settle, decant the liquid and distill. (Check out the arrack section). Be careful, Friday may not be ready for such a powerful drink. Add some coconut water to hers, unless you are ready for a very wild wahine!

Making a grass skirt for Friday is easy and it yields such wonderful scenic opportunities. Cut the leaf at the stem just at the dividing point of four leaves. Weave together one leaf with all its neighbors as the belt and let the others fall as the skirt. Use your fingernails to shred the skirt into as many strings as possible. The thinner the strings, the more alluring! When it gets dirty, make a new one, after all Ti leaves are just about everywhere on tropical islands.

Peanuts

One of my favorite memories of Papua New Guinea was when I walked through the town of Rabaul in East New Britain to get to the market. Rabaul had one of the greatest markets ever. But the best thing about it was the peanuts. These weren't peanuts from the grocery stores in the States. You know the ones, all dried up and oily. Oh, wait. You might think that that is what a peanut is supposed to taste like.

A real peanut, ones like those in Rabaul that were dug up that very morning and still had dirt stuck to the shells, and are divine. You can tell right off why peanuts are legumes rather than nuts. The freshness, the crispness and the explosion of flavor as one bites down on a fresh peanut is enough to make you a fan for life.

Anyway, on the way back to the boat, I would munch on my peanuts. I know, I had no will power. Couldn't wait till lunch. But the thing was is all the other men were eating their peanuts too. And all the women were giving their men dirty looks! It's a guy thing, OK?

The peanut plant likes the sun. When you dig up some, always leave part of a plant in the Ground. In the tropics, you can achieve three crops a year. They like calcium, so if you find your peanuts struggling after a while, mix a little coral in the soil. Not only do peanuts contain considerable proteins but also have as much health benefit as red grapes. Just for the experience, when you first arrive on your deserted isle, one way or the other, explore your surroundings. When you see an area filled with the same kind of plant, dig one up, just to see what kind of roots it has. Almost all islands were at one time or another occupied and cultivated. It would be a shame to be starving to death when you where surrounded by food all over your island. Especially if you were surrounded by the most fabulous peanuts in the world!

Daikon

Daikon or Chinese radish can be found on any island in the tropics that was once inhabited. They are very successful in warm, moist environments. They don't like the salt air but will grow near the lee side of the islands. Daikon are very important for island living as they contain active enzymes that aid digestion of starchy foods. Sorry, Survivor, but you will be eating a lot of starchy foods. Roots don't swim away, there are plenty of them and you can survive quite nicely on them. You can always get back to your Ackins diet after you are rescued!

In the 'real' world you never get to eat Daikon leaves as they yellow and die within a day of being picked. But now you can! Cook them up, especially if they have gone wild (wild Daikon have fuzzy pokers on their stem) as they do contain aggressive chemicals. Even frying in a skillet or hot rock makes them safe to eat. Non-wild Daikon roots are always colored white. Both the root (the radish) and the leaves contain high amounts of vitamin C.

Oh, you won't need vitamin C? There are plenty of fruits on the island? Fruit trees don't bear all year long. Be prepared for the tough times. There is a reason ancient civilizations spent so much of their time preserving food. You should too. Mature Daikon will last for months if you can keep them away from the insects.

Daikon take time to grow. The first year they bear white flowers that quickly turn into a seed pod. There after, the messy business of reproduction over with, they just sit there and grow. A full grown Daikon will tilt the scales at over two pounds. Amazing considering that when they were reproducing, the root would have been only a few ounces. The juice of the Daikon is very healthy and is used to cure kidney stone problems, even in hospitals. Of course, they have some scientific name for it, naturally. Think of all the money you are going to save by being shipwrecked on your island! Plus, you are going to be so healthy when you are rescued!

Lotus Flower

No, this is not the lotus that caused Odysseus in the Odyssey to fall asleep. That type of lotus was a tree in Greece (lets write a book for botanist that includes lots of unused names for new discoveries!) Our lotus came from the Hindus and then to Egypt and then to just about every place on earth that had fresh water. It is a member of the water lily family and as such is considered a very invasive weed. The flowers, seeds and roots are edible cooked or raw.

That would make a hit at a potluck! Bring your salad topped with lotus flowers! They aren't bad either, taste vaguely like watermelon without the juice. The best lotus flowers, if you are so lucky to find some, are the night blooming ones. They are really good and taste ever so much like honeysuckles. After a few days the flower goes away and a single seed takes its place.

To eat the roots, just pull the whole plant out of the water. The roots will be all muddy like, so swirl them around in the water and then cut them off and when you have time, peel 'em. The peel is very fibrous, stop peeling when you get to the softer potato like interior. Some species of locus have very bitter roots. You can still eat them, just cook them for like, forever. Best thing to do is to put the bitter ones in a umu at a luau.

A water chestnut looks almost the same and grows in similar conditions. For some reason it is related to the Eucalyptus tree! Its leaves are much smaller and when you pull it up, it has little nuts with four sharp spines each instead of roots. The water chestnut is also edible raw or cooked. Isn't the natural world strange? And to think that we had to get shipwrecked to find out how really cool the natural world is. National Geographic doesn't tell even a fraction of the good stuff. Like what you can eat when you get there!

Seaweeds

Seaweed is a difficult food source for western people to accept. They look at sea weed as a inedible plant, as something that no normal person would even think of eating. They forget that oriental people have been eating seaweed for thousands of years. They forget that before Cook's arrival Hawaiians ate over a hundred different varieties of seaweed. I guess if Johnny Seaweed Seed had walked the shores of America and Europe tossing seaweed seeds everywhere we would feel different. But he didn't and we don't. And it is to our disadvantage.

Seaweed is incredible. It is loaded with trace elements that humans need daily, it has more digestible protein, pound for pound, than beef. It is the only food that when dried still retains considerable amounts of vitamin C. If all those sailors who died of scurvy had known that all they had to do was eat some of the seaweed that was all around their ship, think of all the discoveries they would have made, all the lives that would have been saved. Sea water is very close, chemically, to human blood, (the main exception being large amounts of salt) and it is in this water that seaweed grows. In fact, one seaweed, when ground up, makes the perfect medium for researchers to explore growth of human bacteria and germs. The diseases grow in the seaweed just like they would in humans.

For us, on our deserted island, far, far from civilization, grocery stores, McDonalds and Dairy Queens, to ignore seaweed as a food source is so reckless, it may be a death sentence. We have to eat seaweed. We will eat seaweed. In fact, if you live on a boat or near the shore, go out and eat some seaweed today. Unless, of course, you don't think it is food unless it is wrapped in plastic, contains who knows what preservatives, antibiotics, curing agents and has been nuked, radiated, blasted, zapped and only the devil knows what else.

Maybe being shipwrecked on this deserted island is the best thing that ever happened to you. Either way, get your trusty machete, a bag (preferably not plastic!) and lets go collect some food!

"OK, not so fast, there buddy. Are you trying to kill off some of your fellow cruisers?" Sorry for the interruption there. That was my conscience talking. It wants me to remind you that there are some poisonous seaweeds out there. "Oh, so now you tell them!" Alright, alright. It isn't a problem. Really.

Any seaweed that has a central vein that runs up the middle AND that has side veins that branch out, you know like any terrestrial leaf, and is brown, should not be eaten. Not that you would. This type is like really yucky. It is loaded with sulfuric acid so it is only good if you want to get stains out of your grass skirt, but it is not so hot for eating!

Any seaweed that is really skinny, skinner than a piece of dry spaghetti, should never be eaten. Sometimes this evil little guy (if you want to swear, its name is Lyngbya, now if you could only pronounce it!) sneaks around and is twisted in with other seaweeds. Keep your eagle eye on alert and you will be alright. It won't hurt your fingers so unwind the strings if you want, or pick some other seaweeds. Check all foods harvested from the wild. Hell, check all foods from the grocery store, too. Those bugs get everywhere!

Other than that, all other seaweeds are harmless. Some are down right delicious. Flip ahead for some of my favorite varieties. Lots of seaweeds grow in the northern climates. They are not covered here as, one, I have absolutely no intention of being shipwrecked where it is cold and, two, as much as it is humanly possible I never sail out of the latitudes of 24°N and 24°S except for New Zealand and Maine which are very special cases. (Best blue lip mussels and blueberries, respectively, in the world, all for the taking. I mean they are everywhere!)

Anyway, back on the subject, don't worry about gathering seaweeds. As always try a little piece first before you stuff your mouth full and swallow. Better yet, unless you have recently become fond of your children, make one of them eat it first, then watch 'em for a few minutes. Hey, I was kidding! Kidding! Damn, what a tough crowd. It really is hell being a writer these days!

Nori

Nori is the seaweed that is wrapped around sushi when you buy it from the Japanese restaurant. You can also buy it in bags from oriental grocery stores. It comes in plastic bags (Oh, well!) and each sheet of pressed together nori is already roasted and seasoned. That is to hide the fact that the nori is old and rotten. Seaweed is either good fresh, good dried or both. Nori is good when you gather it yourself, dry it in the wind, in the shade, by the sea on the limb of a tree. There it can dry slowly in the salt laden air and develop that fabulous taste that created such a stir when Japanese cuisine first became famous in the West.

Only Green Nori grows in the Tropics between the high and low tide lines. It grows to three feet and is attached to the bottom rocks with a coral like holdfast. Don't pick the whole plant. Cut (or tear it, do you really want to put your machete in salt water? Check out making an obsidian knife.) it off the rock leaving four to six inches of plant so it can grow back. Then, in a month, a whole new plant for your dining experience will have regrown just for you! Nori is a flat thin seaweed with float like air filled sections here and there. Cut these out and discard. Trim any damaged sections of plant and throw them back into the sea. Seaweed isn't like an earth plant. It doesn't get any of its nourishment from the ground, everything it needs, it absorbs through its leaves. The parts you throw back into the sea are very likely to make new plants. Seaweed only has holdfasts because, well everything has to have a home, doesn't it?

Once your nori is ready, hang it up in a tree in the shade. Because it is just a thin little plant it doesn't need the power of the sun to dry. After two or three days, you have a choice. Pound it into a powder for a seasoning, toast it on a hot rock and crumble up to add to salads, or wrap some steamed veggies with it and watch your wounds heal! They just needed a few trace elements!

Limu

No Hawaiian luau would be complete without limu. From my earliest days in the islands seaweed was a natural part of my diet. For a kid, feeding myself was as easy a pie. Mangos were a dollar a pound in the stores but the streets were yellow from the cars driving over fallen fruit. Sugar cane grew wild all over the islands and starfruit trees lined the roads. What a place to grow up! The local kids were my reluctant guides but it was easy to see what natural foods they really liked. In their lunch boxes at school they would have jerk pork, poi and limu. I'm sure it was their heritage that made them such outstanding athletes, however having nourishing food to eat didn't hurt, unlike my baloney sandwiches. Eventually, as kids do, I made friends and we traded lunches. To this day one of my favorite foods is poi flavored with limu. It is ono. Whop your jaw! (You didn't know you were going to learn pigeon in reading this book, did you?)

Limu, brown while alive, grows just below the low water line anywhere it can find a place to hold on. At times huge 'forests' of limu hide the ocean floor and harvesting is just a matter of grabbing hold of the twelve inch plants and pulling. One or two handfuls and you have dinner! The leaves have a central vein. (No branches!) Cut the vein out and eat it fresh like a skinny carrot or dice it to add to your salad for a bit of tasty crunch. The leftover part of the leaves can be dried and added to any dish or stewed up fresh and added as a garnish to any meat or fish dish.

Limu is a miracle plant. The tropics are full of such plants that make all other foods taste better. If Marco Polo had discovered Hawaii instead of China, we would all be fatter! Want to spice up a dish? Wrap it in Limu or throw some on top just before serving. I know it sounds weird, putting seaweed on top of pork, but man, oh, man. Once you try it you will never look back. Besides, it is weird putting applesauce on pork, too! Open your mind, grasshopper!

Sea Lettuce

Sea Lettuce looks just like land based lettuce, or at least as close to 'real' lettuce as any seaweed is going to get. It is found one side or the other of the lowest low tide line, so on full and new moons, organize a harvest party down on the beach. Now there is a reason for a party if I ever heard one! "Hey, everyone! Let's get drunk and go down to the beach and eat seaweed!"

Sea Lettuce is easy to find. Twenty inches long, it likes to grow in protected areas between rocks or coral heads where it can't be tossed around by the surf as sea lettuce is a very fragile plant, in fact you can almost see through the leaves, they are so thin. Fragile is good as this plant is very good eaten raw. Again, as always in seaweeds, leave a little of the plant so it can grow back.

At first, it is a good idea to wash your seaweeds off in salt water. Inspect them carefully to make sure no one is living on them. Then until you get used to what your species of seaweed is supposed to look like, drench them in some fresh water. This will kill any stinging micro-organisms that might be hitchhiking. I know you like your food spicy, but mama mia, you eat a stinging zooplankton and you are going to say, "That is one spicy seaweed!"

If you harvested more than you can eat right off, dry the leaves on finely raked sand out of the wind but in the sun for a few hours turning over every hour and then brush the sand off and continue drying in the shade away from the wind until eaten. Don't let the rain get them or you will have to dry in the sun again. Really, really tasty!

When dried cut into strips and add to millionaire's salad for a feast that will knock the socks off anything that New York has to offer. Great for pot lucks when you are still in the 'real' world. Someone is sure to ask, "What is your recipe? It is so good!" Imagine their faces when you tell them!

Gulfweed

Gulfweed is the seaweed that you are most likely to encounter in the Atlantic entangled on your fishing line. I remember all the times I cursed when I pulled in the line just to discover that I had been pulling seaweed all over the ocean when I was trying to catch dinner. Little did I know then that I had caught dinner but didn't know it. This plant is found in all the oceans of the world just drifting around in oceanic currents waiting for you and your dining experience.

Its leaves are all jagged looking and has little floaty round air bladder things that hold it up on the surface. Don't eat these. The whole thing is light to dark brown, the lighter the color, the younger and tastier the seaweed. Just eat the leaves. The stalk is sometimes crisp and tasty and other times, looking just alike as the first, it is yucky. The stalk has little thorn looking parts. Don't eat these raw. If fact, the easiest way to eat gulfweed is to cut it up and add it to a soup or casserole. However, make the extra effort and dry the leaves till they are nice and crisp, then grind them up with a mortar and pestle, or in a coffee grinder. The powder is outstanding. You will give up salt. Food will taste better. Friday will become more (if that is remotely possible) amorous. Hey, what can I say, try it!

MSG was first discovered in gulfweed in 1908. MSG is a sodium salt of glutamic acid, a sister of a building block of DNA. MSG was soon produced and adulterated by a fermentation process that caused a host of negative reactions in users. However, eating the original source, gulfweed, enhances the taste buds without all the side effects.

There are four tastes basic tastes that humans experience: bitter, salty, sour, and sweet. Gulfweed doesn't enhance the individual flavor but does allow you to experience two or more flavors at once. So dry up some gulfweed and start eating some haute cuisine! Imagine gulfweed in sweet and sour parrotfish! Wow!

Spices of Paradise

Survival is based on happiness. It really is. They don't tell you that in survival magazines and books, but it is very true. If you are not happy soon you will fall into depression. Depressed, with nothing and no one to cheer you up, soon thoughts of suicide will creep in like the snake in Eden, whispering evil into your inner ear in the middle of the night. The best way to cheer yourself up is to have good, plentiful and flavorful food. For flavorful, read spicy. And the tropics are filled with spices! How lucky you are to be shipwrecked in the tropics!

Vanilla

The vanilla plant is an orchid. Its flower opens in the morning and if it is not fertilized by noon, it closes and dies and no bean will grow. The next morning another flower opens, the morning after, another and another and another. Few insects and no birds are specific to the orchid, meaning, yes, never again will you be able to say you didn't get any today. Nope, if you grow orchids, you are going to have sex every day of your life, if only with a plant!

The best way is with a Q-tip, however on deserted islands even if you had a Q-tip you would have cleaned your ears with it by now, so get a tiny little twig and crush the end slightly between your teeth, insert the end (are you breathing heavily yet?) into the long flower tube and very gently touch the tip. Do it to another flower then back again. That's it. Oh. You wanted it to last longer? Never mind, a new blossom opens every morning. Well, at least you can tell the newspapers when you are rescued that you had sex every day.

Nine months later (fitting, huh!) the pod is ready to be picked. You will know when it turns golden green on the base. The pod doesn't smell yet. Don't worry. Everyday put it out in the sun and let it sweat. Every night keep it covered so it doesn't get a chill. After about ten days of this, the pod will turn dark chocolate in color. Now you have to dry the pod for 5 months in a cool but airy place, like under an awning that is under a tree. After five months you are ready to give up sex. No, no, no. You are almost there! Drop six or nine pods into a container of alcohol (wine or arrack is good) and let it sit for another month. OK. You are ready! (Did it take too long?)

Chances are you were rescued months ago, but if you weren't, then you have made your very own vanilla for making cookies and cakes, if you had any wheat flour. Just kidding! Now you have some great vanilla to add to your bottle of arrack, just a few drops. After so much work, you know how valuable it is.

When Captain Cook visited Tahiti, he and his crew were enticed by the local wahines, not only for their beauty and sexual lifestyle, but also because of their smell. The women of Tahiti were great perfume makers. You can be too. Friday will be very, very thankful!

Start with a vanilla bean, split lengthwise, add a pinch or three of powered orange rind (cut off thin pieces of the rind, dry in the sun, grind to a powder), a splash or two of coconut oil, a splash of glycerin (see the soap making chapter) and top it off with arrack. It will be ready in a day or two. It is a very powerful perfume. If you are suddenly invaded by a tribe of husky, head hunters from the island just over the horizon and are in danger of losing your life (or at least your head), be prepared for the invaders to throw themselves at Friday's feet and elect her queen, all because of your vanilla growing.

As long as we are on the subject of seduction, don't forget to make up some massage oil. It is easy. A bit of vanilla bean, a bit of ground cinnamon (yes, there is a cinnamon chapter) and top it off with coconut oil. Massage it into sore muscles and Friday, no man will be able to resist you; but better yet, have him massage your tired muscles!

You may be shipwrecked on a deserted island, in danger of your life, struggling to keep body and soul together, but that doesn't mean you can't enjoy it! Think of the stories you will be able to tell at cocktail parties for the rest of your life, especially while wearing your own south seas perfume!

Ginger

The part of the ginger plant you eat is the root. The blossom is good for taking to the waterfall and rubbing it in your hair. It kind of suds and makes your hair smell wonderful! But only eat the unopened bud. (if that, Yuck). Young ginger roots, roots of a little plant are juicy with a great taste. As the plant grows old it is fairly bitter and dry. If you can get some juice out of it, it will be extra potent. After gathering, make sure you keep the root dry, if not it will sprout and will lose all its taste.

The ginger plant likes moist conditions with plenty of water and good soil. If your island has a creek, look for ginger along its banks. There is a belief that ginger likes sunny conditions, not true. It likes a mostly shady spot especially with morning sun.

If you want a pick-me-up during the day, carry some ginger root with you. Chew the root like bubble gum (no, it doesn't make bubbles!) and spit it out when the taste is all gone (Or stick it to the underside of your school desk). The best treat is crystallized ginger. You make this by boiling it in toddy from palm trees. (Check out the Toddy section). How long you boil it depends on how thin the slices are. Give it thirty minutes for a regular bite size piece. When you buy crystallized ginger from the store it is covered with granulated sugar. They are tricking you. What is supposed to happen is, as the ginger cools, some of the sugar from inside the root seeps out. (You can tell the quality of the maker by licking just the sugar on the outside of a piece of crystallized ginger. If it tastes like sugar instead of ginger, you have been had.)

The best part of ginger is making a marinade for your recipes. I know there are a lot of things to eat on deserted islands, but food becomes enormously important when you don't have TV, and movies, and freeways. (Wait. Forget the freeways!) You and Friday will spend a lot of time thinking about food, and inventing new ways to cook it. Ginger will become one of your favorite additions to meals. Those Chinese do know a thing or two!

Cinnamon

For many years Sri Lanka and the East India Company had a monopoly on cinnamon. The West India Company finally broke the secret and grew the spice in the Seychelles. (you didn't know the East and West were enemies back then too, did you) (Hey, I made a rhyme!) From thence cinnamon has spread to tropical islands around the world as has fake cinnamon, cassia.

Cassia, or Chinese cinnamon, has a hotter, less delicate flavor. It is much cheaper to grow, easier to harvest, and a hardier tree. Nothing is wrong with cassia. However, cassia does contain toxic components, (it eventually will destroy your liver and kidneys) so one should always limit one's usage of cassia. Cassia has a thicker, harder bark that cannot be crumbled in one hand. It is the outer bark of a tree that was discovered 400 years ago.

True cinnamon is an ancient spice. It was the secret ingredient that the pharaohs believed would keep their bodies immortal after death. Nero set a funeral pyre for a favorite wife made of cinnamon and Solomon built a cinnamon chest for his beloved's clothes to preserve her beauty. (She would breathe the fumes all day.)

True cinnamon is harvested from shoots off the side roots of the tree. Cut off the shoot, discard the outer bark and rub the inner barks against each other and leave in the sun for an hour. Split the inner bark with a blade and peel it off the shoot. Save the thin inner barks and dry them in the sun for five days, then in the shade for ten more days. When they are a light yellow color and crumbly, save them sticking the curling barks inside of one another and store in a dry cool spot. Cooler spot. Under a tree. Whatever you got.

Cinnamon was used long ago as a food preserver. It has high anti-bacterial activity that prevents food from going bad and is high in antioxidants that prevents people from going mad! Friday will love you for her cinnamon. A tea made from the dried true cinnamon leaves is reported to encourage female sexual response. On second thought, you have enough work to do. Leave the poor girl alone!

Nutmeg   Mace

Nutmeg is the seed of the nutmeg which lives inside a shell. The shell is surrounded by mace, a thin red membrane, and the whole thing covered by the pulp. Mace and nutmeg have similar tastes, nutmeg sweeter and mace, a hotter but a more mild nutmeg taste. Both are dangerous in large quantities. Eating as few as three nutmegs at one sitting is a death sentence. Wait, I can see the movie plot now!

Look for your nutmeg tree in shaded valleys that get morning sun. They like fresh water and hate salt spray. So look inland away from the sea. Wait for the nutmeg to fall to the ground to harvest them. Dry them in the sun until the seed rattles in its shell, then crack it open. In cooking, just scrap a bit into your pot for flavoring, however on deserted islands, far from hospitals the oil is the more important component.

Chop up the nut, along with any mace and stew them under low heat for a couple of hours in water. When the nutmeg is as soft as it is going to get, proceed with distillation. (See the Arrack Section for the apparatus) Oil of Nutmeg is most famous for treatment of toothaches but is just as effective in curing bad breath, (couple of drops in sugar water) and rheumatism (couple drops rubbed on per day).

If the lucky day comes and Friday is going to have a baby, (you gave her too much cinnamon tea!) be sure to massage her tummy for a month before the baby is due with five or six drops of oil a day. It eases labor contractions and encourages early dilation.

It is very important to remember that nutmeg and mace are poisons and that even though they are hallucinogenic, great care should be taken in their usage. These spices encourage a very subtle trip so just sit back and enjoy. Don't take anymore thinking that nothing is happening. It is a very bad way to go, what with convulsions, dementia and finally death. Plus, Friday will never forgive you for leaving her.

Chili Pepper

Chili Peppers have been in cultivation by humans since 7500BC, making them one of human's oldest domesticated plants. They are an incredible source of vitamins and endorphin causing capsaicin. Also, because of the high vitamin C content, humans can absorb much higher amounts of useable iron from food than without them, which is important for holding your breath under water while looking for sea creatures. (and holding your breath when the cave man next to you farts.)

Almost all islands cultivated chili pepper plants. Because insects don't like them, it is likely that many have survived without man's help(?) once the island was abandoned. They don't like salt air at all and do like lots of sun, so look for them in open fields towards the middle of the island. They never grow very big in the tropics. Three feet tall is a big bush. The peppers themselves are a dead giveaway to the identity of the bush. If you don't like hot peppers, young peppers are green and have less of a burning sensation.

Remember that the heat starts first at the stem end and the seeds and inner membrane contain most of the capsaicin. So eat the tips, discard the seeds and either scrap the membrane out of the inside or heat the membrane by spearing the split pod on a stick and holding it over a open fire for a few seconds.

The bad thing about living on a abandoned island is the food supply can be monotonous. Anything we can do to spice up meals is beneficial to our desire to live to the fullest. Oh. You don't think food is that important? You don't think that great food instills a greater desire to be creative, hard working, inventive, early rising and forward planning? All the great empires of the world were based on great cuisine. And when did the American Dream start to fade for you? With the predominance of McDonalds and other fast food eateries? Or perhaps it has returned into full flower on your deserted island?

Betel Nut

Ten percent of the world's population chew betel nut. Yes, it is a filthy habit, but smoking and chewing tobacco aren't? I have tried chewing betel nut and it didn't do much for me. But then smoking anything doesn't ring my bell either. But if you need something to get you through the day, and food, art, crafts and surviving just isn't doing the trick, keep an eye out for your friendly neighborhood betel nut palm.

Full grown the areca palm (to give its real name, rather than an alias) is fifty feet high and about eighteen inches in circumference. The fruit is the size of a small chicken egg, the nut, after you cut away the rind, is grey mixed with brown in appearance. Unfortunately, the nut is yucky if you let it fall to the ground, so just as the fruits are getting big, climb the tree and cut them down, husk 'em, boil 'em, slice 'em thin like a hard boiled egg, and dry 'em in the sun till they are black.

For chewing, wrap a piece of the nut in a pepper leaf along with a bit of lime. (In our case, pounded brain coral) (Dead and bleached white, brain coral, OK? We don't want stinging sea creatures in our mouth, do we?) Your mouth, teeth and lips temporarily turn red which will either turn Friday on or repel her depending if she likes vampire movies or not.

Which pepper leaf you use seems to be a matter of great debate. I guess if one doesn't do it for you, try another. The lime is to make your mouth drool, so when the narcotics in the nut are chewed out of the nut, there is something to swallow. Doesn't that sound great?

Supposedly, betel chewing curbs your hunger, which is good. Do you really want a drooling vampire as a dinner companion?

Hibiscus

Hibiscus is a flowering shrub that lives on just about every island in the tropics. I'm not kidding either! They are everywhere! These are the flowers that the Polynesian wahines put behind their right ear if they are "available" or their left if they are married. You know like in Hollywood, but in this case they got it right. The flowers are also good for other things than just attracting or repelling men. They make a down right fabulous tea.

Pick a dozen or so unopened buds that have turned red (I prefer red hibiscus for tea, but experiment with any color and flavor. Only the red flowers are the "true" hibiscus). Put them in a container and add boiling water. Let them steep for ten minutes or so. That's it. Hard, huh? If you like your tea sweet add some toddy, cane sugar, palm sugar or chew a miracle plant just before drinking.

Kenaf, (guinea hemp) a variety of Hibiscus, (yellow flowers with a purple center) was used during World War II as a jute substitute to make bags and cordage. We can do the same. The lower third of the plant contains the best strands, strip them from the stalk, wash in salt water and sun dry. (See tools section for instructions on rope making.)

Abelmosk (musk mallow) is another variety of Hibiscus. (Yellow flowers with red centers) Its stalk fibers were used by the Polynesians to clarify cane sugar. It seems that regular brown first stage sugar wasn't quite the thing (first stage contains large amounts of molasses), and the nobility wanted whiter sugar. Strip the strands from the stalk and put it in your bowl of liquid cane sugar for two hours before drying the liquid. (Don't wash or dry the strands first, don't ring the strands out when removing. (I much prefer dark first stage sugar, but to each castaway his own!)

Reportedly, musk mallows got their name from their seeds which are a basis for perfume. Personally, I have never found any seeds in a Hibiscus of any color, but if I was stuck on a deserted island with a reluctant Friday, I sure would be looking for them very, hard!

The Marsh Mallow variety of Hibiscus (pink flowers) were in days gone by, used to make marshmallows. (You know, like for putting on a stick, roasting it over a fire until it falls off and burns in the coals, unless you are a girl, theirs always come out beautifully toasted!) Dig up the roots, peel 'em, boil 'em in a joint of bamboo and collect the syrup that floats to the top. Mix the syrup with first stage cane sugar, (here comes the tricky part) get a stick and twirl it in the mixture until a marshmallow forms on the stick. Dry and then roast away. The best part is it won't fall of the stick as easily! Now that is progress! How about that, you had to be shipwrecked before you could toast your first perfect marshmallow!

Curry Leaf

So there you are, sitting on the beach, trying to decide what to have for dinner, and she says, "Either Chinese or Indian." You want to shout at her, you want to tell her to grow up, but then you remember, Mike Riley's 'How to Thrive on a Deserted Island', so you say back at her, "Indian, then." Isn't being a guy great? We get so much pleasure out of getting our way!

Yes, you can make curries on your deserted island. You have all the ingredients, well, except rice will be a bit hard. Coconut milk, coconut cream, grated lime peel (unless you are lucky enough to have a lemon tree), star fruit (for the tart apple), and a wild onion. That's it! Is Friday ever going to be surprised, especially if she is making it and doesn't know about the curry leaf bush you have found. Just smash them up between your hands (three or four leaves for a medium curry) and drop them in the pot when she isn't looking. Will she ever be surprised as curry leaf doesn't keep its flavor once its picked. The ones we get at the grocery store are dried and but a shadow of the flavor of a fresh leaf if you are so lucky to even have a curry leaf in the mixture. Most don't. They substitute cayenne, coriander, cumin and a bunch of other stuff, but no curry. Think how sad you will be once you are rescued and never again will you have a really good curry. (Important Hint: Gather some seeds to take home with you. They will grow in a flower pot in a sunny spot as long as you keep them well watered and then let it dry out completely before watering again..)

Not only are curry leaves tasty but they are also very healthy for oral hygiene. (Check out the Natural Medicine section for more info.)

Coffee Bush

Yes, you can still have coffee in paradise, plus preparing the beans will only increase your enjoyment of the drink. If, sorry, when, they come to rescue you and you actually leave your island paradise, are you ever going to be disappointed when you have to drink Folgers again!

Coffee was first discovered in Muslim Ethiopia where the leaders decided it was intoxicating and banned it. Of course, it instantly became popular and remains so to this day. On deserted islands look for coffee bushes high up on the mountain sides. If you are shipwrecked on an atoll, sorry, coffee doesn't like salt air.

Pick the berries when ripe, red, and bash them with a stick till the pulp is exposed. The pulp sticks to the seed so throw the beans in a pile out of the sun and let them ferment for three days. Wash the pulp off the seeds and dry the seeds in the sun. Straight out of the berry, the seeds have a moisture content of 60 to 70%, we need to get the moisture down to 10 to 15%. This might take up to two weeks. Be sure to cover the seeds during rain showers. Once dry, roast them up. Best way to do that is to build a big, intense fire on the sand. Move the fire away and keep it going. Throw the seeds on the hot sand and keep turning them. As soon as the sand starts to cool, move the fire again and put the beans on the newly hot sand. When the coffee beans become dark brown it is done. For milder coffee keep roasting till they are blackish. Then waking up in the morning will have a brand new and wonderful meaning.

Grinding the coffee beans, (the seeds have enlarged during the heating process and are now called beans) isn't easy. The best thing to do is to smash the beans with a flat rock against a flat piece of wood. The beans turn into shards. Throw the shards into cooking water and let it simmer for at least an hour. Strain the shards out afterwards or to be more traditional, sip the coffee through closed teeth spitting the shards out as needed. The best thing to heat the water in, is half a coconut shell. As long as there is water in the shell and it is on the side of the fire, the shell will not burn.

Paradise wouldn't be paradise without snakes in the trees to resist or surrender to. And coffee is the most enduring of temptations. Alright, second most enduring.

Clove

OK, it has been a long time, and you have been good, and have not smoked a single cigarette since you have been on the island, not that you had a choice or anything, after all. But the yearning just won't leave you alone. You are just dying to light up. Hurrah, you can smoke cloves!

The clove tree likes well drained land (read hillside) up in the mountains away from the salt but not cold or even cool. Harvesting the cloves for smoking is easy, they drop down to the ground when they are ready. (If you really want to try this, rake the leaves etc. from under the tree as the fruit start to fall. It isn't like they are really big or anything). Sun dried, the fruit will they look like, well, a clove! The clove will only be a fourth of the weight of the fruit.

For cooking, harvest the fruit in the tree when it turns red. It starts out very pale, almost white green. If you let the fruit fall seventy percent of the oils are lost. (Which is why you don't smoke the ones you pick. Cloves contain eighty percent eugenol oil which has powerful antiseptic and anesthetic properties. Unless, of course, you want to end up like a zombie. Hey! The next Hollywood hit, "The Zombie From the Tropics.")

In the case of toothache, use the tree picked clove and hold it in your mouth next to the bad tooth. It works really well. When one clove loses its power, pop in a new one. They don't tell you that human teeth keep growing throughout your life. If you can easy the pain, often the tooth will cure its toothache all by itself. I have had fillings fall out on abandoned islands thousands of miles from 'civilization'. On returning to the 'world' and going to the dentist, new enamel had grown in and around the inside of the filling hole. Cloves will ease the pain, so you can continue to live without agony during this process.

Cloves are smoked in Indonesia and Sri Lanka and the cigs are called kretek. In the West, cloves are mixed with marijuana to disguise the smell and to get you mellow faster. Personally, I think cloves really taste yucky, smoked. Plus they don't do a thing for me. But if you haven't had a cigarette for a while, it might help out. Ground the clove into powder, don't try to smoke it whole! I wish someone had told me that, first!

Marine Life

The sea is full of life. But without snorkeling gear most of it is out of our reach. Bummer. Here is a world of life, delicious life, and we can't get any. That is, however, not exactly true. We can catch food by the shore in the shallows and tide pools. Many things you might never think of eating are there in abundance, just waiting for you.

Sea Urchin

Sea Urchins are good eating. Just ask any Frenchmen. Hey, no French jokes, those guys know their way around a galley better than most. The part you eat is the eggs. Don't eat the guts, especially not the gills. The eggs look like fish roe. Well, they are fish roe, kind of. They taste like caviar without the salt.

There are lots of species of Sea Urchin. The urchin with big fat spines is easiest. Turn him over in your hand and break open the bottom of its shell. It is fragile, don't worry. Pick out the pieces of shell and spoon out the eggs. Boy urchins have milt which tastes terrible. Make sure yours has eggs! For spiny sea urchins, the process is more involved. Try to break off the longest spines. (They are very useful as pins, needles, and blow darts. Don't inhale!) Smash the rest of the spines with a rock. Do this in the same place on the island every time, then be careful about walking there with your bare feet!. Once it is safe, or mostly safe, turn the urchin over and proceed as above.

French or not, sea urchin eggs do take a little getting used to. But are you going to sit there starving to death while surrounded by food? Are you a survivor or just the product of your education? Does the blood of your Cro-Magnon ancestors still run in your veins? Think those guys would turn up their nose at free food? After the first three or four urchins, you'll start to like them. Of course everyone is different. I refuse to swallow a live oyster, for instance but love sea urchin roe. Maybe you will, too.

Sea Cucumber

OK, I know it looks like a big ugly worm and if you squeeze it, it squirts all of its guts out of both ends. Gross, huh? But think about this, the long gone locals didn't leave you scuba gear and spear guns and fish hooks, and Hawaiian slings or anything at all useful for killing fish. Until we can get organized, we are going to have to eat from the tide pool. You are going to need the protein just to survive, much less to do all the work this book insists you do to qualify for the 'Castaway of the Year' award. So no more bitching. Eat whatever you catch. Wounds won't heal without protein. So go on down to the tide pool and come back with a Sea Cucumber. It moves so slow, it can't run away. What can be easier?

That wasn't too bad was it? It doesn't have any teeth, it can't bite, it is an invertebrate, like a clam only tastier. Did you squeeze all the guts out back in the tide pool? No? Well, whatever. Cut it lengthwise down the middle, spread it open and wash out all the remaining guts. Skin off the four white muscles that are connected to the inside of the skin. Throw the rest away. Just keep the muscles. There, that wasn't too bad, was it? Not for your first try, anyway. If a lot of skin is still connected to the muscles, slice it off. If your machete isn't sharp enough, you better read up on machete sharpening and obsidian knifes, right?

Ok. Traditionally, Sea Cucumber is the first protein meal castaways eat as they are right there, they don't scream when you clean them and they are delicious. In the Orient, fishermen travel for thousands of miles to catch these babies. To them, they are beche de mer or trepang and are a must at the kind of fancy parties us beachcombers don't get invited to.

Best way to cook the muscles is to lay them on a hot rock by the fire for one or two minutes, or dry them and eat as a snack, or if this really is your first day, eat 'em raw. Delicious. Melt in your mouth. If you have found Friday, even better, the Chinese believe they seriously enhance sexual encounters. My Friday certainly liked them!

Hermit Crabs

On some islands, hermit crabs are everywhere. Other islands have none or just a few on this or that beach. They are a worthwhile food source if you can find some big ones. They are related to the coconut crab and are delicious, if you can get them out of their shells.

Hermit crabs are not the cleanest of animals. In fact they are filthy. When their shells become so gross that even they can't stand it, they just change shells. They are so dirty that throwing them in a pot and boiling them, shell and all will be a waste of time. Instead remove them from their shells.

Hermit crabs are very strong and if you try to pull them out all that is going to happen is they will nip you and then you will break them in half with the edible half still inside the yucky shell. Instead whistle them out. Hold the shell up to your lips, far enough away to avoid any close encounters of claws or searching legs, and whistle with a steady constant tone. If nothing happens change the tone up or down. When you have the right frequency, they will start to come out of their shell. Here comes the tricky part!

Halfway out they will reach out with their legs and grab your fingers. You now have two choices. One, ignore the pain (it is about as painful as an injection) and continue to whistle. As soon as they figure they can't move they will come all the way out to look for a new shell. Or, two, just before they start to pull at your fingers, grab them with your other hand just behind the legs and pull, hard and fast. Almost all of the abdomen will come out. Wash the tail well, and then boil in salt water for two minutes. Don't even think of eating 'em raw. Leave the shell on the beach for other hermit crabs to eat, they are cannibals.

The pinchers and legs are not worth the trouble but the 'tail' is delicious. Be sure to be modest in your harvesting, always leave a breeding population on the beach. Who really knows? Everyone might think you are dead, they have called off the search, grabbed your money and ran. You might well be on this island for a long time to come. Be responsible in your stewardship!

Conch

Conch are among the largest of the snails of the world. Stop! I am not trying to turn you into a Frenchman! These babies have lots and lots of meat in them and are just sitting on the bottom of the ocean waiting to be picked up. So do it. Go get one. Oops. You got a big one, didn't you? It is worthless to eat the little ones, in a year or two they will be huge. Get one that has a pronounced mantle, you know, the beautiful part of the shell that is pink inside that makes you go, ooh! Grown up, there should be three or four inches between the shell and the end of the mantle.

That was fun wasn't it? So now what do you do? I know you already tried to pull him out of his shell. Isn't it embarrassing when a little mollusk can beat you in a arm wrestling contest? Maybe you should have watched more Arnold movies! Don't feel bad. They are just too strong. You will understand when you see the size of the muscle we are dealing with. On one end of the shell are a series of swirls. Trace them with your finger. With the animal sitting normally, find the second swirl from the top and break the shell there. No, you can't use your machete. Stop asking that! Use a pointy rock. This will release the vacuum the conch used to beat you. Ha, you knew he had a secret weapon, didn't you? You now, still with difficultly, will be able to pull him from his shell. He has a black to brown skin that tastes terrible. Either peel the skin off by sneaking your fingers under his skin (it gets easier with practice) or slice it off with your machete.

No, you are not done. Cut the meat, from the foot crossways towards the body, in thin slices. Then pound the slices between a flat rock and a wooden club. Pound hard. Stop just before it becomes jelly!

Ok, now you are finally ready. They can be eaten raw, floured and fried, made into an awesome conch chowder, or my favorite, marinated in lime juice for a couple of hours and then ever so lightly fried on a hot rock on top of the coals. If restaurants in the cities could get produce and sea food like this, as fresh as this, they would make millions. Well, we might as well enjoy the delights of nature as long as we have to stay on our little slice of paradise.

Octopus

Octopus are a delicacy in certain parts of the world, especially in the seafood loving tropics. Stay long enough on the island and you will find you love octopus too. They are everywhere. What? Your reef didn't come with any? You've looked and looked, not one to be found? They are very good at camouflage. What you could swear is a rock might be an octopus. No sense hunting them. They are too smart. We have to outwit them.

Octopus absolutely love cowries. And of all cowries, they love the leopard cowrie the best. Look along the beach. You will find a leopard cowrie, (golden brown with white spots) if not, look along the top of the reef. All shellfish have a mantle, a living bit of flesh that comes out of the bottom and covers the outside of the shell. This disguises them, aids respiration, and allows them to better sense their surroundings. Just because you don't see a cowrie at first doesn't mean they aren't there.

You found your shell. Now you have to build a hook. Yes, you can build one out of coconut shell, or conch shell or wood. It doesn't have to be a really fancy hook as soon as the octopus sees your shell he is not going to let go, at least not till he is pulled out of the water. So here is what you do.

Lash your shell to a little piece of wood with just enough rocks stuck to it with breadfruit sap to sink the wood. On the front attach a line. On the stern attach your hook. Just an inch in front of the hook attach the cowrie shell. Toss your contraption out in front of you on the reef. Don't go deep, if it gets stuck you want to be able to free it. Slowly pull your string towards you and back up towards the beach at the same time. The octopus can see you. It has a more advanced eye than we do. But it is a greedy creature, kind of like us! Keep pulling in, keep backing up. Eventually you will feel a tug, keep pulling, a little faster now. We don't want him to discover there is no one home in our shell. Finally as the shell nears the shore give a big, huge tug and the octopus will come flying thru the air and land on the beach! Wow!

To cook them, pound them against a rock. Their skin will become slimy and peel off. If you have trouble, rub the skin with salt, let it sit for a couple of minutes and then rub the skin off. They are good cooked anyway you wish. If you are not that hungry, just cut off a leg and then throw the octopus back into the sea. He will regenerate completely inside of six months and is great at holding his breath.

Inside the octopus is an ink sack. Keep this when cleaning the animal. It can be used just as it is for keeping a log book or writing a best seller about your tropical experiences. You might be on your way to being a millionaire!

Pipis

Pipis are like snails are on land. They are everywhere, they taste good if you spend a lot of time preparing them, and you get plenty of meat for not a lot of work. If you don't like the idea of escargot, couldn't imagine yourself eating one even if you were starving to death, this might not be the dish to learn about. But if you are in for the adventure, in for the thrills, give it a try.

Pipis are everywhere, really! But the ones you want are on the windward side of the island just inside the reef. These babies get all the good food, the ones on the lee side of the island are eating everyone else's leftovers. Look for them hanging on to rocks. Go at low tide. Pipis don't do a lot of moving around. If the tide goes out, they don't go looking for the water, they just wait for it to come back.

No need to flush them out like clams or land snails. Just throw them on the coals enclosed in wet leaves and bury them in a thin layer of sand. Give it an hour, pull out the leaves and tease out the animal from the shell. Cut them in half, lengthwise, and discard any guts and especially intestines from the creature. When they are all prepared dump them into a joint of bamboo along with coconut milk, a leaf or two of limu, and a nice red chili. Cook them for at least another hour.

While they are cooking cut some limes in half and get ready for a great taste treat.

There are those who believe that they taste best straight from nature. They pull them from the reef and suck them from the shells. All I can say is UCK! On the plus side, for some reason shell fish never suffer from ciguatera. So if the fish on your island are contaminated, fear not, eat the shellfish. That includes lobster, octopus, clams, oysters and yes, pipis!

Clams

Clams are easy to catch when walking along the beach. Wade along at any tide when there isn't a lot of surf and look for a pair of eyes about two feet deep. Really! Clams in the tropics don't spurt like they do up north, but they are still bivalves. That means they have an eating hole and, well, the other kind. And being a bivalve, both valves are right next to each other. What they do is poke their two holes just barely above the surface of the sand and eat and poop (not in unison!) That is what clams do, after all. They are filter feeders.

Everything likes to eat clams. And the clams know it. If you come tromping through the water, splashing, talking, singing, looking for fish, you have very little chance of even seeing a clam. Take your time. Move slowly. Watch for the eyes. They are right next to each other. Think of a very small owl with very black eyes with lashes. Once you see one, move quickly. Clams can dig over a foot in ten seconds. Bring your hands down into the sand on either side of where the eyes were (the second you move the clam will start digging madly) and scoop him up. It is even easier if you have a mask and snorkel. They love to hang out in about ten feet. Hundreds in just a few meters. When you catch 'em put the clams is a tidal pool to spurt out their sand, but be sure to cover them with a leaf or the booby birds will eat them all up. Careful about starfish too. They love to eat clams!

Giant clams are protected world wide, but if you are like, starving to death, it comes down to the survival of the fittest. Don't try to pick one up alive. Once they close their shells there is no opening them, even if a finger or hand is inside. Slide your machete in close to one side (they won't see you coming) and saw the abductor muscle in half. It is very large and will take a while. (Make sure the machete goes all the way in, as once the shell closes, it is either leave the blade or cut the muscle. You won't be able to pull out the machete.) Once the muscle is cut (one on each side) pry the shell apart and cut the muscle off the inside of the shell on both sides. (Make sure the muscles are cut in half, first!) Don't eat the lips or guts unless you are very hungry. But the abductor muscle is great! If it took a while to cut the muscle you might have to pound it like an abalone. Whatever, it is a true taste treat on a lonely deserted beach, far, far from officials! Keep the shell for making salt!

Land Crabs

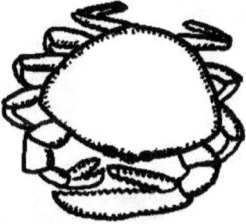

You are a survivor, aren't you? You wouldn't be reading this book if you weren't, right? Nevertheless, if you are squirmish when faced with nature, bloody fangs and all, don't read the following. Give it to your teenage boy to read. He will love it. It is important survivor information, so I include it here.

Land crabs live on almost all tropical islands. They are a very successful life form. There are many species but in all, the males have one big fighting claw (for fighting off other males for the girls) and one smaller eating claw. The fighting claw is often twice as long as the crab is wide, and if the boy loses his claw in combat, his little eating claw becomes the new fighting claw and he grows a new eating claw.

I was taught this by some marines undergoing SEAL training on a little island I anchored off of. They adopted me as I had beer on board and they decided to considered me a sea creature so they could eat on my boat. (I wonder what the drill sergeant thought when these marines came back fat and sassy?)

Anyway, hold down the crab with the flat side of your machete and try to break off his fighting claw. That sounded easy didn't it? Once, it took five really tough marines and me, working together, just to subdue one little crab and he managed to wound all of us! The Marines as hungry as they were (as they were supposed to be) refused to kill the crab first. He was just defending himself. It was not only a matter of honor, but of practicality. The only reason we wanted him was because of his big claw. If we killed him we would take his big fighting claw out of the gene pool and the next year's litter (do crabs have litters?) would have smaller claws. Not good especially after you have tasted these babies.

Forget Maine lobster, forget swordfish, forget Alaskan King Crab, these little island land crabs are so good you will be addicted for life. Plus they are huge! We are talking about a little four inch crab with a claw that will fill you up! No butter, no marinade. Just pure crab that is so, so good. Just boil the claw in water for a few minutes.

But don't forget, no matter how hard they fight, don't kill the crabs. How long are you going to be on this island anyway?

Freshwater crawdads

I know, you are on a deserted island and there are lobster carapaces on the beach, you know they are out there, waiting for you, but without a mask and snorkel, it is going to be tough going. Eventually you will make a spear, build a torch, design some shoes and go out on the reef at night for lobsters. But in the meantime, consider the lowly crawdad. Yes, it is a poor man's lobster but there can be a lot of protein in them and the way you are working during the first month on this deserted island, you are going to need more protein to build all the new muscles you are using. Don't be proud, eat crawfish.

Crawdads or crawfish live in freshwater streams and grow from three inches long to nine pounds and 27 inches (in Tasmania, way south of 24°). They hide under rocks and logs during the day, coming out at night to feed. They are easy to catch. If you have a high pain threshold, put your hand under likely hiding places. Crawdads are very aggressive and will attack you with their Maine lobster like claws. When they bite close your hand around them, pull them out and toss them into a container. (Well, pry their pinchers off your hand and toss them in to the container!) You can capture a good meal in a half an hour this way. If you are squirmy about being bitten, make up a net out of brown coconut webbing and scoop under logs with it. You will get an occasional crawdad to supplement you dinner. The best way of all, is to come back at night when they are walking around and scoop them up as they walk around. Their eyes reflect the light from your torch (check out the candlenut chapter) or flaming stick from the fire.

They are small but good eating. Boil 'em up in a joint of bamboo till they are a bright red. Discard the body, especially the gills which are terribly poisonous, and eat up the tail. Just like lobsters the taste improves if you remove the intestine that runs the length of the tail. If you really want to make a great meal, boil 'em first then stew them in coconut milk with just a squeeze of lime and a just the tip of a chili pepper. Friday will elect you cook after this meal, so make sure she thinks it was her idea, and that she does at least some of the work. Don't worry, after the first bite, next time she will do it all! (Girls, as Karen often tells me, have a much higher pain threshold than men!)

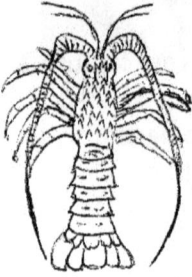

Spiny Lobsters

Why not dine in luxury on your island? You could sit around and eat what easily comes to hand, but why not dine well? Why not eat

lobsters? They are easy to catch if you were born on a solitary island and never heard of a face mask and snorkel. But we weren't and have. Without a mask there is like no chance in hell of catching a lobster by diving. But humans are surprisingly good at stealth. You wouldn't think so would you? But we are.

What you are going to do is walk on the reefs at night during a full moon. (Lobsters like to eat at night. During the new moon they eat during the day.) You will need a spear made out of a sharpened stick at least eight and a half feet long (the length of a javelin). Harden the pointy end in the fire. You will need a torch (Candlenuts will do) and some kind of foot protection. Polynesians walked the reefs at night barefooted, but they had seriously tough feet. Don't try it. Imagine the fire coral, sea urchins with three inch spines, moray eels, whatever. Let's wear some kind of shoes, OK?

The lobsters eyes will ignite with the reflection of the light from your torch. They will just stand there and stare at the light until they see you, then they are history. Be sneaky. Keep the light in front of the spear. Polynesians just stepped on them, waited till they stopped struggling, and picked them up. (Remember the tough feet.) We are going to spear them just behind the eyes. We are not, repeat, not going to pick them up in our hands. The tail of a spiny lobster has very sharp appendages that act like razor sharp scissors when the tail curls shut. If a hand or finger is around the tail then it will be severely shredded if not amputated. Lets just spear the buggers, OK? If it is off season, when the females have eggs, make yourself a little noose out of the spine of a coconut frond leaf. Extend it just behind the lobster and she will back up through it as you approach. Tighten the noose after the tail goes through but before the legs. People will tell you that lobster roe is delicious. Not to me. I would rather have baby lobsters walking around the reef next year.

For cooking, wrap them in seaweed and then leaves and throw them on the fire for five or ten minutes. Don't worry about butter, sauce or whatever, a fresh caught lobster is delicious. If you need a change, sauté them in coconut milk with a little arrack. (With all that protein, you and Friday are going to have a party to end all parties. Might as well skip ahead to the arrack chapter right now!)

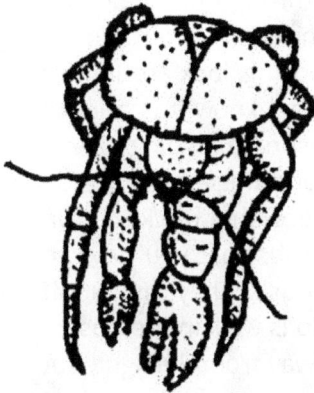

Coconut Crabs

Coconut crabs are a type of land crab that got hold of an exercise book. You know, if you are a 99 pound weakling, become a stud in five easy lessons. They are crabs on steroids. If they weren't absent on the day God was handing out brains they would be ruling the world. However, they are a feast on legs. Grab one of these and guaranteed it will be a night you never forget.

Before we get carried away, you should know that these crabs are protected by every agency on earth, so before you tackle one, look around carefully for agents hiding behind trees. Tackle is the right word. They are very, very strong; they can amputate a finger in a split second; they can seriously wound a leg or arm. A friend got one and put it in a burlap sack and slung it over his back to return to camp. He lost five inches of flesh and muscle. Don't take these babies lightly.

Coconut crabs are nocturnal. During the day they hide in deep holes under the ground or under fallen trees. Their holes always have a back door, so have Friday try to loosen a leg from the back door while you pull on a branch that the crab is slowly demolishing with his eight inch wide (not long) claws! Their legs are each the size of a woman's wrist so it won't be an easy battle. Never, never, never reach in and try to grab a leg. Never, OK? These guys are over a meter across the claws and weigh over forty pounds. Don't put your one and only machete down their hole, you might not get it back!

OK, so, finally, you won the battle and you still have all your fingers and toes. Congratulations! I know, you are lying on the beach exhausted from the battle, but congratulations! Burn the fire down to a nice bed of coals, wrap your crab in a swath of banana leaves just after killing him with a machete straight through his brain (His flesh starts rotting immediately (within minutes) after death, destroying his incredible flavor). While he is cooking, look around for a way to break open his armor plate shell. Yes, I know it is a lot of trouble, but wait till you eat him! There is a reason he is going extinct in most of the world. The only place he is found these days are on deserted islands. Damn, you are lucky you got shipwrecked! On deserted islands there are so many coconut crabs that you have to be very careful walking in the bush at dawn or dusk. They can cut off a toe as easy as pie. One really neat thing to do is walk in the bush a night. The huge crabs in front of you will shy away from the light, but then crawl back behind you, closing off your escape route. Scary! Don't even think of falling! And what if the light went out?

Parrot Fish

Parrot fish are the most inquisitive fish in the sea. If you are wading around the top of the reef with your little javelin (see Tools), they will come around to see what is what. Parrot fish have excellent eye sight, even from water into the air. Once they see your little hunter's hat on your head and the spear in your hand, you won't get within ten feet of them. They have the reactions of a kung fu master so it is of no use throwing your spear at them in the water. They are just too quick. Instead throw a rock or a stick near them and they will jump into the air to get away.

Could you qualify for the javelin throw in the Olympic Games? If they judged for accuracy, you would win hands down after living on your island for a while. You can hit a rapidly moving fish flying in the air, you can! Don't think about it. Just throw the damn spear. You will be surprised how natural the whole thing is. Genetic memory comes to the rescue!

Yes, you can eat parrot fish. They are one of the safe fish to eat as they are primary eaters of the coral which is the home of ciguatera. It takes predators to eat the parrot fish, which then get eaten by other predators to reach a concentration dangerous for humans. By the way, ciguatera does not make a fish act crazy. It is a human disease. It doesn't hurt the fish. Most of the poison resides in the liver of the fish. Don't let the viscera touch the meat of the fish.

Remember how they taught you to clean fish in Sea Scouts? It was all wrong. Don't open the body cavity. Don't let your machete or obsidian knife touch the gills. Don't clean the fish, just remove the filets. Cut the top of the fish on either side of the dorsal fins, cut down to the backbone. Slice behind the gills, behind the pectoral fins, down to the backbone. Slice down by the tail to cut the lateral bones above the backbone and cut through the ventral side of the fish to start removing the fillet. Continue towards the anus (by the forward most ventral fin, then stop. Remove the meat and discard the skeleton. The body cavity is never exposed to air or touched by your blade. Always do this for all fish. Unless you like to eat guts and other yucky stuff when what you want, is to eat pure fish meat? Living on a deserted island is not a good time to get sick. Practice makes perfect, why not start practicing cleaning fish properly now?

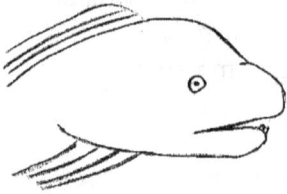

Moray eels

Moray eels are delicious but dangerous. They hide in small caves throughout the reef, including under small coral heads atop the fringing reef. Make it a habit to bend over and look under rocks when looking for food on the reef. I don't advise lifting the rocks with your hands however. Morays do not have a poisonous bite but their teeth are so loaded with bacteria that infection is evitable. Morays also have backward slanted teeth which makes it impossible for them to release their prey if the prey, you, is fighting to get clear. As a result, if a moray bites your finger, and you pull your hand away, your flesh will be sliced into ribbons. Because of their bacteria and your lack of powerful antibiotics, the best thing to do at that point is to amputate your finger. Failure to do so could easily lead to death from gangrene. Adding to the danger of their main teeth, morays have a second set of teeth in their throat which are thrust forward when attacking ever so much like the monster in the Alien movies. It is the only known creature on earth to have 'alien' jaws.

Morays are delicious. They do have lots of small bones, so the best way to cook them is in an umu (Hawaiian underground oven). After a few hours in there the entire skeleton can be removed in one piece. Morays share with groupers and barracudas a high likelihood of being contaminated with ciguatera. This is because the spend their lives eating smaller reef eating fish, and they live a long time. There are other eels on the reef, the white eel being the most common. He seems to have no teeth, but that is only because his teeth are smaller than the Moray's impressive dental work. White eels are down right great eating, but share all of the morays other negative traits. In some species of both eels, the mucous on their skin contains a toxin which scientists are still struggling to understand.

Perhaps, the best thing to do on your island, is to leave the eels alone. Yes, they taste good. The morays probably think the same thing about you!

Chitons

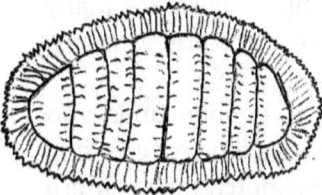

Chitons are everywhere on some reefs, and don't exist on others. They are an abalone type creature that wears its shell on its back and hugs the rocks with its bare foot. When the tide goes out, the chiton doesn't hide. He just sucks himself onto the rock and waits for the water to come back. Like the abalone, he is delicious and very difficult to remove from the rock. The best thing to do is to wait quietly till he is moving then quickly slip the point of your machete under his shell and flip him over onto his back before he knows what is going on. To cook them, turn them on their back and squeeze some lime juice on the foot. After an hour, pry them out of their shell, clean the guts out, slice them thin and then pound them till they are soft, much like an abalone.

Chiton have one of the most beautiful shells in the animal kingdom. They used to be made into gorgeous earrings in days gone by. As long as you don't have anything else to do on your deserted island, you might as well make Friday happy exercising your artistic talent!

Cones

No, not the ones we used in driving class, Cones are shellfish that have a wicked barbed stinger that fires with incredible swiftness from the end on the triangle like shell. Never pick any shellfish up by the ends. Always grab them around the middle. There are many species of shell fish, most are edible. Because there are so many, let's not pick the dangerous ones, OK?

Just when you thought you know how to handle cones, you should know that there are some shells that have a little notch along the side on the shell along the lip. Through this notch they can fire an equally evil stinger. So don't pick them up by the ends, don't pick them up around the middle area of the lip. Maybe we just shouldn't pick them up? There are lots of other shellfish in the sea.

Other Foods

People out in the wilderness have to do what it takes to survive. You can't let lessons learned in civilization guide you now, at least as far as what is proper to eat. Eat what you can. Stay healthy. Become the master and ultimate predator of your island. If you have to force yourself to eat some of the following, remember without food you will die. Plus you will get like very bored. (Sorry, as a youth I had this thing about California teenage surfer girls. It took many years to exorcize it from my brain.) It may be that I have not been totally successful.

Termites

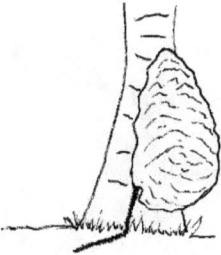

Termites are a great food source, high in protein, easy to gather, renewable with no planting, watering or weeding involved. In times of storm or shortage, we have to be resourceful in our choices of food on our deserted island. Plus, they don't taste all that bad, a bit like a cross between carrots and celery. Really! Just pop them in your mouth and eat them raw. Think of all the vitamins! No, they don't crawl around inside your mouth or bite your tongue.

So what you do is go up to your termite nest and punch a hole in it. No big deal. The walls are very thin. Inside are hundreds of passages with thousands of termites. Insert your hand and scoop out the internal walls and termites. Squeeze a bit, then open your hand and lightly blow all the mud walls away and pop all the remaining termites into your mouth. Yum! What a nice snack! And much better for you than a candy bar! The good part is by the time you come back the next day the nest and walls are rebuilt, and new delicious termites hatched. All ready for another healthy and nutritious snack.

If there are hundreds of termite nests all around your shack, take termite eating to the next level. The most delicious part of the nest is the queen. She is full of eggs and is gigantic compared to the workers. However to get to her you will be attacked by the warrior termites who practice chemical warfare. They try to spit acid in your eyes! Yikes! To avoid being blinded for life, (or at least wearing facial scars for years) pry the nest off the tree and throw it into the sea. Termites are not swimmers, can't hold their breath and hate salt. It will only take ten minutes to drown the whole nest. Drag it back to the beach, cut the nest apart until you find the queen right in the middle. She will likely be covered with dead defending termites. Throw her in a pot and boil her for ten minutes. She tastes like scrambled eggs.

Termite eating is a normal thing to do in primitive societies. If things get bad on the island during the rainy season, we have to get primitive too. But the best part of all, is telling everyone after you got rescued, that you ate termites for dinner!

Bird Eggs

I know, birds are so cute and the baby eggs are darling, but you have to remember how many chicken eggs you might have eaten in your life. Eggs are a traditional food source for islanders. Up on the upper cliffs on the central peak if you are on a tall island, the terns live and thrive. Good for them. I say let them live. Not for humanitarian reasons, but because you will have to risk life and limb to get at those well protected eggs.

If you want to be an egg gatherer, watch the skies for boobies. These are large sea birds which gained their nickname, gooney birds, on Midway Island during WWII when they insisted on flying into the path of incoming planes and nesting on the runways. Not that they are stupid, wait, I take that back, they are less than bright. On some abandoned islands in the Pacific where American Forces built airfields in their leap frog attack on Japan, the airfields have now become the exclusive property of the boobies. On those islands, egg gathering is a pleasure.   The hermit crabs have turned into an army and travel from
one end of the runway to the other and then turn around and go back again eating any eggs they can get their claws on. One or two hermit crabs would easily be handled by the boobies but faced with an army, they just move to another part of the runway and have another egg. More intelligent would be to build a nest elsewhere on the island, but these are boobies after all. They got the low end of the stick when it came time to hand out brains. The advantage for us, the egg gatherers, is we know which eggs have just been laid. They are the ones just behind the advancing army. Fresh eggs are ever so much nicer to cook with, much nicer than cracking open an egg and having a half grown chick fall out.

We can do the same thing on any island on a lesser scale. Boobies like flat areas to build nests as they are terrible at landings and take offs and need all the help they can get. It's likely that on your island the hermit crabs have not yet unionized into an army but still we find them searching thru the breeding grounds for rotten eggs in a ragtag group. Follow behind them looking for new nests. Don't be shy in picking up the Booby mothers to look under them. They have absolutely no fear of man. Lift them off their nest by the neck, lift their eggs up to the sun to candle them. (Hold them up to the sun to see the shadow of whatever is inside.) If it has a growing yolk inside, replace the egg and plop the mama back on her nest. You haven't hurt her, she won't be fussed you touched her egg. These are boobies, after all. Boobies are used to diving into the water at speeds up to fifty miles an hour, hundreds of times a day.

They are as indestructible as any of God's creatures. No wonder He made them stupid; otherwise they would be ruling the earth. The eggs you found will continue to develop so use them within a day. Need eggs later in the week? Go gather more then. They will still be there. No matter what time of year it is, there will always be food to eat on tropical deserted islands. Isn't that great? Well, except in storms.

If you do want to add adventure to your life, wait till the terns or swiftlets nesting in the cliffs on high islands have finished breeding and left for the year. Then suspend yourself with the ropes you have made and collect their nests. These are the main ingredient for bird nest soup. Boil the nests in water and be prepared to be amazed! Interestingly, swiftlets are the only birds that use echo-location (like bats) to find their way in the large caves on tropical islands.

Turtles

There is this big myth that turtle eggs are supposed to be this delicious wonder food. It isn't true. They can't even be cooked as eggs, they don't fry up, don't bake well, if fact they are pretty useless as an egg. As a food source they are very important, but not as an egg.

Personally I have a problem with harvesting turtle eggs as I hate jelly fish. I really do. And turtles eat jelly fish. Turtles are friends, not food to paraphrase Nemo's shark friend. However, if you are starving to death and you find some turtle tracks going up the beach early in the morning, here is what you do.

It is worthless to try to dig holes to find the eggs. Turtles haven't been around since the time of dinosaurs without being tricky. Instead of digging, find a thin strong stick, carve a point on the end and push the point into the sand around the tracks. When the stick hits the nest it will break some of the eggs (they don't have a shell, but a leather like membrane covering them) and the wood spear will come up covered in sand stuck on with egg glue.

Generally the mother turtle goes to some length to lay down false trails so put on your Sherlock Holmes hat and go sleuthing. The nest is usually two to five feet under the sand and the top sand is almost always smoothed over to look untouched.

The best way to eat turtle eggs is in soup. Heat up some water and when it is close to boiling, cut the shell (they don't crack) and dump the insides into the water while stirring. Add whatever other ingredients you have handy and you will have yourself a fine meal, as long as you can digest it with a belly full of guilt!

Turtles are a good protein source. Their meat doesn't dry well and a turtle might tip the scales at fifteen hundred pounds, so you and Friday better be mighty hungry if you eat one of these babies. Please don't tip an egg laying mother over on the sand and eat her. She is a breeder. Find a small turtle on the fringing reef. Don't kill more than you can eat. Don't eat more than you need. Don't need more than the day requires.

Salt

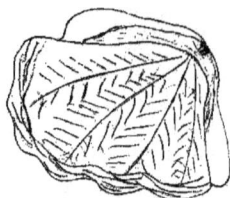

We are lucky, living on a deserted island, because we have lots of salt. In the Himalayas in the past, long ago, salt was a precious commodity that sold for the value of a sheep for a pound of salt, mostly because the salt train started in India on the other side of the tallest mountains on earth. For us, we are surrounded by salt, liquid salt, for us salt is everywhere.

But how can we turn the liquid into dry crystal salt like in the grocery store? The Polynesians, as usual, do it the best. They collect large shells, usually giant clam shells, cleaned and dried, and lay them around the cooking hut angled up like a basin, and fill them with salt water every day. Whenever they want salt, they just let one shell dry out that day, take as many pinches as they wish, and when it is empty, fill it with saltwater again. Easy, hey?

The salt we make this way is sea salt (naturally) the most healthy of salts, full of the trace elements that are so important to good health. Besides cooking with salt we are also going to preserve food with it for those nasty wild days during hurricane season (unless, of course, we get rescued first!).

Generally it takes two or three sunny days for all the water to evaporate from the shell. Don't worry about rainstorms. The fresh water will float on top of the brine and if the shell overfills with rain, only the fresh water will spill out.

I first experienced collecting salt this way on one of the outlaying islands of Indonesia. Beautiful young teenage girls did the collecting and filling of the shells. All the young men of the island followed them around gazing in awe as they tossed their ankle length, long hair out of the way before leaning over to fill each shell. I followed too as I was in my early 20's and single handing. For some reason the men were not aloud to speak, just stare, well, maybe drool a bit. Or else they were speechless! Of course in those days, I really liked salt, that must have been it. That is why I followed the girls around. Cruising is such a great experience. A real eye opener!

Chickens

Every tropical island of halfway decent size always has chickens on it, but you wouldn't know it. Wild chickens are fey creatures and difficult to see much less catch. They are great fliers and yet spend most of their time running around on the ground along little trails that they built that go under every fallen tree on the island.

They aren't plump like store bought chicken and tend to be tough and gamey, but never the less, they are chickens. The best time to spot them is at dusk when the fly up into the trees to hide for the night. Once you know about where they are, look for their trails and set a few snares. Don't be disappointed if you don't meet with immediate success. Just get trickier with your snares. Wild tropical chickens don't sit on their eggs. They lay them in the sun and let them hatch by themselves. Every day the hen will pass by to check on her egg. If you find an egg on the ground, don't touch it! Set up a couple of snares around the egg and hope for the best.

Actually the very best chicken catcher is a Jack Russell Terrier, but it is unlikely that you stowed one of them in your ditch bag so you will just have to do it the old fashion way!

Once you have your chicken, once you have cut his throat and hung him upside down to drain all the blood, pull out all the big feathers. Under the big feathers is a matt of downy feathers that are nigh on impossible to remove. Either swing the chicken into the fire on a rope tied to his legs to burn off the feathers or throw him into a boiling water for one minute. The feathers will be easy to remove then. My favorite method is just to skin the bird, but you do loose all that delicious skin. You don't eat the skin? Have you ever been starving to death hungry on a deserted island before? You may find you will be willing to eat things that would make your nose turn up in a city full of fast food joints that, in reality, sell things much worse than gamey chickens.

Flying Foxes

Flying foxes are fruit bats that grow to sixteen inches in body length with a wing span of five feet. They rely on vision rather than echo location as their prey are flowers and fruit. Their range has increased in recent years from southeast Asia and Madagascar to cover all tropical Indian Ocean islands and coastal lands and have also spread into the Pacific to Fiji and the Caroline islands.

They feed at night and sleep during the day, hanging upside down from shady trees or rocky overhangs. They can rarely be approached during the day but the ancestral Madagascar natives used breadfruit sap as a glue on the bat's preferred sleeping spots. Today in the Western Pacific flying foxes are always featured on the menus in high class restaurants. If you have foxes on your island you should make an effort to enjoy a fancy dinner.

Most wild mammals are infected with fleas and ticks. As soon as you have captured and cut the throat of your fox (Bleeding is important in mammals) roast him whole in the fire for a minute to rid him of pests. Afterwards prepare him much like a rabbit. Skin, discard feet, wings, guts, feet and head, and boil and roast for 'normal' tasting meat or just roast for a venison taste. I could tell you that they taste like chicken, but they don't. They taste like flying foxes. They are always the most expensive entrée on the menu. If you find such a restaurant, try 'em. If you have 'em on your island, enjoy a meal that will knock your socks off.

Flying foxes have no natural enemies. Do your island a favor, eat a few foxes just to kill off the less successful bats. At least now, you will have a better chance at finding ripe fruit still on the tree.

Cooking Methods

I'm sure you have been dying to read this chapter. After all we have built houses, lit fires, (you have peeked ahead, haven't you?) caught marine life, picked seaweeds, harvested veggies, netted foxes, but how are we going to cook all of the food we have gathered? Or are we going to survive cave man style and just throw it on the fire.

Somehow on picking the island we happened to get shipwrecked on, we forgot to order the one with all the pots, pans, ovens, rotisserie, silverware, mixing bowls and the like. So there we are, stuck in the middle again. Finally we found some wild grains but what are we going to do, throw it on the fire and look for the grains in the sand and burnt wood later? Are we just going to burn everything to a crisp in the fire? Isn't there hope of making soup or a nice bouillabaisse? Are we going to eat everything raw? Isn't there any hope for haute cuisine?

Fear not fellow explorer, adventurer and beachcombing castaway. Help is on the way!

Cooking food in Bamboo

If you are ever rescued, sorry, when you are rescued, you will regret cooking for the rest of your life. You are about to be spoiled rotten. You are about to be introduced to a delicacy rarely enjoyed in this civilized world of ours. And you are going to do it on your little fire on the beach on an island in the middle of an ocean, somewhere in the back of beyond.

When you are exploring the island keep and eye out for stands of bamboo. Oh, you already did that in building the hut? OK. But now we are going to use bamboo to cook with. Cut a section off of a fairly large yellow stalk (3 or 4 inches wide) cutting below any joint and then just barely below the joint above. Dump any water out into a coconut bowl for use later. The inside of green and yellow bamboo sections has a membrane lining the walls. It can be poisonous, often it isn't but just for fun, scrape it out with a stick. It comes out easy. Wash it out with seawater and we are ready to start. Every bamboo stalk will have twenty or more such 'pots'.

Collect some banana leaves (Any leaves can be used instead of the banana. In Indonesia, the locals use papaya leaves as they impart a resistance to malaria. In Polynesia, Ti leaves are used as often as papaya) and place your food in the middle of the leaf before folding it over and carefully shoving it down inside the bamboo tube. (We are making a lining for the food and we don't want any to escape.) Add one and a half times (allowing for steam and absorption by the bamboo) as much water by volume as there is food, (Too much water is way better than too little) add whatever other flavors you might think of. A little dried seaweed would be good, a little coconut milk added instead of water, a piece of fish or lobster, a slice of mango. The island is your larder, your imagination provides the spice, your taste buds get the enjoyment.

Stuff a few more of the banana leaves into the top of the bamboo. (Don't cover completely with the top of the bamboo. We really don't want our bamboo to explode!) and stick the bottom of the tube into the coals of a fire. (Coals, not a living flame!) It will take longer to cook than on a stove at home. But boy, will it taste better!

When it is done, when the steam is no longer coming out of the top as quickly, when the fire has turned the bamboo black (it won't burn as long as there is water in the tube), remove from the fire and carefully slice down both sides of the bamboo. Don't cut into the banana leaves. It will be very, very hot. Let it cool and then slice open the leaves and enjoy a nectar of the gods.

Many foods can be cooked in your bamboo pots. If you get tired of having roasted sweet potatoes, throw them in and boil them.

Add your seafood, veggies and sauce and make a really great bouillabaisse. And guess what the best part is? No dishes! Throw your pots on the fire and jump on the hammock for a rest after a job well done.

Cooking on a stick

Let's get down to basics now. Cooking caveman style is a favorite of every kid who grew up roasting hot dogs and marshmallows over an open fire. Such techniques have been little improved since you were a kid. The only thing we have to look for is to make sure the type of wood we use as a skewer is not poisonous, and to not cook over a roaring fire. Successful survivors let the fire burn down to a bed of coals then move the still half unburnt logs a few feet away to start a new fire going and to create a new future bed of coals. Food is just too hard to come by and takes too much of our day harvesting to just drop it into a roaring fire after the twig we are holding burns through and our dinner turns into a sacrifice to the gods who, after all, marooned us here in the first place.

Most food is cooked more efficiently boiled in water or coconut milk, baked in an underground oven, fried on a stone in hot coals or dried in the sun than cooked on a stick. But a lot has to be said for the pure fun of holding a piece of food over a living fire on a skewer. And the truth of the matter is if you don't have fun you are not going to survive for long. We are the otters of the primates, the ape that laughs, the noble savage smiling at a fresh kill (if not roaring and beating his chest!), the animal that sacrifices good food to a distant God. Make sure you laugh everyday that you are shipwrecked, even if you have to play practical jokes on yourself!

Good skewers are hard to come by. Forget any evergreen, any piece of wood that smells piney when the bark is stripped off. Ignore any branch that is too bendy or any wood that snaps in half easily. I like to carve the butt end of the center part of an old coconut frond. They truly are fire resistant. Don't carve them too thin.

It is really fun to cook bread this way. Wrap the dough around your branch and hold it over the fire. Make sure Friday is watching so she knows who cooked!

Making your own luau

It isn't hard to make a luau, you know like in Hawaii. Hawaiians had the same problems back then, before the white man came, as we do now on our deserted island. No metals. They got around it by using steam. Here is how you can cook on a deserted island, Hawaiian style, of course as always, with modifications. Don't forget the leis!

There are two difficulties we are going to face, digging a big enough hole and finding the right rocks. Oh, so you think it is easy to dig a hole in the sand? Ha! Try it! First, the edges are always falling in when the hole starts to get deep, you can't throw the sand far enough out of the hole to keep it from falling back in and third, the water level isn't that far under the sand on a beach. We don't want water in our hole, we want to steam things, not half boil them. The Hawaiians got around that by making their luaus in earth, not sand. We could do that if we had shovels, picks and a diesel back hoe. Have I told you NOT to use your machete for stupid things like digging holes and chopping down huge trees to make a canoe? I haven't? OK. Don't do it. Without your machete, life is going to become very hard on the island, indeed. It was a gift from the gods, given to you on your first day on the beach. Don't abuse it.

The second difficulty we are going to face is finding the right rocks. What we are going to do is heat rocks up in the fire and then bury them with our food wrapped in wet leaves. Sounds great doesn't it! The only problem we face is rocks have a bad habit of EXPLODING when heated. Violently! Sure, that is all we need. There we are sitting around the fire heating our rocks, having a sing-a-long with Friday and rocks start exploding and we are blinded for life by rock fragments with the nearest hospital in the next galaxy for all the help we are going to get from it.

What the Hawaiians did was gather a certain kind of lava. This lava looks just like a smooth granite like rock. No. that isn't a stupid thing to say. Most lava is all jagged looking. Most lava rocks have big holes where the molten lava released gases while it was cooling. This kind of lava will explode when heated with dramatic results and razor edged fragments! The rock kind of lava has no holes and a smooth surface. This is the kind we have to be on the lookout for as we explore our island. It will be up on the lava flows, in the middle of the flow, not on the edges. It really will look like a regular rock. Get ten or twenty of them, about six inches long or slightly longer. (So your island doesn't have a volcano. Bummer. However brain coral is the next best alternative. Make sure it is totally dry before proofing. All atolls used to be volcanos. The volcanos sank but often in the middle of the island you can still find left over lava.) Now comes the tricky part, we have to test or proof our rocks. We don't want them exploding while we are busy cooking. Build a fire, make it a good one, and throw five or six rocks right into the middle of the fire and run! Run really far away! Don't put all your rocks in at once. One rock exploding might crack a perfectly good rock next to it, making it undependable in the future. If no rocks exploded, put those rocks aside and when your nerves return to normal, your legs have stopped quivering so that you CAN run away again, and your nightmares have eased off; it is time to proof another batch. When you have at least ten good rocks, you are ready. Remember, you are going to use these rocks over and over again, so don't lose them in the eating frenzy to come. They are an important part of survival on a deserted island.

Have you dug your hole? For your first try, it doesn't have to be huge. Fingers and spear like sticks work well. Umus are the best way to cook food. If you haven't, read on, there is hope for you yet. Line your hole with leaves to insulate it from the cold earth or sand. Banana leaves are great for this. Everytime you pick a stalk of bananas you have to cut down the mother tree to make room for its children. Banana trees only bear fruit once. (Don't forget to harvest the heart of the tree. Read the banana section.) That means you are going to have a LOT of banana leaves laying around. This is a good time to use some. Almost any leaf can be used. Don't use taro or dasheen leaves. They are very bitter (They actually will burn and blister your mouth if not properly prepared) and will ruin your dinner and Friday's mood. OK. The hole is lined with leaves. Right next to the hole you have been building a fire where you have been heating up your rocks. You are going to pick up your rocks and lay them in the fire carefully. It will help if the fire is really close to the hole. I know those yogis teach people to walk over sizzling hot burning rocks. They don't seem to be harmed by the experience. But somehow I don't think I have reached enough enlightenment to lift a hot rock up in my hands. Then do it again and again. Sorry if I am a stick in the mud, but I just ain't going to do it! Go ahead, say it. I don't have enough faith. Its true, I can't even stand on one foot for longer than a couple seconds.

You are going to have to build some pinchers. Long ones as these rocks are so hot you are not going to want to get all that close to them. Palm fronds are really fire proof, especially their fat ends. The ends are so hard to burn I don't even put them in the fire any more, just leave them hanging out. They have a kind of reverse scoop on them which doesn't help us as the damn rock will just roll out. So cut a notch in the ends of two of them and pick up the hot rock between them, wedging the rock between the convex sides. When the rocks are good and hot, lift them out and lay half of the rocks carefully around the bottom of the hole, throw some more leaves on top, put in the food, throw some more leaves on top, carefully lay the rest of the rocks on top, throw some more leaves on top and bury the whole thing in sand or dirt. Then go and have a nice rest under a coconut tree in your hammock. You deserve it. That was hard, hot work.

I kind of jumped over the put the food in bit, didn't I? Sorry. That is the most important part. Making a luau is such hard work, you are not going to want to do it every day. You are not going to want to do it every other day. Maybe full moons and Christmas will do. It is a lot of work but you can cook a lot of food in them AND if you are careful, the food will keep a long time. Leftovers is the key to survival on a deserted island. Carefully wrap all your food in batches to be eaten in a single day. Like a pound or two of taro in one wrapping of banana leaves. (Try papaya leaves too. They give a pleasant tang, or yucky bitterness if you used old leaves. Some people believe they promote a resistance against malaria. That's important if you have mosquitos on your island.) Wrap up a serving or two of fish in seaweed and then leaves. Even wrap your breadfruit, which comes in its own built in covering. As long as you do not disturb the covering in the next few days, the food will stay good. All the germs have been wiped out. No new germs can get in. (Maybe eat the fish right off.) Make sure the leaves covering the food are slightly damp when you start out.

So you have been sleeping for five or six hours under the trees in your hammock. It is time to open the umu. OK. First we carefully remove the dirt from the mound of soil (or sand) covering the pit. When we reach the first layer of leaves, watch out! I know it has been a long time but the heat has had no where to go. It is still intensely hot under those leaves. Get a long stick and kind of pull the leaves apart so that the steam can start to escape. Don't be a hero. Don't say "It don't hurt." Steam takes a while to penetrate to the nerves when you stick your hand into the umu, but it is burning flesh the whole time. As soon as the steam starts to escape, remember that you haven't taken your afternoon swim. If fact, you missed your afternoon nap. Now is a good time to do both.

An hour later return to your feast. Remove more of the covering leaves, now cooler, push aside the top rocks (they don't look like it but they are still intensely hot) pull out enough food for tonight's feast and recover the rest with your leaves right away. Don't worry. Insects are a lot smarter then humans. They won't go into a still hot caldron. Not even a buried one.

The only other tricks? Remember to wrap your food really well. The leaves are supplying the moisture to steam the food. Put plenty in there. Don't open it too soon. It can't over cook. Hawaiian food is supposed to fall apart when touched. Besides, there is only so much steam in the leaves. If you open it too soon, when the steam is really, really hot, you can get very badly burnt. Enjoy your hammock.

So you couldn't dig a hole, anywhere? Bummer. Not to worry. The Pacific Northwest Indians who lived in present day British Columbia and Washington State, had great big huge feasts like wars where they tried to out do each other in gift giving called a potlatch. (Who ever gave the best gifts won the war. Exactly why did we start killing people off in wars?) To prepare the marine food for these feasts, (salmon, crabs, clams, and a few roots and berries for fun) they dug a shallow hole in the sand, lined it with seaweed, built a hell of a big fire on top, let it burn down, drenched it with seaweed, put the food on top, covered it with seaweed and dumped mounds of sand on top, and waited five or six hours before opening it up. They avoided digging a deep hole because it is easier to pile sand up than it is to dig a hole and they have big tides up there. The bad part of this technique is you have to eat all the food up as the heat is not sealed in as well as in the Hawaiian umu and if you wait too long the waves and tide will steal your food. But it is a lot easier to dig a shallow hole in the sand than a deep hole in the earth, and to build a fire instead of looking for all those pesky rocks. But if you ask me, Hawaiian food is so ono, it break the mouth, bra.

So what happens if it is the rainy season and every piece of wood on the whole island is soaking wet, Friday is shivering, your arthritis is acting up and it doesn't look like the rain has any intention of stopping, and you are damn tired of cold food. If you are not prepared you are screwed. But hopefully, you are prepared with a dry load of charcoal. Charcoal is easy to make, burns hotter than wood, takes less space to store out of the weather, and gives the food a more exotic taste. To make charcoal, make a big fire of hardwood (mangrove wood is by far the best, much better than hickory) let the fire really get going and then bury it all under at least a foot of sand. The fire won't go out. (I know the boy scouts told you it would, but believe me, it won't). It will continue to smolder under ground for three days, when you take most of the sand off and dump tons of water on the embers. Make sure it is all out. The wood has now turned black and the surface of the wood is carbon black. Store it in its own hut. (Please not next to your sleeping hut. You are going to be working so hard you won't want any 2 AM wake up calls during lightning storms that Friday thinks are too close to the charcoal.)

Remember, in the earth you only have to dig the hole once for an umu. (In the sand, the hole fills back in.) You only have to find the rocks once, and those rocks are going to be mighty useful in the future, especially for canoe making. Once you are set up, really you could have an umu, what, once a month? Once a month for a full moon party if Friday is a big help? Hey, if you can't find some reason to have a feast once a month, you simply just aren't trying hard enough!

Drying is the new Baking

So you have been all over the island and you still haven't found a Holiday Inn or a McDonalds. What kind of island did you pick to be shipwrecked on anyway? And you have looked in your grass shack, looked everywhere, but you still can't find the oven. How can you possibly survive. I mean you can only play at being on a boy scout campout jamboree for so long and then it gets really boring. Really, really boring. So boring you would happily kill for a chocolate cake. But all is not lost.

Baking is really a very stupid idea. Hey, it is! Would I lie to you? It is stupid because it is based on the idea that to preserve and prepare food, you have to heat it to the state that all life is terminated. Kill the damn cake to make sure there are no germs left. Heat it so high that every vitamin or enzyme in there is blown apart into a million useless pieces.   Heat it so high that any protein becomes an indigestible mass of something filling our intestines. Of course, we can't be eating food that might make us sick from germs. But does that mean that will have to kill our food so lethally that even germs won't eat it? And this is the stuff that we hope will keep us alive? Do you really think that Twinkies are good for you? They taste the same now as they will twenty years from now, and this can be described as food? One of the mysteries of modern science is the drunk sitting on the park bench in the middle of winter, wrapped in newspaper, and not dying. Any one of us would be sick in a few hours, dead in two days. Why not the drunk? I figure it is because the food we eat (and he isn't), is making us sick. As bad as alcohol is, the food we eat is worse! And this is progress? Isn't there another way?

Aren't you lucky you got shipwrecked! You are being forced to invent a whole new way of life, or rather rediscover an ancient way of cooking. When foods are dried the cell walls become very solid and impermeable. Germs can normally enter cells because of the water in the cells creates passages in the cell wall, but when dried those walls are like electrified fences with machine guns and Dobermans to invading germs. By drying foods we not only can make them safe for storage but also change their chemical structure and taste, much like baking does. By drying, we can make, well, cakes!

Actually, lets start easy and make crackers and breads first and work our way up to cakes. Whichever one we start with, one thing is sure, I am not going out and looking for non-existent wild wheat plants to harvest their tiny seeds. There is just no way. That would definitely cut into my hammock time. But there are lots of flours on islands in the tropics, you just have to know where to look.

If you are lucky you might find some corn plants on your island if it was previously inhabited. If you do, don't eat them! Replant the kernels. Fertilizing with seaweed just under the surface and the guts of one small fish deep in the seed hole. When you have a crop, grind the kernels into a meal (coarse flour) and enjoy. Sago on the other hand is so productive in the tropics that you could eat cake every day and never run out.

Recipe-- Corn or sago crackers

Combine one coconut shell of starch meal, two pinches of salt, two splashes of palm syrup, and a splash of coconut oil. Mix in a fresh bird egg, (if a tern egg add two) then pour in a coconut shell of hot water. Blend together well. Make into little patties keeping your hands wet. Place on a banana leaf and dry in the hot sun for two or three hours or until hard on the outside.

Drying is a lost art. To do it well, think of a convection oven. The food is heated up and the air, moist from the food, is removed with new drier air taking its place. It doesn't help to dry by the sea as the salt air is loaded with moisture. However, trees and bushes are great moisture removers so set up your dryer a hundred yards or so in from the sea, in a sunny area. Make sure there are no trees or structures around your drying place so that the moist air can rise as it is heated. Try to make the rock you are drying on as dark as possible. Black lava, no micro-holes, is perfect. Start drying after the rock is really hot. Temperatures of a 120° and over are possible on a good day.

To be more effective at drying, create walls of black lava around your big stone that will reflect the heat back into the center of the food. If you want to dream, a piece of slanted plexiglas on top sure would be great. It would let the sunlight in and as a plus we could have a vent to draw out the moisture. Actually as long as we are dreaming, let's add solar panels, dc refrigeration, DVDs and a television. Dreams. It's hell being shipwrecked, isn't it?

For sure somewhere on the island, no matter which island it is, there will be cassava. Cassava root (read about cassava in the root section) is what we in the west call tapioca. Tapioca flour is sold in the west as pearl tapioca and is made into puddings, but it doesn't have to be so. Cassava is unique in that it carries its own yeast with it from the ground. Here is what you do to make cassava bread. Boil the root in a bamboo section. (Don't roast it in the fire. Cassava is great roasted, but for bread, it has to be boiled.) After about thirty minutes, decant the water into an ant hill. Don't throw it away! Carefully slice the root down the center from end to end and bend the skin away from the insides. Try not to let the outside peel touch the inside root. Squeeze the root between your hands into a container and save the water that comes out. If you want to make bread right away proceed with the squished cassava otherwise smash it into very thin patties and dry in the sun to make crackers right away or to save it.

To make cake, add the yeast to any starch. All of the yeasts will work. Add a sugar source (toddy, palm sugar, sugar cane). Mix well, and set it somewhere warm to rise. Like all yeasted breads or cakes, the dough must be bashed down again and again to distribute the yeast cells throughout the dough. If you don't you will end up with big holes in your cake. If you have found chocolate, make chocolate cake. Always add vanilla to any frosting as well as boiled down starfruit juice.

Baking is easy. Store bought cakes are altered to cook quickly because the average housewife doesn't want to spend all day in the galley. The slower the cake cooks the longer it has a last chance to rise. In the end the yeast has to die off, either from the heat or old age. If old age kills the yeast your cake will have a yeasty taste. Don't cook for too long. The other advantage an oven has is it dries the cake out uniformly. We can get around that in drying by making pancake size cakes and then gluing them together with frosting or fruit puree.

After you have dried the cake or bread for a least a couple of hours, fire it on a hot rock by the fire for a couple minutes just to drive off the last bit of moisture.

Have fun. If noting else works, make cookies!

Bread

Before we can make bread we have to make the flour. Not a problem. Most deserted islands have lots of cassava. Check out the cassava section to identify it. When you have found your plant dig it up and gather the roots. The outside of the roots are toxic. Do not peel the root. The chemicals from the outside of the root will be spread to the delicious insides. Instead, scribe the outside of the root to a depth of a quarter of an inch. Make the scribe a wavy line going down the length of the root. Then grab the skin on either side of the line and peel the skin off in one smooth motion. The skin will not harm you. It is only toxic if you eat it, but be sure to wash your hands after the de-skinning is done. Afterwards, boil the root for two hours.

Find a coconut tree with some of the brown lacy burlap looking material by the lower branches. Wrap your boiled root into this material and wring the water out of the cassava. Save the water. Cut the root into thin slices like a carrot and set out to dry.

That wasn't too bad was it? The good part is cassava plants have lots of roots so there are plenty to practice on. What we have to do now is pulverize our root. The easiest way is to use our pounder. (Following) But a couple of flat rocks will work as well. When it is as powdery as it will ever be, mix it up with the water we squeezed from the root, (it is like potato water, it ferments naturally.) mix in some sugar water, some salt and knead it into a dough like substance and set aside in a sunny spot covered up in a couple of banana leaves. In a couple of hours you are ready to cook your bread!

Cassava will not form a loaf like wheat will, so take a little in your hand and form it into a pancake let it raise again in your sunny spot. In an hour lay it on your hot flat rock on the coals flipping it over after 10 minutes or wrap the pancake around a stick and support the stick above the coals turning now and then. Enjoy one of the blessings of civilization, fresh hot bread!

The Pounder

Pounders have been around since the age of cavemen but that doesn't mean that they are easy to make. As usual Polynesians made the most beautiful, partly because they are a very artistic race, partly because their civilization only joined ours a couple of centuries ago and they haven't forgotten their survivor skills and partly because they really liked to eat pounded food, like poi. They made their pounders out of lava rock mostly because lava and coral were the only two rocks they had available. This is important as we, very likely, only have lava and coral available to us also.

There is tremendous skill involved in sculpture. That is what you are doing, you know, acting like Michelangelo. There are two types of art. Adding stuff and taking away stuff. Painting is adding paint to a canvas till it looks like something. Sculpture is taking away pieces of rock till it looks like something. At least that is what Sister Ann Margaret told me in seventh grade. I don't know why I remembered that while I have forgotten so much math.

So find a nice rock that vaguely looks like a pounder and hit it with other rocks till it looks like a pounder. Easy, huh? Well, maybe not. If you are artistically challenged like me, it will really help if you find a rock that really, really looks like a pounder to start. Then the trick is to hit your pounder with glancing blows with your hammer rock. After a while as it gets closer to the right shape, start tapping instead of hitting and eventually find a nice sandy tide pool with no easy exit and leave your pounder in there for a week or two to get a nice smooth finish.

In Micronesia, the long gone pre-blender locals hollowed out a section of tree trunk, as a pounding bowl, and pounded roots and the like with a long limb of a tree while standing up. It is much less tiring that way. Who wants to be bending over pounding all day?

Survival Techniques

OK, you know what to eat and maybe what not to eat, but how do you create the superstructure, the bones of civilization, the details of survival? How do you start a fire, build a house, where do you dig a well or erect a signal fire? How do you build a grass shack or weave a coconut leaf hat? How do you tie and weave your own hammock?

These are all important and crucial questions. The skills of survival are what we most have to learn. Do you have your survival hat on? Ready? Start surviving!

Beachcombing

Traditionally, beachcombing is the heart and soul of surviving on a deserted island. The amount of jetsam and flotsam that drifts up on the beaches of deserted islands is amazing. Some of it might even be useful. For the purposes of this book, we are assuming that you never find anything useful on your island's beaches and that you have to make or harvest everything yourself. However, in the interest of being fair, just in case you do find yourself shipwrecked, beachcombing may well be an all important asset to survival.

To beachcomb effectively first determine when high tide occurs. This is easily done by sticking various pieces of wood six inches apart in the sand from the water's edge leading up towards the trees. As the day goes by, notice how high the water gets and when. (Well, as your watch didn't survive the shipwreck, approximately when.) Everyday the tides are on the average, 50 minutes, we can call it an hour, later in the day. If high tide was at noon today, it will be at ten to one tomorrow. This is important as valuable items can be buried in the sand in a surprising amount of time, sometimes in an hour. Just after high tide is the best time for beachcombing, interesting things are then swept over the reef but haven't had the time to get buried.

I never understood why Tom Hanks in the movie Castaway didn't have an easier time of it. So much stuff is swept up on to islands. The most obvious are shoes and plastic bottles. Flip flops, slippers, go aheads whatever you might call them, are everywhere but more important is the stock that they are cut out of. These are big pieces of dense foam, sometimes an inch thick, that shoe shapes have been cut from, but plenty material is left. What a find! What a bed! When we return to civilization we can all be millionaires making a new style of bed! We'll call it survival foam. It is super comfortable, especially if baby shoes were cut from it!

Plastic bottles are a great resource for storing food and supplies away from the rain, salt air and insects. The best ones are wide mouth gallon jugs, but the ones that survive crossing the seas and reefs best are booze bottles. Gather what you can. Whatever you find, it will be more effective than coconut shells, but no where near as cool. As you get more and more efficient at survival, the more you will need containers to store medicines, food, compounds to make soap, seeds, liquor that is brewing or aging or is ready to be drunk.

The cod end of fishing nets, which are made out of heavy polypropylene, always survive. They are almost always green (at least the nets that survive are) and make great hammocks with almost no extra work. They are scratchy, so a coconut leaf or ti mat will keep skin scrapes and infections down. Sometimes they are buried deep in the sand but are definitely worth the effort to dig them out.

Long line equipment washes up with fair frequency. At first it looks like a jumble of worthless sun damaged line. But wait! In the middle of the jumble you might find the leader. This is an almost indestructible 500 pound monofilament line with a clasp on one end that attaches the leader to the longline (a continuous line maybe 20 miles, or more, in length. The clasp is a stainless heavy duty closable hook that can easily support your weight while climbing trees, exploring for bird nests and the like. The other end of the leader where the hook should be is almost always missing as the whole thing was broken off by some gigantic dweller of the abyss. The leader, surprisingly, is of little use. It is almost impossible to tie a knot that will hold in it, the only knot that might be successful if the line is old enough, is a figure eight.

A fair amount of boat equipment washes up. Things like destroyed hatches but with the hinges still intact. Here is a quandary. Do you chance ruining the point of your one and only machete removing the rusty screws in a maybe useful hinge? My feeling is no.

Your machete is so important to your survival. Better to burn the wood and recover the hinge the next day.

Occasionally a bottle washes up half full with something. Hard to say what it is as the label dissolved the first day in the sea. Personally, I never even open these bottles. Chances are they have been exposed to germs when first opened and are now germ warfare time bombs just waiting to go off. There is enough food on islands if you have the knowledge to know where to look.

Plastic fishing floats are fairly common. They make great bowls, if you can cut them in half. A broken heavy duty conch shell makes a passable if incredibly slow saw. Use the other half as the base, gluing the two ends together with a glue made of breadfruit sap boiled in coconut milk. Otherwise, they make great, if monotonous, musical instruments when you tire of your own voice!

The Grass Shack

Lets face it, if you don't build a grass shack as a shipwrecked or adventurous sailor, you are not going to be thriving, you will be just surviving. And not surviving very well at that. Its like a rule, if you are castaway, shipwrecked, marooned, or just practicing, you are going to have to make a house. Stop beating around the bush. All you will need is your trusty machete, so lets get the lead out and get going. Everything you need is right around you. Ready?

The Framework Supplies

As long as we are going to be building a house we might as well make a good one. That means erecting a decent framework first. It can be built out of most anything, but traditionally it is made out of either flotsam, bamboo or rattan. Gathering flotsam is always fun. You get to take long walks along the beach, kicking at stuff and throwing the odd rock out into the sea. Tell Friday, you are not wasting time, you are building her a shack! Any tall, strong, somewhat straight, timber will do. You will need four solid posts for the corners that are at least ten feet long, four mostly straight beams for the roof at least ten feet long, and the odd seven footers for the doors and the windows. This is really the hardest part of the shack, finding the material. Might as well start looking on day one. Part of successful thriving is being observant during your scouting adventures.

Flotsam logs are pre-salted which discourages termites from eating your shack as fast as you build it. Termites are the enemy of houses in the tropics. But they hate to eat grass shacks if you build them right.

Bamboo is strong and light, termites don't like to eat it, and geckos like to live in it. (You do want geckos in your grass shack. We don't have to spray DDT all over creation to kill bugs—we just have to co-inhabit with a few hungry geckos.)

Rattan branches grow upwards whilst the trunks grow sideways along the land. They grow very straight must be cut and dried before use to prevent them from taking whatever curve they feel like. Take the bark off first in strips. This is the rattan they use to make cane seats. Set it out to soak in the tide pools by the sea. We will need it after a bit. But the part we are after now is the straight branches.

The rafters for the roof can be made out of anything. Don't worry about them yet. We are going to make the walls first to get in a little practice and to strengthen the framework before we thatch the roof.

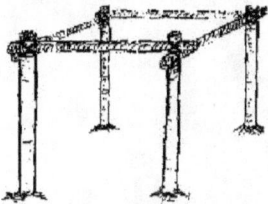

Building the framework

Yes, we have to dig holes for the corner posts. Deep holes and no, you are not suddenly supplied with shovels or a back hoe. When coconut tree fronds get old, drop off and sit for a few years, all that is left is the base of the frond, which is shaped, yes you got it, like a backwards shovel. Look around, they are everywhere. It's good enough to dig a hole in the sand if we cut the bottom backward part off. Yes, we are building our shack in the sand. There are way less bugs there. You may not believe that, but after being bitten by hundreds of sand flies, I do. (**Valuable personal experience**--don't build your shack on a sunset beach, one facing the west. I did once. I didn't realize sand flies, no-nos, no-see-ems, flying teeth are sun worshippers. I was so bitten, so in agony by the next day that I didn't leave the boat for weeks. The eastern side of the island, the windward side in the tropics, is where you want to build your shack. The wind is your friend. But you will have to build your framework posts deep to resist the trades.) We are going to make the posts as far apart as the longer coconut fronds that you can find on the island are long. We are making our starter shack for now. Our Hollywood, three bedroom palace will have to wait for the second edition!

Ok, you dug your holes, dug 'em deep, maybe 3 feet. Now you have to set it in place with rocks and pieces of coral.. (In *Grass Shack, The Sequel*, we will cement the posts in place. Ancient Romans built their palaces and roads out of cement made out of burnt coral mixed with volcanic ash which set after some time when in the presence of water. The dead old coral found along the beach is best and the ash is found high up on volcanic cones, if you are lucky enough to be shipwrecked on such an island. The coral is roasted over a fire till it turns to ash, then the two are mixed well, throw in a few rocks to make concrete and there you are. Who said us castaways aren't civilized?)

Once the corner posts are up we lash on the girders to connect all four posts. It is best to lash them to the outside of the corner posts to increase interior size and to make it easier to eventually mount the trusses of the roof. You can lash them with anything that comes to hand, but if you have found rattan trees during your explorations, and have the rattan bark soaking in the salt water, the rattan will be your best bet as it is very strong and it shrinks as it dries. Other possibilities are the central petiole or spine of the coconut frond leaf. It is easy to slice off the leaf part and when green the petiole is flexible and easy to lash, and there are certainly enough of them. If you really want to get carried away, coir, a very strong and flexible rope is made from coconut husks. This takes a little skill in braiding, but after a while you will get better at it. See the chapter on making rope. Far better, if you can't find rattan and you want a rope rather than a coconut "stalk" to tie together your framework, see if you can find some sisal plants. Sisal makes beautiful white line by cutting off a mature leaf at the base, pounding the leaf, scrapping off the pulp, soaking in salt water and then weaving together the

strands. The strands are up to 50 inches long so each leaf can easily do a corner post. Sisal looks ever so much like Mother-in-Law tongue, only bigger and greener. Again see the chapter on rope making. If all else fails, you can always find polypropylene rope washed up on any tropical beach in the world. Use lots as it will be sun damaged by the time you get it after floating for thousands of miles and who knows how many years.

Now tie in the smaller posts for the door on one side and the window on the two other sides. You don't have to bury them three feet deep. Maybe a foot will do. Leave the leeward, the western side, a solid wall. This is the direction that the hurricanes are most likely to come from in the tropics. Let's not make it too easy for them to destroy our shack. Give the west side a couple of upright posts too, just for luck, well tied in.

weaving the sides

Alright, you have your framework finished. It is nice and strong. Time to weave up the sides. The easiest and I think the prettiest is to weave together coconut fronds. It is easy to do, here is how. Grab yourself a coconut frond, you will see it has a central branch like spine and equal sets of leaves on either side. Strip off each set of leaves from the central spine leaving only a quarter to a half an inch of spine to keep the individual leaves connected. Lay the two halves down with the top one angling opposite the bottom both aiming down so that the individual leaflets are open side down so they won't collect water. As you can see the frond leaflets are just begging to be weaved together. Right over left, left over right. No need to get too carried away. Weave them together for a foot or two. Coconut fronds are fairly long. You will need long ones and short ones. Let's start with the back wall, the one without doors or windows. Lash the two branch spines together and to the corner posts. There, doesn't that look great? Ok. Weave together another set. Tie it behind the first set, just above the height where the first sets' weaving stopped. Lash it on. Weave the first ones' left over leaves into the seconds ones' upper leaves so that it covers the spines of the second set. Anal personalities can continue to weave them together till both inside and out are flush and beautiful. Continue lashing and weaving until you reach the sand. Dig a ditch. Bury the last set of fronds. Wow! You just made a wall!

The other three sides are much the same except you can use shorter sets between the corners and the door and windows. To finish off the sides of the door and windows take a untrimmed frond, almost slice it through the middle, bend it apart and weave the opposite leaves into the wall and each other. To make the shutters and door, proceed much the same, build a frame, weave the fronds, tie it together, lash it to the frame work, you have just finished the lower part of your shack! If you really enjoy seeing the stars at night, and don't mind midnight showers, stop right here. To build your roof, read on.

The roof

Trusses are easy. Really. I don't know why they are so expensive in the real world. Wait a minute. We are in the real world. Those other poor slaves, those on the freeways, land of taxes, artificial smiles, ulcers and heart attacks are living in some far away imaginary place. Isn't it obvious?

Trusses are dead easy. Start with a flat piece of land or sand. Lay down the two straight strong pieces of wood, let's call them beams, on the sand at a pleasing angle, at least 40 degrees. The way it works is, the higher the angle the easier the thatch will shed water. If the angle is too low the rain will soak through the thatch before the roof sheds it. Make sure that the ends will reach over the framework of the walls. Now comes the hard part. Make two more just the same as the first. Don't get carried away. A little error here and there will add character to your shack. Now to mount them. This is going to be difficult if you are by yourself and Friday hasn't wandered by leaving her foot prints all over your beach, but don't give up hope.

It can be done easiest by locating your shack under a coconut tree and finding or weaving a long piece of rope. (*Valuable Personal Experience*, climbing a coconut tree. They do this so easy on TV and at Waikiki. But they cheat. Yes, sorry, they do, not that it will help us. They tie a short piece of line between their ankles and brace their feet on opposite sides of the tree, the rope holding their feet tight to the tree. Sounds easy doesn't it? Forget about it. The pain of your entire weight bearing against the sides of your shins or ankles is incredible. Trust me. Even climbing ten feet will cripple you for a week. Far better to do it like the locals used to do it when your island was occupied years ago. They took their machetes and cut a series of alternating notches in the tree on opposite sides of the tree. At first, you might find this difficult, but no one said you had to reach the top in one day. Take your time. Most likely you have months before the rainy season hits. It won't hurt the tree). The bad part of building your shack under a coconut tree is the certainty of bombardment of coconuts. Make the roof strong!

Anyway, plop up your truss, (pull them up with a rope hanging from your coconut tree. If you really don't want to climb up the tree to hang the rope, try throwing a rock tied to a light string over the top of the palm, then use the string to pull up a thicker line, and then your rope), measure where the pieces of roof beams and wall girders will meet. Take it down again and lash in another length of wood, longer than the roof is wide, just above where the beams touch. This will stop your roof from sinking down lower as you add the weight of the thatch and it is the start of the bedding storage loft. This is where we will keep our bedding during the day. Nothing is so miserable as sharing your bed with ants, bed bugs, cockroaches, termites, centipedes, scorpions, and things we don't even want to think about. Remember that geckos are our friends? That we want them to live in our thatch roof? We want them to come down during the day and eat any bugs in our bedding. It is so much easier to build and live in a tropical paradise when you can get a good night's sleep, bug free. So, the trusses are up. You tie them to the girders. You run a roof beam on the top, connecting them to each other. You will have to stand on your walls to tie a lot of this in. This is a good thing. If your walls can't hold your weight, don't waste anymore time on this shack, or turn it into a cook house. Cook houses are always built far away from the sleeping house and have to be burnt down every couple of years as they become infested with bugs waiting for their next meal. So, your walls are strong enough. Time to start the thatch.

The thatch is best made from pandanas leaves. The tops of these leaves have to be bent double and then dried. As usual the sea is your best place to soak the leaves before doubling them. Lay weights over the wet pandanas leaves after doubling the them and let them dry. They are ready for thatching as soon as they loose their limpness but before they become hard and brittle.

While the thatch is drying run thin lathes across the trusses horizontally and about two feet apart. Ok, we are finally ready. Start from the bottom. The pandanas leaves go around the lathes, the bottom half goes below the lathe. It has to be long enough to get stuck under the next lathe. The top half goes above the lathe down roof (below) the one we are working on. On the bottom layer we start at one lathe up roof (above) from the bottom. Shove the leaf together with its neighbor, horizontally, all of them against the trusses. Continue until that row is finished. Start on the next row. Again the leaves go one half of the doubled leaf above the lathe, one half below, but both haves above the lathe down roof. Finally, really finally, this may take many days but try to complete one lathe completely until you quit for the day. The closer you shove the leaves together along the lathes the more watertight the roof will be. You are finally at the peak of the roof, both sides thatched. On the last lathe fold the pandanas leaf in half, half of the leaf going under the lathe and half over (both over the thatch below it) with the stem pointing up. At the peak of the roof you will now have twin sets of stems poking up above the roof. Tie these sets together. Lay a lathe between the sets of stems and tie it to the stems also for extra strength. Lay bundled leaves in the vee formed by the stems if needed for water tightness. You most likely won't need it. This kind of roof is very water tight and will last for twenty years or more. You can now see why the framework had to be built strong, what with all this climbing all over it.

The area below the peak of the roof and above the window beam can be left open for ventilation but normally is thatched to protect against rain and squalls. It can be thatched with coconut leaves like the walls but now that you are all practiced up and all, might as well thatch it with pandanas. It will look better and will be much stronger.

Congratulations. You have just built a grass shack that will likely stand at least for years. You should be proud of yourself. Go have a drink of arrack. Or if you haven't made any yet, open this book to the brewing section right away and get going!

How to Open a Coconut

You may not think so after a few abortive attempts, but coconuts are easy to open. How you do it depends on what kind of coconut you are opening and what you are going to use it for. On your island, you are going to be opening a lot of coconuts. You need to know how. Let's start with the easiest.

The drinking nut is easy to open. Lay it on its side on a log. Hold it with your left hand if you are right handed and slice off wedges of the pointy end with your sharp machete, the end that was not attached to the tree. Rotate the fruit as you cut. Don't take mighty whacks at it. Chances are you will only cut off a finger. Hold the machete a foot or so above the coconut and chop away. Eventually you will hit something solid. This is the shell. Continue all the way around the fruit until the shell's top is exposed. (Try not to hit the shell, it will only dull your machete.) Hold the coconut upright in your left hand, exposed shell up, and using the BACK of the machete tap the top inch of the shell all around turning it in your hand. (*Important Personal Experience:* Don't use the sharp edge of the machete if you have recently become fond of having complete fingers. They are really hard to sew back on straight. But I don't want to talk about it.) If you are accurate the shell will crack as perfectly as if a power saw had cut it. With the tip of the machete pry open the

155

shell and drink the fizzy water inside. (Note the white fibers in the husk you just cut. These drinking nut fibers are the ones you are going to use later to make coir rope. Double note: In WWII medics used these fibers to sew up wounds and reattach limbs as the drinking nut fibers are sterile and strong. Careful slicing of the nut will insure you don't have to make immediate use of this information.)

      The eating nut is opened with a stake. Find yourself a small sturdy tree about an inch and a half in diameter and cut it down about three feet from the ground. Make sure there is good flat land around the tree, so you don't loose your balance at a crucial moment. Sharpen the end of the tree with upwards flicks of the machete until it forms a point Remember, the eating nut is much the same as the drinking nut but a later stage in growth when the husk has become harder and dryer. While the drinking nut is a beautiful pure green, the eating nut has at least some brown streaks and may be all brown but still on the tree. After the nut has been laying on the ground for a week or two, it is growing past the best meat eating nut stage.

      Hold the nut in two hands, one on each end, and slam the nut down onto the pointed stake just missing the interior nut. (I know, I know, but you will get better at it.) Push and twist the nut down until the impaled husk separates from the rest of the nut. Pull up the nut off the stake, rotate slightly and impale again. I am sure I do not have to say to take every effort possible not to impale your hand. But not to worry. It is one of those things that comes very natural and easy to humans, almost as if we have a genetic memory. Continue to rotate, impale and twist until all the husk is removed from the nut. Note that on the end of the nut that was attached to the tree there are three soft spots. These are the eyes. Resist the temptation to dig out the eyes to get at the water. Instead, hold the nut in your hand, just like you did for the drinking nut and whack with the back part of the machete all around the equator of the shell until it breaks evenly in half. Pry the shell apart, (the interior meat will be holding it together), above what ever receptacle comes to hand to catch the water. The eating nuts water isn't bad. It tastes a bit more of coconut but lacks the refreshing fizz of the drinking nut. If you cracked the nut carefully around the equator you will have a perfect bowl from the pointy end of the nut after you remove the meat.

Don't worry about cleaning all the meat from the shell. If you leave the shell on the ground hermit crabs will clean it out perfectly by the next morning. (*Important Personal Information:* Unless you want your shack overrun by night roaming hermit crabs, crabs that will climb in to bed with you, that will pinch at any protruding part of your anatomy, don't leave the open shells anywhere near the shack. In fact, leave them on the other side of the island. Hey, don't laugh, their pinching hurts!)

Copra nuts are a different kind of coconut. They are more elongated, thinner and often seem to have a crease around the equator. While these nuts also have water inside it is definitely inferior in taste. Just throw this water away. The meat tastes like coconut but lacks the indescribably milky flavor that bursts in your mouth like the eating nut. The Copra nut does have an essential trait. It's meat is chockablock full of oil. The nut is opened like the eating nut using the stake to pry the husk off the nut then cracking the nut into two hemispheres. After it is opened the hemispheres are left coconut side up in the sun to dry out in preparation for making oil.

Uu's are the sprout stage of the coconut. This stage starts when the coconut has been resting on the ground for so long that it has sent roots out of two of it's eyes and a stalk out of the third. The uu is best when the stalk is about eighteen inches long and the roots can still be easily pulled from the dirt. Place the nut on a log, raise your machete up above your head and bring it down in one fell swoop, splitting the rotting husk and shell in half. (You are cutting with the grain? From pointy end to stem end?) The interior is filled with a sponge like fibrous center that is fairly tasteless but will grow on you. Check out the Coconut Palm chapter for a recipe for making UU burgers, delicious!

It could be that the pointed stake is just too much for your nerves. Very understandable. The thing is it is easy to make. That is good. However there is another way. Tongs were created way back is the beginning of civilization. They were a good tool for removing things from the fire. It took almost to millennia for human inventive mind to come up with the reverse tong, however. This tool is about four feet long and the pivot is three inches from the bottom. As you separate the handles, the two metal plates tear open the coconut husk. It is very quick and keeps your hands far from pointed objects. Here is how you do it. Put the handles together and jab the blades, now together, into the coconut husk. Open the handles and the husk splits open as easy as pie. Jab it again and again. For a completely clean coconut shell it might take ten jabs, maybe thirty seconds of your time. How cool is that! However, we don't have any metal on our island. But if we found some harder wood that had died (wood becomes very hard a couple years after it has been chopped down), we could make our own coconut tongs, if we had a pivot. Did some metal screws come washing up on the beach in some flotsam? Worth looking!

How To Climb A Coconut Tree

You really have been wanting to get some of those drinking nuts. They are just sitting there on top of the tree, laughing at you. I know, I know. You have been throwing rocks, trying to poke long sticks at them, whatever you do, it isn't succeeding. And it won't. The only way to get at those nuts is to wait for them to fall on their own or to climb the tree. Yes, I know that you have a thing about heights, it is a very useful trait. It will make sure you hold on tight as you climb!

Traditionally, natives walk up trees, hands behind the trees, forearms balancing against the trunk, feet in front. With a little practice and a lot of youth, this works pretty well, for going up. Be prepared to lose serious amounts of skin if you try this going down until you have had a lot of practice. Try not to lose all of your youth or important body parts while practicing.

Alternately, natives, sorry, locals, tie a coarse sarong between their ankles with enough distance so the feet can grab either side of the tree and the friction of the rough sarong keeps them from falling. Your hands are just for balance and for holding on while your feet jump up a few feet at a time going up or down when falling. Sorry, again. I meant going down. If your sarong is of fine, slippery material or because you don't have a sarong and are using a plaited coconut leaves or some old rotten polypropylene line you found on the beach that had been sitting out in the sun, weakening for decades, you will be going down the tree, quickly. The scariest part of falling is how fast it is. Read the last sentence again. That is how long it takes to fall from 50 feet. No doubt my immortal words will be echoing in your head as you fall, echoing once that is. The other problem is that the coconut tree is skinnier on the top than the bottom. You sarong might be the perfect size for the base of the tree, but it won't be as useful on the top.

More modern techniques, for those who have recently become fond of their chest and stomach skin is to build yourself a ladder. Ladders are easy. Two long sides, lots of steps between, lots of line to tie the steps on. Trouble is, 20 feet is about as long as a ladder can be and still move it from tree to tree. Plus, coconut trees are not oaks. They sway in the wind, a lot. At twenty feet the tree is not swaying so much that the base of your ladder is going to become cockeyed. At thirty feet it will. 20 feet is not much use when most trees are over 60 feet. There are younger, shorter trees. For these your ladder will work well. See if your island has some rattan trees. Slice the bark off one of the trunk/branches and dry in the sun for 3 days. The branches (rattan trunks grow parallel to the ground while their branches grow straight up into the air. Isn't nature wonderful?) grow very, very straight. They make wonderful ladders and later even better spars for your canoe that you will soon make. (Don't tell Friday that your are working with rattan. She will have you making chairs and beds and locker doors until, well, forever. Don't tell!) The dried bark makes wonderful ladder making material. Tie it on when slightly wet and it will dry rock solid. You will never use an aluminum ladder again. However, there are usually not a lot of coconut producing trees under 30 feet.

Next technique is the most traditional one in the Indian Ocean. Whack a series of steps into either side of the coconut tree. It works really well in climbing and descending. It means that you don't have to take all the coconuts when you finally get to the top of a tree. There is no reason not to leave some for tomorrow. However, there is a problem, you knew there would be, didn't you? It takes a long time to cut notches into a coconut tree. The best I have ever done is 20 feet of notches a day, working very hard. Plus, there is the fact that your machete is going to get dull. It will need to be sharpened. You will need to find your sharpening stone first. The notches are cut with a downward and slightly inward slice first then a sideways whack to form the step. It will take a lot of whacks to form one step. Coconut trees are tough. As long as you alternate steps from one side of the tree to the other, not two steps right across from each other, you will not hurt the tree. Really. I have climbed trees on deserted islands in the Indian Ocean over 50 years old in perfect health with notches cut in them so long ago that the steps resembled slips.

If you have already built your ladder, you won't have to start cutting notches until you are at the top of the ladder. That will save a lot of headache and even more sprained wrists. Cutting notches on the right hand side if you are right handed is ok. Harder is cutting on the opposite side of the tree. Perhaps now is the time to develop your opposite hand to become ambidextrous. Just think, when you are rescued, you could try out with the pros as a pitch hitter! If you never wanted to play baseball, circle around to the opposite side of the tree. Now the next step to be cut is on your dominate side. Thank goodness.

I do hope you have read this far, as there is a better way. It is my own personal invention developed after falling from far too many coconut trees. I really don't know why Tom Hanks in the movie Castaway had such a hard time building a raft. Islands in the middle of the ocean are trash magnets. Wait. Let me rephrase that. Abandoned tropical islands in the middle of the oceans, collect a lot of useful items mixed in with the trash. There that is better. It is amazing what washes up. It is Christmas every day you go for an explore! In this case, what we are looking for is closed cell foam or plastic floats and tarred fishing rope. Fishing floats seem to delight in washing up on islands, You won't have any trouble finding any. The big plastic balls that wash up are from the longliners that throw hundreds of miles of fishing gear into the ocean every morning and pick it up the next day. They attach a float every hundred feet, a ball with a flag on it every thousand feet. That is a lot of floats. It is understandable that some get lost. (If we had a hacksaw, the plastic floats would make beautiful bowls that Friday would go gaga over. But we don't so unless you want to spend days scratching with sea shells, forget it.) I really don't know why Tom didn't make a raft out of longliner floats and go-ahead shoes. I guess Hollywood has never visited a deserted tropical island!

Attached to the floats is a blackish colored line. This is sisal line that has been coated with tar. (I know that tequila is made from a Mexican version of the same African plant that sisal is made from, however, tequila can't be made from the line. Bummer, huh?) This rope is impervious to sun and salt. Always collect this line when you happen upon it. You might find some polypropylene line that has just washed up. Grab this too. If it has little pieces of line sticking out sideways or has lost its shiny appearance, ignore it. It will break with the slightest load.

OK! You have floats of some kind and lots of line, you are almost there! Now tie the float to the line and the line to the tree. Tie the line around the tree at least twice, better three times. You have just made a step! Try it out. Cool, huh! Make another a few feet above the first, you are making your own installed ladder! The trick here is two fold. Because the coconut tree gets skinnier as it goes up the line won't slip down the trunk. And two, because the tree has a trunk built not smooth, but wavy, with bark bulging out and then wearing a girdle just above, the line has a hard time slipping anywhere. When you are finished with one tree, untie your ladder and retie it on a new tree! Who needs to be cutting notches? Who needs to be searching for rattan trees all over the island. This is beachcombing at its best!

OK, you have made it to the top of your coconut tree. Now what? First don't go around and take mighty swings at the bunches of coconuts up there. It is a long way to the ground. First wrap your legs around and tie a rope around the tree and either hold it in between your teeth, or tie it around your waist. Then reach up to the bottom of each coconut and twist it around and around. Usually it only takes two or three circles and it will fall obediently to the ground

However, no doubt you know by now that there are always snakes in Edens. If not snakes then bugs. The crown of a coconut tree is usually a home for thousands of bugs. Don't work your way up between the fronds to sit up on top of the tree. It isn't worth it. The insects will not be happy at your unwarranted incursion and will let you know about it. It is really hard to descend safely from a coconut tree when being attacked by hundreds of biting insects. Stay below. Take what coconuts you want, cut what fronds you need for your projects, from below, climb down. Leave the crown of the tree to its rightful owners.

In the Indian Ocean there lives a green ant. They look about the same as a black ant only bigger, almost the size of a driver ant. If you see some of these, run don't walk, to the nearest bit of water and jump in! They don't like water. Green ants share with killer bees the ability to swarm and attack any intrusion into their home. If your coconut tree is inhabited with green ants, leave it alone. A coconut is not worth hundreds of bites all over your body. And take it from me, their bite really, really hurts!

In Central and South America, coconut trees are inhabited by tarantulas. Don't worry. They don't live on islands. There, see? ~~Survival~~ Thriving isn't all that bad, is it?

Signal Fire

You have to have a signal fire. All the best castaways do. They won't understand at the Adventurer's Club afterwards if you didn't make one. It doesn't take long. Soon as you have a free afternoon, just after your siesta, lunch, your swim, a snooze, afternoon tea and a swing in the hammock, get right to it.

Don't put your fire on top of a mountain. Please don't. I mean, there you are fishing on the reef for lunch when you see a ship passing on the horizon. Off you go, running as hard as you can up little trails, leaping over streams, avoiding evil little ankle breaking holes, sweat pouring off your skin only to find that on arriving on the mountain top that the ship is over the horizon, you forgot to bring the fire with you up the mountain and when you try to start the fire with two sticks the sweat from your brow keeps putting it out. Instead build your signal fire on the beach, next to your camp but far away so you don't destroy your shacks upon ignition. Keep it handy to your camp fire so all you have to do is stroll over to the signal fire with a flaming stick from the cook fire and set it off. Much better than broken ankles, cardiac seizures and hearts broken in two as the ship sails off.

Signal fires should always have black or dark smoke. The classical way to do this is to throw green leaves on top of a roaring fire. It is very exhausting to be constantly cutting green leaves every morning so as to always have a ready supply, just in case. It is far easier to build your fire (Boy Scout style, like a teepee), make a big one, then build a roof over it with open sides (to let the air in and the rain out, and then have a lot of husked copra coconuts around. When the shell breaks open in the heat, the oil in the coconut meat mixed with the coconut water, produces a very satisfactory black smoke. The roof will go up in flames when the fire is ignited.

The trouble is that you might really be having a good time playing castaway on your little island and you might not want to be rescued right now, especially as Friday just showed up, but you never know when you might break a leg, suffer a stroke, break up with Friday or some other terrible disaster. Build a signal fire when you have the time, just in case. Just in case.

Digging a Well

Wells are not that hard to dig on atolls. Under the sand lies a lens. A lens is a layer of fresh water which is either trapped by a rock formation under the sand or much more likely floats on top of the underlying salt water. All the plants on the island feed off of this lens for their fresh water needs.

At low tide as you walk along the beach you will see little rivulets of water running down the sand and into the water. This is fresh water that has escaped the lens. Walk straight up into the island along the likely path of the rivulet and start digging at a low spot in the sand. It will not take long. The lens usually lies just fourteen to twenty inches under the sand. Taste the water. It is always fresh so don't worry!

The water in your new well might be cloudy and yucky (a highly technical water collecting term), if so, bail the water out of the well and throw it onto the sand or dirt around the well. OK. Stop freaking. I know you are thirsty. No, you won't die. The water is not lost. There is no place for it to go except back down thru the sand and into the lens but now, it will be filtered by the sand.

On larger islands you may well find a little creek that is active when it is raining but disappears when the sun comes out. Not to worry. The reason the creek is there in the first place is the ground under it is solid rock and the water can't be absorbed by the ground under the creek. Watch carefully. Somewhere as you walk along the creek you will find a spot where the water seems to disappear. This is where you want to dig your well, but not in the creek bed! Build it there and you will have to rebuild it every time it rains and the well is washed away and filled up with dirt and rocks. Build it to one side or the other. Probe in the dirt with a pointed stick to try to find a less rocky area.

After you dig your well you might want to line it to stop erosion adding to the yuckiness of the water. You could use rocks.

You could use non-poisonous dried sticks, but the easiest, if not official (you didn't read it here) way is to find a plastic fifty five gallon barrel, cut off the top and cut holes in the bottom and insert it into the well hole. I know it is beachcombing, but, hey, it really, really works great!

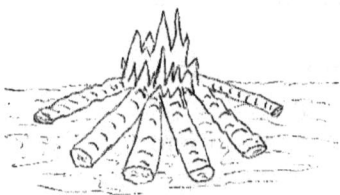

Starting a Fire

The Boy Scouts got it all wrong. Everything they taught us about making a cooking fire was wrong for a deserted island. Really! Don't set your wood up like a teepee. Don't cook your food on skewers above the roaring fire. Don't put a ring of rocks around the fire. Don't keep throwing logs on top to feed the fire. Don't throw water on the fire when you are done. That is all wrong. Survival wrong. Here is how to make a fire on a deserted island.

The idea is to create coals like a charcoal barbeque, and then cook the food on the coals. This is the way islanders, who luckily were never Boy Scouts, have been successfully cooking on fires for centuries. First, they build a fire with the larger logs flat on the ground to be pushed into the center of the fire. As the center of the fire burns up the wood, the logs are pushed in from the sides. When you are ready to cook, the unburnt ends of the logs are dragged over to a new patch of sand a few feet away, the lit ends pushed into a becoming a new fire and leaving a nice bed of coals to cook on back at the old fire. The moved fire is kept going as the log's lit ends, once they are pushed together, will ignite into a new fire. As the bed of coals starts to cool, the fire is moved again, moving the logs by their cool outer ends, leaving a brand new bed of coals after each move. Eventually if you keep your fire going all day, you'll return to your first cooking spot which then is cool to the touch. Worried about the fire spreading out of control? You are on a sand beach. There is no where for it to spread. You really like skewers? Put them over flameless coals like anyone barbequing on a weekend would do. An alternative method is to heat lava stones that can be found high on the central peak of volcanic islands. These stones are then buried underground with food in a kind of oven. (See Making your own luau).

First we have to start a fire. Essentially, you shouldn't have to as there should be a few live coals in last night's fire that you didn't throw water on. We are on a sand beach where the only burnables are introduced by us. Poke up the live coals, blow on them, introduce some kindling, voila. Sure, yes, I got it, I know; how do we start a fire the first time or after a huge rain squall drenches our fire?

Fire is easy to start. Just ask any fireman. All we need is heat and some combustible materials. Most wood starts to burn at 650° Fahrenheit which produces a flame temperature of 1800° F. Some woods are easier to ignite than others. Wood that contains larger amounts of resin are easier to start as it is really the vapors of the internal oils of the wood that start the fire. Easier to start, but harder to keep going. To aid in the release of the wood's vapors, place the wood you want to use to start the fire in a warm spot with no wind and exposed to direct sunlight. It may take an hour for the wood to reach its highest temperature. This can be enhanced by a mirror, reading glasses, magnifying glass, etc. (But you don't have to cheat!) This harder, oilier wood is hard to burn as it is more dense, so around it we are going to place more combustible material, kindling. One of the Polynesians favorites is the dried brown webbing-like material found around the lower branches of a coconut tree mixed with the dried flower of the breadfruit tree. Confused yet? Ok, let's go step by step.

1. You find yourself a piece of oily hardwood and a skinnier piece of soft wood about an inch in diameter. Carve an indentation in the hardwood as perfectly as you can that will match the rounded end of the softwood. (Don't worry about it. If it is perfect, you will be able to start a fire in seconds. If it isn't, it will take a little longer. Eventually the softwood will

wear down to the right shape. But believe me, it is amazing how quick it is to start a fire.) Put both pieces of wood in the sun and in a place protected from the wind. What we are trying to do is create spontaneous combustion. When a hay stack is left out in the field too long in the rain and then, in the sun, the wet hay inside the stack starts to ferment. The fermentation releases methyl alcohol and the weight of the hay produces heat and since alcohol ignites at 149°F (just a little above boiling water), the resultant fire is said to be caused by spontaneous combustion. This is how we are going to start our fire, kind of.

2. When our woods are nice and hot from the sun, we twirl the thin wood between our hands while pushing the thin wood down into the hardwood's hole with the friction of our hands. I want to emphasis that we are not trying to cause a spark. Sparks require a very high temperature, we don't want a spark, we just want a fire. As we twirl the thin wood, more heat is produced in the hard bottom wood which releases yet more oil vapors. Around the hole in the hardwood we have already placed our kindling. By far the best kindling on tropical islands is the web like material found in the branches of the coconut tree. Look around on the ground, I am sure you will find some nicely dried material. However, the stuff still in the tree works even better. Make sure you put some shredded up webbing in the sun when you are heating up the other woods. Next you will need a bed to put the fire in once it is started.

3. The bed is easy to make. We are going to make it right next to our twirling machine as the fire it starts will only last a few seconds before it burns up all our kindling. Small branches intertwined with coconut webbing form the bed. The whole bed sits on a layer of very dry chopped coconut husks. Anything that is easily burnable can be added. Bigger branches should be close at hand to feed the fire as it grows.

4. Twirl fast, back and forth, don't stop, push down as you twirl. This sounds like someone telling you how to swing a golf club! But it is easy once you get the hang of it. Really! Yes, your hands work their way down the soft wood's length as you twirl, but we are only talking about a few seconds here. As the oily vapors start to smoke you are almost there. Don't blow on it! You will just disperse the vapors.   We want vapors and heat.

5. Finally the fire will start by itself almost, by spontaneous combustion. When a flame starts and ignites the kindling around the twirler, dump the kindling, softly and gently, into the bed and now you can gently blow on it. Prepare to be admired. The fire maker!

6. We can always cheat.   Did I actually say that?   We can especially cheat for the signal fire. In making arrack we will generate significant amounts of wood alcohol. We will be making coconut oil. We can press the oils of kukui nuts. All of this assumes we already started a fire. The first fire is all guts, and grit. But, you can do it. I can do it, so I am sure you can!

Have you given up? Hands are rubbed raw? Not even a glimmer of a spark? There is hope still. An easier way to start a fire, but not anyway as cool, is to shine sunlight through a clear glass bottle or a very clean clear plastic bottle. Where are you going to find stuff like that? On any beach in the world. The stuff that washes up!

OK, try it at home first. Don't use white paper to shine your light on. It won't work. The white reflects too much of the heat. Find dark paper, use a pencil to darken your paper or to be more traditional, use dark, dry leaves.

Move you bottle closer or farther away to try to get you reflected sun image as tight as you can. Keep your hands steady. It will take a couple minutes to heat up your leaves. Be ready to add kindling.

And there you go! Actually, after you practice up and all, two pieces of wood is easier!

Sounds hard doesn't it. Might be a good idea if you are going to be shipwrecked to be sure to include a few matches and a Bic lighter! Either that or practice at home first. Actually, if you are going to grab something as the boat is sinking under you, a lighter is like the last thing you need. You can manually start your own fire now!

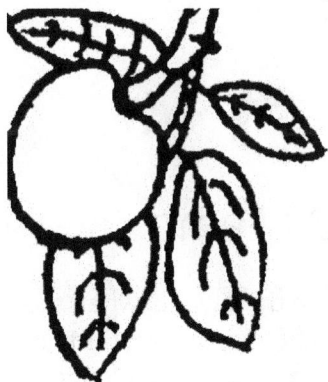

Candlenut Torch

The candlenut (kukui in Polynesian) tree is one of the tung oil (Euphorbiaceae) family of trees which produce nuts full of flammable oil. We in the West express the oil from the nuts and use it as an oily type of varnish. Not so the Polynesians.

They strung the nuts along a midrib of a coconut leaf and ignited the top one as it started to get dark. Each nut burnt for about ten minutes, so when one nut started to run out, a slave would invert the midrib, ignite the next nut in line and return it to an upright position. In normal everyday life the torches were not used, but for feasts and high councils, they were an important part of the ambiance.

The Polynesians did husk and grate the candlenuts, heat the shavings and squeeze out the oil. They used the oil for covering the lashings of their canoes to make them more waterproof and to paint over the tapa cloth to make it waterproof to use as raingear.

Kukui nuts can be eaten after roasting but often have a laxative effect which limits their usage! The large tree is found worldwide in the tropics and sub tropics. Before the rise of petroleum, tung oil was a major source of lighting oil. The leaves have a slight blue tint and the limbs of the tree don't branch out for the first fifteen feet of the tree, so it is a good thing that we can harvest the nuts on the ground. When you want some nuts, get a stick and dig around under the candlenut trees. Soon, you will find some nuts which outer skin has rotted away and are ready for cracking. See waiting in our hammock is a virtue! Crack them open with a couple of big rocks.

If you are walking the reef looking for dinner and your fish or lobster has hidden himself under a coral head, take a handful of crushed kukui bits and lay them on the up current side of the coral head. Your prey will soon scoot out, so be ready for him!

Kukui nuts also have medical properties. Check out the Natural Medicines section.

The Coconut Oil Lamp

Normally in the more basic parts of the third world, when the sun goes down, you go to sleep and at first light, maybe four thirty in the morning, you are up and at 'em. As a product of Western Civilization, you might find this difficult to do and incredibly boring. But not to worry. Just because you don't have electricity, doesn't mean you haven't any lights.

The coconut lamp is simplicity in itself. A bowl of oil with a floating wick will do fine. However, remember you are living in a dried leaf house. Dried leaves burn very well and very, very quickly. Our coconut lamp better be as safe as it can be. It can't be allowed to fall over. If it does, the oil will spill, the wick will ignite the oil, and your whole shack will burn down with you sleeping in it. Yikes! The best way to keep the lamp from falling over is to make the base really heavy.

A coconut shell makes a good coconut lamp. Kind of keeps it in the family. To make the base, find a rock with an indentation in it that will vaguely fit the shell and fill in the voids with sand, clay, rocks, anything nonflammable. Your coconut oil is not refined, so it will be smoky. That isn't bad as it will help to keep away blood sucking bugs that are attracted by the light.

The best thing to use as a wick is rolled up coconut gauze. To keep it from burning up in one night, it has to be rolled very tightly. Keep it afloat in the oil by inserting it through a small hole in a piece of wood and you are in business. Now if we only had something to read!

Soap

Life is so much more enjoyable when our skin and clothes are clean. Living on a deserted island is a fairly dirty experience, that cannot be denied, but we have an endless supply of water in the ocean and under waterfalls especially in the rainy season, if you have a waterfall. All we need is soap.

People have been making soap for hundreds of years. You can make it too. First we need an oil source. Need you ask? Again we rely on the coconut oil we squeezed from copra. Added to this is the root of the beehive ginger which grows in the forest along the stream below the (one can only hope) waterfall. This root only supplies a touch of oil but its perfume makes the final product so much more enjoyable. To turn the oil into soap we need caustic soda.

On your island caustic soda is best created by turning seaweed into dust. We do this by drying the seaweed and then burning it on our bed of coals. Before the seaweed flies away in little leaves and dust, (leaving us with our mouths open) we bury it under a thin layer of sand. (We don't want sand mixed in so burn enough for a thick layer) When it finally cools off, maybe a couple of days, scoop up the layer of seaweed caustic soda. We are now ready to make soap.

We will need a cooking bowl. The bigger the easier, but if you have to use a half a coconut shell or a section of bamboo, that is ok. (it won't burn in the fire, if there is liquid inside) But the best thing to do is find the little glen by the river that has the deposit of clay and fire up your own flatware and pots.

Add water and coconut oil in equal amounts, throw in a few diced ginger roots and heat it up. As it heats, start adding in the seaweed soda. Slowly the oil will start to solidify into a mass of soap and glycerin. After it solidifies as much as it is going to, we add salt water (Luckily, we have plenty) to the heated mixture which causes the soap/lye to rise and the glycerin to settle to the bottom of the bowl. Since we are playing with caustic soda and creating lye at this point, let's not put our hands or other body parts into the solution, shall we?

Separate the soap/lye and save the glycerin in a different container. Our soap is still filled with dirt and solid particles of coconut and ginger. Put it back into the bamboo section, clay pot, whatever, and heat it up and add an equal amount of water and seaweed soda and heat it up. The purer soap will rise to the surface, the dirtier soap will sink to the bottom. Discard the dirty soap. Careful now, there is now a lot of lye in the mixture.

Our purer soap will now be laced with lye and can be used to wash clothes with a paddle in a container, for body soap return the soap to the vat and boil several times with new salt water each time and then strain and pore the soap/lye into a container of coconut oil, stirring constantly, don't be in a hurry. Take your time. Don't rush. Lye is very dangerous and hospitals are far, far away. Keep stirring until it is uniform in consistency. If it is too greasy, put your container in the shade; if it is lumpy, put your container in the sun. Finally pour the mixture into coconut shell molds. It will take several days to solidify and then, why then you have your very own soap bar!

Before you start, a few warnings.

1. Have a container of vinegar (wine gone sour) to pour on the skin if you get some lye on it. Vinegar will neutralize it. Lye will burn, watch out!
2. Always start with cool water in making soap.
3. Always pour the lye into the coconut oil, not the other way around.

Other Types of Soap

Glycerin soap is very gentle on your hands and face. Really you should be cautious using homemade soap first on your skin until you have tried it on clothes and galley ware. To make glycerin soap simply add ten percent by volume of glycerin back into the mixture just after adding the lye into the coconut oil but before it has set. I love using beehive ginger blossoms to wash my hair and face, but really it is more of a cool thing to do than a way to really get clean!

Avocado pit soap is great when you have really gotten dirty, deep into your pores. Pound the pits into marble size pieces, dry, then pound into powder. Mix the powder into soap solution after adding the lye. Works really well on seriously dirty hands.

How to sharpen a Machete

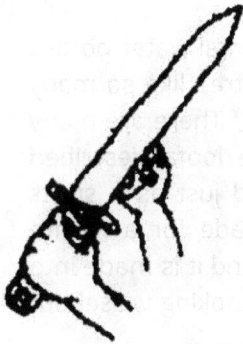

Sooner or later your Excalibur in the stone that you were rewarded with as you crawled out of the unforgiving sea on your first day on your island, will get dull. Dull machetes are good for nothing except glancing off the coconut and smacking your leg. You are going to have to sharpen it. I'm sure your first thought is to look around for an internet café to order a new one, but wait. It really isn't that hard to sharpen things. Here is how to do it.

First climb up the central peak if you are on a tall island, up to where the lava fields are still exposed. Don't go to the top of the mountain. Up there is only aa lava, cinders and clinker. We want a basalt type lava which has been cooled down slowly to get rid of its internal air bubbles. This is called pahoehoe lava. Look in the middle of a lava flow for a flattish, more polygon piece of lava. It is fragile if dropped but abrasive to steel. Find a safe place near the stream to install it.

We are going to sharpen the machete with a wet stone method. The lava has to be kept wet. Don't get carried away. The microscopic pieces of metal that will slide from the blade, help in the sharpening process. Don't wash them away. Start at the top of the stone and drag the blade towards you as you hold the blade at the same angle to the stone. Try to mirror the same angle that the original makers set in the blade. If anything make the angle a little steeper as no doubt, use has worn the edge down a little. Hold your hand nearer the handle of the blade, closer to your body than the tip. Hold the tip farther away. You want the metal scrapings to flow off the tip, not accumulate by the handle. Press down on the blade while you pull it towards you. If it is better for you to push away than pull, go for it, but try to always use the same motion. Your kneecaps and fingers will thank you!

Calabash Gourd

The Calabash Gourd is one of the fundamental water bottles of the castaway. It grows out of the trunk of the tree like so many tropical plants and grows to a globe a foot across. There are many types of gourds in the tropics, for example the loofa described elsewhere in this volume. The calabash is picked just as it starts loosing its green color and then dried in the shade for a month before the top is cut open, it is cleaned out inside and it is made into a water bottle. The gourds can also be used as a cooking vessel but don't last long considering the labor in drying them.

Another good use for the calabash is as a fishing float. Once the top is glued onto the cleaned gourd it is to all practical purposes water proof. One doesn't need much imagination to envision gourds used as lunch boxes, as tupperware, as life jackets, or as cocktail mixers.

Gourds can be made into musical instruments by inserting small rocks into the dried gourd and re-attaching the top with breadfruit sap. Small gourds with a single rock inside have been thought to have magical protective powers by ancient cultures when tied to the legs or arms. A useful thing to know when your island is invaded my head shrinking cannibals!

Plates and Bowls

While banana leaves are the traditional plates in Polynesia; disposable, plentiful, recyclable, they have their limits when it comes to fine dining. And after all, why do we have to eat like savages (oops, sorry, local inhabitants) just because we are abandoned on a deserted island? Surely the first step out of the stone age was a fine set of flatware?

Gourds grow on trees throughout the tropics. It is easy to find the trees. They are the ones that have broken gourds strewn around the ground below the tree. When the gourds start to grow, don't pick them until they reach the size you require. Left alone, they develop into the size of a basketball before they self destruct. Carefully saw them across appropriately depending if you want a water container or a soup dish. Use a sharpened spider conch or your obsidian knife as a saw (see the Tool section).

Coconut shells are the best flatware ever invented. They look good, they are water proof, they are probably dishwasher proof. They are totally plentifully. You will be opening at least one if not ten coconuts every day on the island. We always drink at least two coconuts for cocktail hour, maybe more if we have arrack! Use the back end of the machete to tap the shell where you want it to break. You might have to circle the shell ten times, tapping away to get a perfect crack, smooth all the way around. Don't be dismayed if you don't get it perfect the first try. You have lots of time and material for practice.

Clay bowls were once the in thing. Keep a good lookout for clay deposits on your explorations. (Always have a stick or your javelin in your hand and just stick it in any likely spots. Clay won't stick to your stick, but feels spongy when pushed. In your hand it feels like, well, play dough!) Directions under Galley Tools.

Paper Mulberry

Tapa cloth was made from the paper mulberry tree, a tree closely related to the breadfruit tree. The tree which resembles the breadfruit after too much sun bathing. The bark seems to be almost peeling off the tree. Polynesians took this peeling bark, peeled it to its smallest width, and pounded the bark between a flat board and a stone pounder until it started to resemble cloth. After pounding for a while, it is soaked in salt water, and then pounded again. Layers of bark are then laid ninety degrees to each other and pounded yet again. Eventually, when dried, it becomes somewhat flexible. (Don't expect silk! Closer to new denim jeans, back when they were still made of denim!)

The tapa was painted in various designs and worn as clothing or used as wall decorations and curtains by the ancient Polynesians, in fact, it is still made and sold in Tonga and Fiji.

The paper mulberry, like mulberries in northern climes bears a cherry. In the tropics this cherry is pit less, and is red when ripe. Some trees are much sweeter than others. If the first mulberry you eat is so sour your mouth puckers, don't give up. Keep trying! In any case, the sour ones do make nice jams if you have a lot of sugar laying around!

Salt Water

Never drink salt water. It says that in every survival book ever printed but it isn't true. Salt water is full of the trace elements that our bodies need to operate and to keep us in good health. Salt water is chemically almost identical to human blood, with the exception of large amounts of various salts. Far more salts than the kidneys can eliminate. But we sure could use those trace elements.

Do drink salt water, but just in a single, little, tiny sip once a day. And only drink it if you have abundant fresh water available as a chaser. If even this is too much for your kidneys, if it makes them hurt, just rinse your mouth out with some salt water a couple times a day. Not only is this a good dental hygiene, but the skin under your tongue is a very effective semi-permeable membrane, that excels at absorbing trace elements.

Never drink salt water if you don't drink fresh water just after at least ten times in volume of the salt water. Some authorities believe that your skin absorbs trace elements while bathing in the sea. That this is why in years past, doctors advised patients to visit the beach to complete their medical recovery even if they were only exposed to the salt air. If this is true, by the time you are rescued you will be one of the healthiest people on earth!

Weaving Rope

When you get down to weaving your own rope, you are definitely no longer squatting on your island, you are becoming a resident. Nothing shows the desire to set yourself up as a survivor as a length or two of well weaved rope holding up a woven shade mat of coconut fronds hanging from coconut and breadfruit trees to make gathering the daily fruit and toddy an easier task. And when you get right down to it, rope making is not difficult. There are three plants on almost every island in the tropics that grow excellent rope making substances, coconut, ti and sisal.

Sisal making still survives and indeed is making a comeback due to the increasing cost of petroleum, the basis of synthetic ropes. Its advantages are: it floats, it is unharmed by solar radiation, it is very strong, it is very resistant to chaff. You have seen examples of this rope many times. Remember the fiber matting that used to cover the floor of your grandparent's (great grandparent's?) beach house? Or the fiber door mat by your front door? Both are made of sisal. The advantages of making rope from sisal is the fibers are up to fifty inches long making it easy to introduce new fibers in the splicing process and there are hundreds of fibers in each leaf. The disadvantages are to get at the fibers you will have to scrape the vegetable matter off the leaves, soak them and scrape some more until just the long fibers are left. Scraping is easily done with sea shells. Walk down the beach, there are hundreds. Conch shells are good. Biologists don't believe it, but I assure you, conch are world wide. Soaking is best done in the tide pools formed at low tide at the end of the beach.

Coconut husks make coir rope. Coir has fallen out of favor in the last fifty years. I don't know why. Years ago the main sheet on a sail boat was always made out of coir. Its advantages were that you only had to lead the rope thru a block, then hold the two lengths together in your hand to keep the sail close hauled. The line was so strong and bristly that it would not slip. You are not going to be making the bristly rope of old. We are going to weave a beautiful line that will make Friday stare in astonishment. And we are going to make it out of the husk of coconuts. The disadvantage of making coir rope is the individual fibers are only five or six inches long. However there are thousands of them in one coconut and they are easy to separate.

Ti leaves are easy. They are a thin, tough leaf that is easily separated into thinner strings with your thumb nail. The narrower your original strings, the finer the rope will be. Ti is the least abrasive material of the three but is still very strong. Use it around your shack and as a belt and bra string for Friday (not that she needs one).

OK, one way or another you have your material. Start with three unequal lengths. Weave them together like a woman's hair braid, left over right, right over left until you almost reach the end of the shortest length. Add another length to the short one and continue to braid holding the new to the old until it is well meshed in. Continue this way until you reach the required length. You have made string. Make three strings. Tie the three together at one end and then weave those three together just as you did in making string. You now have twine, useful for fishing and the like. Make three twine and weave them together and you have made your first rope. Congratulations!

However, real sailors don't make rope this way, only castaways. If you want to make a real rope you will need a flyer. Hey, I don't invent these names! Don't blame me! The flyer, basically, is a piece of wood with three holes in it, through which your yarns of sisal or coir are run. You will need three flyers. The flyer is twisted and then spun in opposite directions. It is the opposing twists that give a rope its shape and elasticity.

So, spin each flyer to clockwise while wrapping each flyer around each other to counterclockwise. Easy, huh? Maybe we should just stick to weaving rope till we have been on the island for a few years and need new projects!

Health

Without your health you are going to have a hard time on your abandoned island just staying alive, much less thriving. Be careful with your body. Keep your mind sane and active with building projects. Don't eat strange fruits unless you know they are healthy for you.

Ciguatera

Ciguatera, just the name sends waves of apprehension up my spine. Fish poisoning, vomiting, diarrhea, weakness, numbness, muscle pain, your skin becomes so itchy you want to scratch it all off. Death occurs ten percent of the time. No, thank you. What is so wrong with fruit and veggies? Alright, I understand, you need the protein. But you must know that if you eat just one more coconut you can't be held responsible for your actions.

The first hurdle is catching the fish. Without a facemask, your options are limited, however, reef fish often visit the top of the fringing reef, looking for food. I have speared three foot long parrotfish while walking along reefs with my trusty throwing javelin. (It did take practice!) But how can you tell if the fish has ciguatera?

Short and sweet, you can't. Best thing to do is feed some to Friday, first. Sorry, scratch that. Who knows? She might be reading this! How ciguatera works is bigger fish eat littler fish, littler fish eat the blue-green algae which causes it. Each time bigger fish eat a smaller fish the amount of ciguatera increases in the big fish. Eventually, some fish are so toxic that they can infect humans with just a mouthful. Never eat a fish bigger than your forearm. Smaller humans, (and the semi humans otherwise known as kids) must eat only smaller fish that match their own forearm. (So when the huge Polynesian Chief gets the biggest fish it is not a sign of respect!) Parrot fish and grunts rarely are contaminated with enough poison to affect a human as they are eating the algae itself so the concentration of poison going up the food chain has not happened. I know, I know, but it is true!

If you do come down with symptoms of ciguatera, never eat reef fish again for at least a year and especially from that reef. The concentration of poison will slowly increase in you just as it will in the bigger fish. Ciguatera doesn't hurt the fish. It is a human disease. If a fish is acting weird, it doesn't mean he has ciguatera, but don't eat him anyway. Some say that if you leave the fish on the deck and he becomes stiff and rigid in 45 minutes, he doesn't have ciguatera. (They do have an injection in hospitals that is an antidote now, not that it will help us!

Oral Care

Many diseases enter the body through the mouth. It is important to keep the mouth as clean as you can especially as the nearest dentist is looking right at you from the other side of the mirror, if you have a mirror.

The primary tool for oral hygiene is the tooth brush. What? You didn't get shipwrecked while carrying your tooth brush? Not to worry, nature will provide. A perfectly workable tooth brush can be made from a twig sharpened on one end and split into a featherlike end. When it gets used up and needs to be replaced, make a new one. There are a lot of twigs on the island. Personally I prefer eucalyptus twigs for their taste, casuarinas for their clean after taste and neem twigs for their antiseptic and healing oils. The sharpened end is for using between your teeth as if you did have any dental floss you would be tying lures with it.

The tongue is one of the windows into the health of your body, and one of the portals thru which the body eliminates its wastes. It often is covered with a white scum when you wake in the morning (especially after a hard night drinking arrack). As you eat and drink and swallow during the day these poisons are reintroduced into the body. Far wiser to scrape your tongue first thing in the morning to eliminate these wastes. In civilization this is best performed with the edge of a teaspoon. In an abandoned island teaspoons are hard to come by. However, a perfectly good substitute can be made from the broken edge of a sea shell or of a trimmed coconut shell.

The tonsils gather bacteria and kill them. The debris from the bacteria quickly cover the surface of the tonsils diminishing their effectiveness. The best way to counter this in the wild, far away from mouthwash and gargles is to clear your throat early in the morning. Ancient Chinese believed a demon lived in the throat and the louder the throat was cleared in the morning the more likely the demon would be scared away. In any case, clear your throat as loud as you like. After all, there is no one to hear you, is there? Afterwards, salt water makes one of the best gargles there is, and we do have lots and lots of salt water!

If you still don't feel clean, try chewing a small piece of dried torch ginger root. Swallow the spit if you like. It won't hurt you. Spit out the remains of the root after ten minutes or so.

If you really miss toothpaste, make up your own with salt mixed with the dried ground up zest on an orange. Don't brush too hard until the salt has dissolved a bit.

If you really miss your mouthwash find a curry leaf tree. The leaves contain beta carotene, folic acid, riboflavin, calcium and zinc. Chew 2 or 4 leaves after brushing with a bit of water then swish it all around. Yes, Friday will wonder why you smell like curry, but she will get used to it!

Ok, she can't get used to it. A great stopper of bad breath, if you consider curry breath, bad, is nutmeg. Chew just a little bit, a sliver. Really! Eating just two nutmeg in one day can be lethal. Besides just a sliver is highly hallucinogenic. It is very subtle. You probably won't even notice. And you thought eating all that pumpkin pie for Thanksgiving is why everyone unbuttoned their pants and fell asleep during the game!

Insect Repellant

The most effective insect repellant is mud. Really, it is the newest thing in Paris! Very retro, like the mud men of New Guinea. We do have lots of mud by rivers and creeks in tropical islands, but somehow being covered in mud doesn't play well with my idea of a tropical paradise. There has to be a better way.

The Thais came up with the best idea. They planted Neem trees all around their houses. The Neem is a beautiful tree and flowers with an indescribably beautiful scent. The leaves put out their own undetectable odor that mosquitoes and sand flies hate. Who needs screens when the bugs refuse to come anywhere near your grass shack?

When traveling farther afield or if you didn't find a grove of Neem trees to build your shack in, we can make a repellant out of the juice of the leaves. Here is how.

The Neem is a big tree with lots and lots of leaves. Pick the young ones, they are loaded with the juice we want. Crush the leaves in your hands and drop them into a bowl of coconut oil and slowly simmer over coals for a few hours. Strain the leaves out and voila!

Spread the heavenly scented lotion on an exposed skin. Bugs are a thing of the past! But what happens if you can't find any neem and are being eaten alive?

You are not living on the western beach, are you? The sunset beach? Sand flies love the sunset. They go there to dine, knowing that every day large biped mammals migrate there to perform primitive mating rituals while watching the sun set and ignore any bugs that happen to want a little blood, just a little bite, mind you. If you really have to perform the rituals, start a fire and dance around it staying in the smoke for the more dramatic movements to repel any bugs. Insects are attracted by carbon dioxide that mammals expel when breathing, so try to keep the heavy panting down.

After a few weeks saltwater bathes just aren't doing the job anymore. Time to visit the waterfall, home of the mosquitos. Try to get there in the middle of the day. Mosquitos are most active in the morning and the evening. On your way there pick the blossom of a beehive ginger. Not only does it have slight anti-insect properties but it has a beautiful scent and suds up slightly when used as a shampoo.

As always, clothes are the first line of defense. Take a look at the tapa making chapter. By the lower branches of coconut tree grows a brown gauze like material. It makes a great mosquito screen if you sew pieces together.

So what happens if the bugs already bit you? The last thing you want to do is scratch. Don't do it! The tropics are no place to have an open wound. Staph is epidemic and antibiotics are thousands of miles away, kind of. We do have natural antibiotics in the tropics. Some that are still undiscovered by modern doctors. Read more in the Natural Medicine chapter.

So what do you do after you are bit? Slapping the bite site is always useful. It supplies three things: it brings blood to the surface of the skin to help wash away the poison, it stuns the synapses in the nerves so the itching stops, and it feels good to do something about the bite since you are not allowed to itch.

A little coconut oil dripped on a stick and then set afire keeps bugs away as does a smoldering coconut husk, for extra effectiveness, leave the coconut meat in the open nut as you are burning it.

At night, is when you are most defenseless. They can dine at their leisure while you are sleeping. To prevent attracting bugs, never cook near your sleeping shack. The heat and odors will attract all manners of bugs. Remember on the American frontier- like the old Daniel Boone series? They never cooked in the main house. Make yourself a cooking shed.

If your island has really bad bugs, considering building your own island. No, I am not being delusional. Everytime you find a big rock bring it over to the fringing reef on the windward side of the island. You don't need a big island, just enough for a sleeping hut, maybe a hundred feet away from the beach. It is OK if the spring tides come over the top of the rocks, they will keep your island clean. Plus you need a night ashore on the big island every once in awhile to remind yourself why you went to so much trouble to begin with.

Latrines and galley waste

Relieving yourself is not the most pleasant subject, but it is an important one. You don't want to contaminate your island, camp, creek, waterfront or shack. Most likely there will be no flies when you arrive on the island as there will be no large animals to act as a vector. There are always baby flies being born from a reservoir of hibernating larva, but without a large animal to supply the poop, they won't be able to mate and lay eggs.

Polynesians never dug latrines. Instead they walked into the ocean, squatted down and did their business there. Even their barkless poi dogs were trained to do the same. That way they kept their islands sweet smelling paradises. The currents around the island soon dispersed any residue that was not eaten up by sea creatures. I know what you are going to say. "And now you expect me to eat things that have been eating my poop?" Yes, I do.

When I was a boy in San Diego, every weekend we went down to the Tijuana Estuary and dug up clams, caught fish and had a marvelous time. The estuary led straight from the slums of Mexico where every sickness known to man killed people daily. But those clams. They were the juiciest, fattest clams ever! No, we never got sick. The clams were filter feeders; they turned bacteria into clam meat without any cross contamination. It is the same on coral reefs. The coral will love your poop.

Never bury or leave galley waste on the island. Just throw it into the ocean. The biggest dangers on deserted islands are not sharks, moray eels or cannibals; the biggest danger is sand flies. These flies, also called nonos, no see'ums, flying teeth can so de-capacitate you that you might well starve to death in the midst of plenty. They breed on the beach and on any food source. Never leave food on the beach. Always rake any seaweed that floats up by your camp back into the water or better, bury it inland to start improving the soil of the island. Eventually you will develop a partial resistance to sand flies. The operative word is partial. There are always snakes in edens. Don't encourage yours.

Filtering fresh Water

Fresh water is not always clean in nature. That doesn't mean dirty water is bad. Watch any dog and cat. If they are offered a choice between standard house water or rain water with leaves in it, they will pick the leaves every time. If you are getting your water from a well or a stream it may well have sediment in it if not other things as well.

The worse thing to have in a fresh water stream is a dead animal. In this we are luckier than most. You can back walk the length of the stream making sure there are no unwelcome guests. If you do find something, bury it at least a hundred feet from the stream.

Generally, you are just going to find leaves, sediment, the rare fish roe and insects in the water. The best thing to do is to build yourself a filter system. I like to build mine out of calabash gourds. Carve a large hole on the top, a very little one on the bottom and fill it with sand with a rock on the bottom to keep the sand inside. When you scoop water from the stream or well, pour it into the top of the calabash with another container below to catch the purified water. Once a week, change the sand. This kind of filter really works well.

I know you are going to turn into a rooting tooting beachcomber, but even tough guys need pure water to keep going, and especially to use as a mixer with their arrack!

Natural Medicines

Your island is full of natural medicines. Really. The forest is a great big pharmacy. The prepared islander need not fear being injured or falling sick. Like much in life all we need is knowledge. Presented here are a few of the many natural remedies that I have tried myself with good results or have been told about by islanders around the world.

Aloe Vera

Long time sailors need no introduction to Aloe Vera. Even though it originated in Africa, it no longer has any original natural occurring populations. It has spread worldwide. There is much contradictory information about aloe's usefulness in beauty products, but it has been proven time and again that not only is Aloe Vera gel from inside the leaves effective against fungi and bacteria but it also is the only plant on atolls that is effective against streptococcus. The gel is also very effective in healing burns. The Reader may wonder why the long distant former inhabitants of many islands have grown so many plants that were effective against burns. Alas, The Reader will soon find out that cooking over a wood fire on a windy beach may not be the safest thing to do. But we are prepared when we do get burned.

For protecting the lips from the sun and wind, mix the gel from inside an aloe vera plant with fifty percent coconut oil. Heat together until uniform, pour into a container and cool. Great for hot days on the beach or windy days in the canoe.

Avocado

Eating avocados has been proven (I forget by whom) to prevent high blood pressure, heart disease and stroke. Of course they can't charge you $100 a pill so there is no huge cry to eat more avocados, is there? Because of their high concentration of carotenoids and tocopherols they are also effective against prostrate cancer. Think of it. Being shipwrecked might well save your life!

Bamboo

Inside of the joints of bamboo, (for who knows what reason), resides elemental silica. Silica is essential for healthy nails, hair and teeth, organs that have a really hard time of it in the wild. Elemental silica can be absorbed directly into the blood stream by placing it under your tongue and letting it dissolve. Crack open the joint, the part separating two lengths of bamboo of a young green plant. Inside find a few drops of syrupy liquid. Drop the drops into a clean coconut shell and dry it in the sun. Avoid the salt air, don't let the rain get into the shell. Once dry, take a pinch and place under the tongue, you will be able to tear open coconuts with your bear hands!

Bananas

The inside of the banana peel contains a natural anti-biotic which is quite effective against both oral infections and skin infections. For the mouth, tooth, throat, ears, sinus and eyes, chew the inside of the banana skin swallowing the saliva. Chew one skin per hour. Good results will be obtained within a day. Don't eat the skin. For skin rashes, cuts, scraps and burns, lash the inside of the peel against the injured skin, replace every four hours after thoroughly cleaning the wound with fresh water and allowing to air dry, except for burns which should not be washed. Results will be gradual but improvement will be noticed within a couple of days.

The sap of the banana plant is effective in cases of leprosy, good to know just in case, or so I was told on Molokai. Hey, if those guys don't know, who would?

Betel Nut

I can hear you from here, no your teeth won't be stained black! Really! The main ingredient of betel nuts is arecoline, which is a worming agent used by veterinarians. Listen, I know you aren't an animal, and chewing betel is a nasty habit, but until you find garlic, how are you going to get rid of worms?

Breadfruit Leaves

A tea made of young breadfruit leaves reduces blood pressure and I have been told but cannot confirm that it also controls asthma. The roasted flowers can be rubbed on an aching tooth for temporary relief. The ashes of the burnt leaves are said to help skin infections, but I really didn't see that much improvement myself. It did help a little.

Cattails

To make a salve for healing sand fly bites and jelly fish stings, pound up the younger leaves and baby cattails. Keep the jelly like juice and throw away the plant part. It keeps well so make up some extra for emergencies. Use it like using aloe vera.

Cayenne Pepper

Cayenne pepper is not a pepper. For a while, back when, pepper was a very expensive commodity and merchants labeled anything they could as pepper to increase profits. However, cayenne is a fantastic medicine. Almost for sure' who ever lived on your island before, would have grown cayenne. It's there, it's free, just find it. It's not hard. They are small bushes with small red peppers on it. (Uh, oh, I just said peppers!)

Unfortunately we don't have quinine or Peruvian bark on the island so we have no cures for malaria or dengue. However, cayenne does a good job of jazzing up the bodies own defenses to enable it to fight disease. Because both malaria and dengue require a mammalian host to continue the disease, and the only likely mammals on a deserted island are rats and flying foxes (fruit bats), the chances of you coming in contact with either are limited but possible.

Clove

The oil of cloves not only has exceptional anesthetic and antiseptic properties but it is also useful in that most dreaded of all health problems, toothache. OK, being eaten by a Great White, stung by a box jellyfish, a foot seized by a giant clam might be worse, but hey, we can avoid those! Now we can stick a clove in our tooth if the filling falls out or rub the gums with the oil if it just hurts.

Coconut Oil

Coconut oil is good to treat saltwater sores and sunburn. Saltwater sores are caused by having your skin always damp with salt water. Try to get up to the waterfall at least once a week if not every day, or at least jump in for a swim in a river or creek. Get into the habit of never running away from rain squalls, shower in them instead. After, rub coconut oil into your skin and hair. It isn't greasy, it absorbs right into the skin.

If you drench a stick with coconut oil, light it, and then stick it into the sand, it repels mosquitos. Burning a coconut husk also does a fair job at keeping mossies away. Sew together the gauzelike fibers at the coconut palm leaf bases to make a mosquito net.

Ginger Root

There are two main types of ginger in the tropics; torch ginger, the one with the flame like flower, the most common and beehive ginger, the one with the flower that looks like, well, a beehive! This is the flower you can use as a shampoo. Both type's roots are good, not only for eating but also for medicine.

Chewing a fresh, peeled, young root really eases a sore throat. It also helps a sour stomach, and stomach problems. If because of the stress of living on a deserted island, Friday's menstruation stops, a hot ginger root tea taken daily will get her back to normal.

Ginger dried and ground into powder, then melted with sugar with a little coconut milk makes an awesome candy. Just the thing when you are feeling blue or a little depressed.

One day when you have been on the island for a year or two, you will tire of waiting to be rescued and build yourself a canoe, study navigation and go voyaging yet again. When that day comes remember that chewing ginger root is great in combating sea sickness and easing mental tension.

Jack Fruit

The Chinese think that jack fruit seeds are not only a cure for hangovers but also an aphrodisiac. Don't laugh. They have, by far, the largest population of earth. Maybe they know something we don't? They also burn the young leaves until they are just ashes, and then sprinkle the powder on ulcers caused by insect bites.

Kapok

Kapok was used as absorbent material during surgery before artificial materials became more available. When the kapok tree is throwing its seeds you will find more absorbent material than you could ever use under the tree and flying in the wind. Make pillows and softer beds in case you or Friday get sick, but mostly use it to get all that sand out of your eyes on windy days.

Kava

Kava, a brewed drink popular in the South Pacific is made out of pepper plant roots that are mashed (or even chewed by virgins then spit in to a pot, a story I think the locals made up and told to Margaret Mead!), water is added or traditionally, coconut milk and the pot then is left to ferment. It is normally drunk before a tribal meeting as kava reduces stress and aggression.

Kukui Nuts

Burn the flowers and the nuts into a charcoal. This powder is very effective against fungus and fungal diseases of the skin and scalp. It also works well on athletes foot and crotch itch.

Limes

Limes are a wonderful medicine. The juice is great for easing the sting of mosquito and sand fly bites. Taken internally, it is a diuretic for the liver, a stimulant for stomach, a cure for hemorrhoids. The juice eases heart palpitations, headaches, coughs, arthritis, bad breath and thinning hair. The pharmaceutical companies would love to get a corner on the market. Stay tuned!

Mountain Apple and Banana

The crushed flowers of the mountain apple are an excellent astringent and are useful for lowering fever and to halt diarrhea. The fruit is full of vitamins and the bright red color never fails to raise the spirits of the infirm.

The ashes of the burnt unripe peel of a banana works well in cases of diarrhea, best taken with coconut water. The sap of the banana plant is useful for insect bites and hemorrhoids while the cooked flowers are useful in easing bronchitis. Eat one flower an hour.

Noni

Noni is the Polynesian miracle drug that in part explains how they were able to survive deep sea explorations, endemic coral cuts, falls from hundred foot coconut trees, shark attacks and strange diseases encountered in new islands. The plant has been transplanted by islanders during their voyages until today it grows throughout the tropics, worldwide. Modern science has ignored the Noni. I don't know why. It cures just about everything that can go wrong with the human body including some types of cancer. The only downside is it really tastes bad.

I mean bad. Terrible. Outrageous. Imagine a hobo with athlete's foot and jungle rot wearing a pair of socks for ten years then giving them to you to smell. It is much worse than that. But it is good for you and it is a little alcoholic! You can make it yourself. Here is how. (The enhancement to your sex life alone is worth the effort!)

When the fruit becomes ripe, it turns white, pick it and put it in a container. A coconut shell that cracked completely in half with both sides whole, will work. (We don't want any flies or bugs getting into our brew.) Leave it in a cool, dark place and wait. That is it. After a few weeks all the juice will have run out of the fruit and fermented. Throw the fruit remains away or eat it if you are really, really hardcore. Drink an ounce or two of the juice in the morning before eating. Mix it with some other kind of juice. Aficionados insist that it should be drunk straight, but not by this writer. The taste is really bad. Prepare a list of projects. A long list. You will have so much energy that you will go crazy without something to do. Sounds great? You haven't tasted it yet!

For a good tasting Noni without the throw up tendencies, make a tea out of the new leaves. Pick them and dry them in the sun. After a day, crush them in your hands and dry them for a couple more days. Very good flavor, but not containing most of the totally mind blowing effects of the juice.

Noni juice is also excellent for curing burns. Pour it on and cover with young noni leaves. Change only once a day. Keep out of the saltwater.

The green fruit can be eaten during the hurricane season when food might not be as easy to come by. Again, not tasty, and not with the health kick of the juice. But it will keep you alive.

Okra

Use the young leaves to wrap around the wound for a really outstanding pain reliever. Crush the leaves first between your hands then cover the wound at least three inches past any pain. Replace as needed.

Papaya Seeds

Papaya seeds dried, crushed up and ingested with water are a somewhat effective cure for worms. Eaten whole, papaya seeds keep the intestinal tract clean of poisons and fatty deposits that can lead to future diseases. Overweight persons are in danger to a large degree because of the fat deposits inside the abdominal cavity not just because of the fat beneath the skin. Papaya seeds eaten whole on an empty stomach do a good job of regulating these fats. Indeed there are health farms in Polynesia that restrict your diet to papaya seeds, cayenne pepper and activated carbon for two weeks. Sounds dramatic doesn't it? It does work. I have seen people at death's door, confined to their beds, get up and walk out of the health farm two weeks later, laughing and smiling at their friends. (*Personal Comment:* An interesting activity at these farms is laying in an open casket under the trees for two hours a day. Sounds weird, huh? I tried it and it was so peaceful. Unbelievably pleasant watching the trees sway in the wind high above me. My two hours went by in a flash. Makes you wonder why we rail so hard about death. Depends if you go up or down, I guess!)

Papaya Skin

For some reason skin boils are a problem in the tropics. Whether it is the constant trade winds that keep our skins slightly salty and thus moist or the fact that dry towels are a benefit of civilization. On your island the best thing to do is to take a quick swim once or twice a day in the stream or waterfall, (if you are lucky) washing yourself with the flower of the beehive ginger, and then air dry. Advocates of the perfect tan will appreciate this, for others, it far wiser to air dry under a tree with just enough sunlight coming through the branches to keep you warm. In any case the papain in green papaya skins excel in dissolving and softening meat including the skin over the top of a boil. Lancing a boil in the tropics is an invitation for infection. A sterile lance is an impossibility and the boil is sure to heal over the punch mark inviting streptococcus. (*Important Personal Hint:* Strep lives just inside the lip of the nostrils. Determined effort should be made not to pick your nose and then touch a wound before washing well. No one knows why strep lives there, it just does.) (Well, everything has to have a home, doesn't it?)

Pineapple

OK, the worse thing in the world has happened and you have gotten Friday pregnant. OK, it isn't the worse thing. In fact it is kind of cool. You know, really, creating new life in a new world. The worse thing is the baby won't come out. You've looked at the edge on your machete and decided that a caesarean operation is out of the question. But it has been over 10 months and something has to be done. Guess what! Pineapple juice, the real stuff, not juice from Dole but juice from a ripe pineapple, expedites labor. A cup every hour.

Watch out! Don't eat very young pineapples! Not only are they toxic but the flesh eaten (one teaspoon) every morning for 3 days causes an abortion! Baby pineapples are very, very poisonous and the nearest hospital is far, far beyond the horizon.

Starfruit Juice

The skin takes a beating in the tropics, especially along the beach where there is always salt on the skin keeping it slightly moist. Great for keeping the wrinkles at bay, not so good for jungle rot. Ring worm is the most well known of the fungal diseases but all of them respond well to a syrup of Starfruit juice applied twice a day. Life is so much better when we look and feel sexy, you know, like the Polynesian natives Captain Cook discovered on Tahiti, living in perfect health, benefit of tropical plants and distance from the disease pits of Europe.

Tamarind

Boil up a bunch of leaves and flowers with just enough water to cover and keep boiling until the water is reduced to at least half. The strained liquid is then a useful antibiotic as well as a treatment for dysentery.

Adventure and romance

Let's face it, we are all suckers for Hollywood. Our lives revolve around adventure and romance. Whether it is office politics, going fishing, daytime soaps, the newest blockbuster, that guy/girl down the block, beating all the lights on the way to work, whatever; we live for romance and adventure. And just because we are suddenly stranded on an island in the middle of nowhere, doesn't mean we are going to become new, more placid, people.

Not that we should. The human race's love for what is exciting and fun and titillating and uplifting is what keeps us human. And it is going to take a bit of adventure and romance to get us off this rock, eventually. But let's start slow and build work our way up to lettering in survival varsity.

Making a Hammock

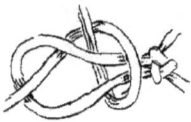

You have to make a hammock, it says so right there in the castaway's handbook. And it is easy to do, kind of. The easiest way is to find a piece of netting while beachcombing. They wash up routinely, but bury themselves rapidly in the sand equally as quickly. If you do find one, watch out. The polypropylene they are made of is very rough and can easily cause deep scratches on your skin (very much a no-no in the tropics). So be sure to line your hammock with banana leaves. Yes, it will be hotter, but Friday will definitely be appreciative.

However, the proper way to make a hammock is to weave one up out of rope you made yourself. It isn't that hard to do. There are endless books of rope tying and weaving, but here is my own secret method for tying up hammocks.

The best of hammocks have a spreader bar at both ends. This is a piece of wood that keeps the hammock spread open making egress and entry far easier, plus it simplifies the construction by keeping the lines in their proper places. Burn and carve holes in both spreader bars at about one inch intervals.

Run your first line, doubled, right in the middle of a spreader bar, attaching with a lark's head. We are going to tie a series of sheet bends. Nettings are made in finger sizes. The mesh of the net is described as being so many fingers wide. For example, a good size for a hammock is a mesh size having a 2¼ inch eye. The hole in the mesh is 2¼ inches long when it is elongated. This is a three finger eye as the net is made by placing three fingers next to a line and tying a sheet bend around them. Put three fingers right between the doubled line and tie a sheet bend around them. Put your fingers below your new knot and tie another sheet bend around them. Continue until you reach at least the length of hammock you desire. Don't cut off the ends.

Lead another doubled line right next to your initial line. Bring one side of the line down to the middle of the first eye you made in

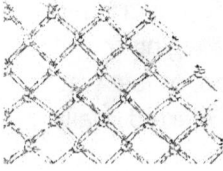

your first set of lines and tie a sheet bend in the middle of the eye. Continue down and tie it to (I'm not going to say sheet bend any more!) its mate. Continue down, first tying to the eye then to its mate until you reach the end of the first line.

The idea here is we are limiting the number of lines we have to deal with at any one time. This way the maximum number of lines that are ever in your hands is two, and you can stop at any time, and then continue later with no mental gymnastics. Keep adding additional lines until you get to half the width you desire. The last line on the end is run tighter to give the hammock a safety factor. Falling overboard while sleeping between two waving palms is not fun.

On the far spreader bar, continue the weaving (knot tying) making the center looser and each line outwards a little tighter until the last line is almost straight. If you are a heavy person, don't make the middle as loose. The lines will stretch to accommodate you!

Tie a harness to each spreader bar that leads to your friendly neighborhood coconut palm tree. Be careful not to rig your hammock directly under a coconut palm. Those falling nuts really hurt when they land!

Beauty Tips on Deserted Islands

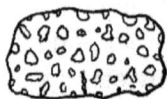

Just because you are temporarily living on a deserted island doesn't mean that you are going to let yourself go to the dogs. Certain standards of beauty have to be maintained especially for the kinder, gentler sex. Not to worry. Nature will provide.

Pumice stones are from volcanos. Even if your deserted island isn't 'blessed' with a volcano, chances are you will find pumice stones on the beach on the windward side of the island as they are so light, they will float across oceans. Rub the stone all over your body removing old skin, scabs that are ready to come off, ingrained dirt, and toxins from civilization your body is finally managing to get rid of. Use it under the waterfall, on the beach, with soap, or just wet. Imagine that, you had to get shipwrecked before you started really taking care of your body!

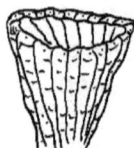

Sea Sponges live on the bottom of the sea. They are a colony of millions of different animals and plants living together under one roof. Eventually they die and the skeleton of their house washes up on to the beach. They are the best thing for washing your body in the river. First though, pound them between two rocks to be sure everything is dead in there, we don't want any surprises while in the shower, do we? Besides, sometimes there are little spines inside made when the little animals started building high rises. Make sure it is nice and soft before washing more delicate sections of your anatomy.

Sand is great for the feet. Just walking along the beach makes our feet feel so much better. And this is important as without happy feet we are going to starve amidst plenty on our deserted island! Keep them doggies happy, dry, and as clean as you can.

The shell of a spider conch makes a romantic picture when used as a comb. If you really want to pose as a wild wahine sitting on a coconut tree angled over a black sand beach with blue water just beyond, long hair hanging over one ear, a hibiscus flower in the other, a thin slip of coconut gauze as your only garment and a lei around your neck, then you have to have a spider conch comb in one hand. It is a rule or something. Either way, you definitely will make the cover of Cosmo.

Making Leis

Lei making is the ultimate art of the Hawaiian wahine and the thing everyone most remembers about their trip to the islands. There isn't a trick to it. You can make leis too. It is easy!

The easy way to make leis is to have a lei needle, a very long, stainless needle that can hold ten blossoms at a time. But it isn't a necessity. But lets start at the beginning.

Find a plumeria tree, (Frangipani in Tahitian) and pick all the blossoms you think you will need. Bring them over to a stream or fresh water supply and let them soak. This will keep the flowers fresh longer. Find yourself a string at least three feet or more long. Whether it is the spine of a coconut frond leaf, a thin piece of ti leaf, a woven section of sisal, a string made of coconut husk (coir), it doesn't matter. If the string is strong enough, it can be threaded right threw the blossom in the end and out the flower part. A needle from a Waree palm will work fine if needed. String the blossoms one after the other and after reaching the required length, tie a knot, or use a smaller string to lash everything together. Put the lei back into the water. The more you handle flowers the worse they look. Kind of like women?

When the time comes, lead Friday to a secluded grove, have her close her eyes and slip the lei over her head and give her the required kiss. If you were having trouble with Friday before, forget it. She will now go native. You have created a Wahine!   Traditionally, the bigger, more important, the occasion, the more leis the honored one wears. The flowers are going to die anyway, pile the leis on up to her nose! The smell of Frangipani is so unforgettable, so romantic. Your girl will love you passionately for the rest of your life and forgive you anything!

Coconut Head Band

Just surviving on a deserted island isn't really enough. Life is more than eating, sleeping, working, sex and offspring. Where is the romance and adventure and beauty?   We need the arts, music, and dancing. Even if we are only hitting coconut shells against each other and stomping on the sand around the fire just after dusk. Humans need artistic expression to stay sane. Let's start with something simple. Something kind of easy. A coconut leaf head band. This band can be made more effectively with other longer lasting leaves, but we have lots of coconut fronds and making this band is good practice for weaving the Grass Shack and making the coconut leaf hat.

By now you have become experienced at climbing coconut trees for the nuts, the green fronds, and gathering toddy. If not, see the index. You will only need three longish frond leaves but you might need the whole frond, what with practice and all. Remove two leaves from the frond and cut the central stem out leaving four halves. Fold one leaf at an forty five degree angle so that one half is about six inches longer that the other. Lay a second leaf between the halves of the first and bend one end at a forty five degree angle so that it parallels the longer end of the first leaf. (All angles are going to be forty fives so I am not going to say it anymore. Having one end shorter that the other is to ensure the splice will not be in just one place when we come around in a circle.)

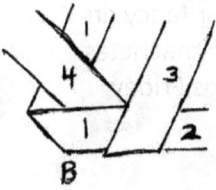

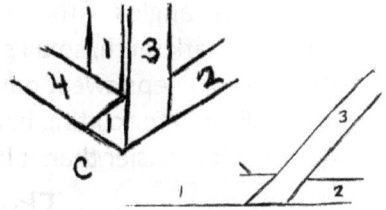

OK, now it is easy. The outer leaf goes over and under the inner leaves after making an angle at the edge of the inner leaf and in itself becomes an inner leaf. Your art work should be forming a kind of hexagon. If it isn't you didn't rotate the outer leaf that is to be folded next. Right and then left, fold it over and under. After a foot and a half begin to wrap it around your head to see how much farther you have to go. When the two end meet start splicing the new leaves into the old by sistering the new to the old, tuck once or twice then cut off.

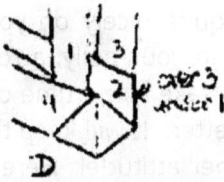

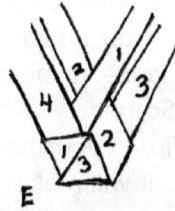

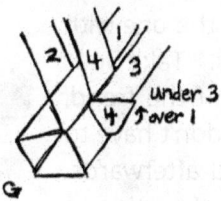

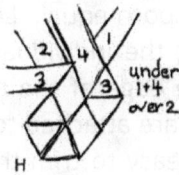

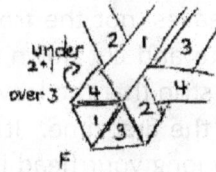

The angles of the head band make it very easy to insert flowers, shark teeth, small shells, or whatever meets your fancy on that day. It keeps sweat out of your eyes, your long hair (machetes are really bad for cutting hair) out of your eyes, and keeps Friday ecstatic. It is easier than it looks, try it!

The Coconut Hat

There are few things that are required to be a castaway, a ship wrecked sailor or a beachcomber; but the most important of all is making and wearing your own coconut leaf hat. It is the classic image of the desperado living on a tropical island and abandoning civilization in favor of a better way of life. When you first land on your island, you are not going to be a happy little ex-sailor. In fact you might be just a bit crazed and desperate. You may have a wild look about you that resembles a trapped rat in a corner of a maze. But not to worry. You bought this book. If you are not instantly rescued, you are going to be able to survive quite nicely on your deserted island. So once you have some food in your belly, a roof over your bed, a fire in your hearth (OK, beach), take some time out and make the hat. It will make you feel much better. It will keep the sun out of your eyes. It will give you the proper attitude! Here is how to do it. (Useful Hint, try making the Coconut Head Band first as practice.)

Not all coconut fronds are born equal. Look for the one with the longest leaves, not the frond, the individual leaves. Take your trusty machete and cut down the edge of the middle of the frond, just leaving a strip that the leaves are attached to. You don't have to cut too close the first time. It is easy to trim the frond afterwards. Measure how long your head is around and cut your leaf section to fit, but don't cut it exactly. Between your head and the remainder of the frond, you are going to weave a layer of palm leaves. How much room to leave for the leaves depends on how tightly you can weave. As a general rule of thumb, stick one finger between the frond and the head as you are measuring the hat band. Grab a green, limber, section of leaf and cut the leaf away from the spine. Bend the frond around your head and tie it together with the attached spine.

Now comes a judgment call. The longer the leaf is, the wider the brim can be. But if you weave too much into the brim, you won't have enough left over for the crown. But don't worry, if your first attempt doesn't work, you can turn it into a visor. If you are relatively un-artistic, like me, you are in trouble. However, I always liked painting by numbers. It was way cool. Not that my stabs at immortality were going to win any prizes, but I was content. On our island that is what is most important. After all who is going to see it. (Actually, when you get rescued, they will ask you to put it on for the TV cameras, so try hard.) Anyway, here is how to make a coconut hat as easy as it gets, by the numbers.

As Easy as It Gets

Let's assume you are normal. (Big assumption, who else do you know who lives on an island all by themselves?) Normal people's heads are about twenty one to twenty three inches in circumference. Coconut hats always have to have an odd number of leaves. If you want to make a hat twenty two and a half inches around, (the hat band will stretch about an inch) you will need a frond with fifteen leaves, more or less.

How it works is each leaf circles the hat band. It goes one third the way around for the visor part and two thirds for the crown. Hold the hat band in your left hand with the leaves going away from you. (The leaves have a natural twist, they don't come away from the hat band at a ninety degree angle.) Hold five of the leaves lightly in your left hand all nice and flat and next to each other, all with the spines facing out, the hat band closest to your hand. OK? The leaves are lined up, going away from your body, getting ready to be weaved. They think they are leaves, we know they are a hat!

Take the leaf inside your left hand fingers. You are going to slide it between the fourth and fifth leaf (away from you) in your left hand. Can you see it? However, before it gets there it is going to be weaved in place. The trick is it is only going to weave coming in from the edge of the visor. (Don't worry. It will work out. You have to have faith, like the church says!)

The leaf you are weaving goes out to the brim, turns in after skipping two leaves (the spine of the leaf stays on the outside at all times) and goes under, over, under, over, then tucks in between the

fourth and fifth leaves and sticks out below the hat band. It is really straight forward, weaving wise, with the exception that we only weave going in. This is because we are making a circle, the 'in' weaving will be done as we come around the mountain as they say.

Now you have to hold the leaf you just wove in your left hand too. You can do it. If your hand isn't big enough just tell it to stay. If it refuses to stay, you have to work on your command skills. (Aren't I helpful!)

Now, it will start to get easy. Take the next leaf that is towards you, the one closer to you than the leaf you just wove, and do the same thing as the first leaf. It goes out to the edge, spine out, goes under the leaf you just finished with, then over, under, over and tucks in. (It goes under the hat band as we are going to bend it up inside to protect Friday's lovely hair. This leaf will be much more obedient about staying. Your command skills are improving! Continue along, turning the hat as you need to get to new leaves. Eventually you will come to the splice where you connected the hat band together. If there is a gap there just fudge it. This is a coconut hat. Funky is good. The join can always go in the back of your head if you get fussy and all, however you will find when you finish, that the join won't even be visible.

Then you will come to the leaves you started with and that your left hand is still (hopefully) holding. Each one in its turn gets woven from the brim to the band. It is finished! That wasn't hard was it? Did you get it the first time? If it takes a couple stabs to get it right, use your attempts as little fruit bowls or something! Are you ready to make the top of the hat?

The Going Gets Easier

Now that you are all practiced up, the top will be easy. If you wove your brim away from your body, the top will turn and be woven towards your body. Again grab five leaves. Bend them up inside the hat band. Make sure they are all lined up properly, all in a row. They should be slanted to the right if you have been using your right hand to weave, left hand to hold. Hold the hat, topside up, and the leaves in your right hand facing away from you, and with your left, grab the next leaf that is away from you. It goes up in the air, turns, comes down and tucks under the first leaf that is closest to you. The spine of the leaf is now facing down and away from the top of the hat. After you tuck it under the leaf that is closest to you (of the five leaves in your hand), it goes over the top of the hat band (to hide it) and then tucks into the leaves of the brim to hold it in place. This first leaf will determine the height of the crown. Play with it till you are happy. As a general rule the crown is twice as high as the brim is wide.

Ok, grab the next leaf away from you, next to the one you just wove. It goes up in the air, follows the height of the first leaf, goes over the leaf the first leaf went under, then under the next, then over the hat band and tucks into the brim. Continue leaf by leaf all the way around the brim. The very tip top part of the hat will not be wove (unless you made that first leaf really low). This is good as it will form a nice aeration hole in the top of the hat. Cut off any leaves that came out the end of the brim, or leave them there for added funkiness!

You did it! You made your very own coconut hat! If you want to try again there is no lack of raw materials, but there is no need. Coconut hats last for years and years as long as you don't sit on them or they don't fly off to windward while sailing your canoe.

Brewing and distilling

Making alcoholic drinks is as old as mankind. It has developed hand in hand with civilization, if fact some authorities believe that civilization developed around early breweries. Rather than ignore the history of our species and forbid anything to do with drinking alcohol, we should utilize alcohol as our forefathers did, as a preservative. Fruit could be preserved for years by fermenting it and then storing it in bottles, clay amphora, gourds, or any flotsam that washed up.

In the old days, alcohol had two uses. It provided a food (well, energy, anyway) during the winter and it reduced the desire to eat. This way the women and children received most of the real food during the winter and the men spent most of the time sleeping rather than messing up the cave by trying to help.

On a deserted island, alcohol also has two uses. Man cannot live the day to day grind without hope of some kind. For most men, that hope is the party next week. The hope is that they will have a great time drinking, maybe get lucky, most definitely laugh a lot and if they don't get into a fight it is only because they are watching other men fighting on TV. On a deserted island, the cable man still hasn't arrived but Friday, hopefully, has showed up and if there are no fights to be had at least you can go out and kill a fish.

Wine Making

Wine is easy to make. In the real world it is made in the vineyard in laboratory like conditions. Everything is sterile, hairnets on tight and vacuum doors sealed. Not at all like our island. There we have leaves blowing around every which way, insects peeking into our vat and if we had a hairnet, we would have used it to catch bait long since. The only way to make wine on an island is fast. We have to make it so fast that any contaminates never get a chance to grow until the level of alcohol is high enough to kill them off. We have to encourage our fruit to brew as fast as it can.

The first thing to do is to dice and slice whatever fruit we are using as fine as we can get it. Try to make sure your cutting board is as clean as it can get. Scrub it with sand on the water's edge. Scrub it hard. Don't worry, no one will think you are a sissy. This is wine we are talking about here!

Add a secondary sugar source. In the wine world, this is considered adulteration. On a deserted island, it is considered wisdom. Add any toddy you made, any sugar to centrifuged out of cane sugar water, (fill a beach bottle or piece of bamboo with sugar water and tie a string around the end. Spin it hard around and around for at least fifteen minutes then pour off the fairly pure water on top of the bottle. What is left is concentrated cane syrup. And just dare Friday to ask you what you are doing! We are talking about getting ready for a party!)

Add a yeast to the brew. Fruit carries its own yeast on its skin. It will ferment very nicely on its own, but not very quickly. Add some yeast extracted from cassava.

Cover the brew with brown webbing from a coconut tree and let it do its own thing. Try not to look. Every time you open it, you introduce other life forms, many of which will fight the yeast for the sugars in your brew. Let it sit for two to three days before your first peek. (You can listen from the outside. No doubt with the absence of TV, boom boxes, freeways and neighbors you will notice that your hearing has improved.) After it has stopped bubbling, cover the top with a board, cork, whatever you have to prevent contact to the outside world. The wine is resting. Let it rest for two to seven days.

At the end of resting all of the fruit's remains have sunk to the bottom of the container and the wine is waiting for you on top. Decant the wine into smaller containers and seal it up tight. Let it rest again for a least a month. If you really can't wait, at least try to last for a week. For distilling, two weeks is enough.

After it is all over, have one hell of a full moon party!

Toddy

Toddy is produced all over the tropical world. The less civilized a place is, the more likely you can buy some toddy there. Before soda and beer, there was toddy. We made a bad choice getting civilized, we really did. I remember with such fondness walking under the coconut palms on the small islands of Indonesia, and having the toddy gatherers lower down coconut shells filled to the brim with delicious toddy. And the taste! Wow! These days, it is hard to find any islanders under twenty that even know how to gather toddy. They want to be modern. They want to drink coke and beer. We just want to get away, to get back to the roots of our genetic memories. We want to live the natural life.

It was a lucky day when you were marooned on that island, though I know you didn't think so at the time. But now! The quality of life is so much better! And you can drink toddy anytime you want! It is easy to harvest. Every coconut tree not only has coconuts and fronds but also a flower stalk. When the stalk is young, before it has baby coconuts on it, slice a couple of inches off the stalk. Bruise the end of the stalk with the flat side of your machete. That is it, for now. The next day go back and cut a very, very thin slice off of your last cut, lightly bruise the end of the stalk again. On the third day, after cutting the stalk again, it will start seeping. In a week, you will be getting up to a liter of toddy a day! When the stalk first comes out of the coconut tree it is facing upwards. You have to bend this stalk down so it drips into your coconut shell instead. It is covered in a sheath that looks like a brand new leaf coming out of the top of the plant. It isn't. All of a sudden the sheath bursts open and a pale white stalk hangs out with little seed like flowers hanging all over it. Insects are irresistibly attracted to the flowers and within a couple of days you have yourself some brand new coconuts growing. This is too late. You want to cut the stalk before the coconut flowers are fertilized. Toddy will flow if you are a couple of days late but not as abundantly.

Anyway, the stalk is originally growing upwards. (Under normal conditions, the weight of the coconuts reverses the direction of the stalk.) There is no way to cut the stalk and not have it drip all over itself. Just tie a piece of string to the end of the stalk and tie the other end to a hanging rock. Sugar palms, are coconut like trees whose stalk comes out already pointed down! Lucky you if you have some of these trees.

So your twice daily routine is to climb your first coconut tree, dump your toddy into a joint of bamboo, cut the stem again, replace the cup and climb over to the next tree. If you are serious about this, connect your toddy trees with strong ropes up by the tops of the tree. That way you only have to climb up one tree and down another. Be sure you have one rope for your feet and another for your hands. While you are up there, don't forget to drink some of your toddy. It is most delicious straight from the tree. (For some reason toddy gatherers are some of the most beautiful people on earth. Does the Polynesian secret of beauty lie in the drink of toddy?) The bad part of toddy is it only lasts a short time. Its high sugar content ensures that microbes will love to grow in there. Bummer. To prevent that, we can make a wine out of whatever we don't drink right off.

If you were careful to keep everything a sterile as possible (on a deserted island), just put some coconut gauze over your container and you will have palm wine in a day and a half. By then it will reach about eight percent alcohol level, enough to prevent the growth of any microbes looking for a new home. If you are worried about contaminates, you will have to give your brew a head start. Do this with some of your cassava yeast. Put a drop in your brew for every coconut shell of liquid. This will ferment your toddy much faster and prevent other microbes from getting a start.

I don't want you to feel you have to be alcoholic to be a beachcomber. Of course you don't. The best use of toddy, besides drinking it right out of the tree, is to make jaggery out of it. Jaggery is a natural sugar that was first discovered in the pyramids of Egypt. The first step to make jaggery is to make a syrup. Heat up your toddy on a well controlled bed of coals, proceed slowly as you don't want to boil your mixture over and waste it all. It has to be heated just below the boiling temperature of water until it is reduced by three quarters. The resultant syrup is just as sweet as maple syrup (from the sap of another tree) and is great on your bread or crackers. But still, insects and microbes will love your syrup. Boil your syrup again. It will form a froth on the surface, skim this off. (Spread it and eat it on some handy dried breadfruit.) The syrup won't crack (form candy) because of the molasses content, however it will form a fairly solid sticky mass that is microbe proof. Did you know that too much sugar is a poison? That is why Hostess Twinkies last forever. Nothing will eat them, well except humans! Pour your jaggery into a half a coconut shell for storage. Keep it out of reach of the rain and ants. Ants share with humans a fascination with sugar. To keep ants away fill a larger container with water and island-ize your jaggery in the middle, or just simply share. Solid sugar is a preservative.

If you don't like the taste of molasses, pour a liter of hot syrup into a bamboo joint that has a rope attached to the top. Spin it around and around and the molasses will sink to the bottom of the bamboo after ten minutes. Pour off the light sugar liquid on the top of the bamboo and save the molasses. It is full of vitamins. Put hibiscus wood in this liquid to absorb the rest of the molasses, and it becomes jaggery. Pour your jaggery into a half a coconut shell for storage. If you were careful in making it, the other half of the shell will fit perfectly! Use jaggery anytime you want sugar. It has its own unique taste.

If you do want to make a wine out of your toddy, welcome to a new and wonderful world of bootlegging! No, just joking! While the wine is fine, it does have a bad habit of turning into vinegar if left too long. Instead, you should consider turning your wine into a liquor. Rum or vodka or whiskey last forever. Nothing eats alcoholic beverages, except of course, humans and elephants. (They do! They eat the fermented fallen fruit of the marula tree which produces a state of intoxication in which the elephants do things like sliding down muddy river banks on their backs! Really! I am not making this up!)

Arrack

Arrack is traditionally made by the distillation of cane wine, however, on deserted islands, arrack is the distillate of any alcoholic liquid. As castaways, we can't be too picky about what we brew, you know, use whatever bubbles, (a wine that can be distilled, can be made out of any fruit, producing a brandy. A grain or root crop, fermented and distilled will produce an alcohol flavored by its origin. Thus potatos produce vodka; cane sugar, rum; barley, scotch; corn, bourbon; and so on.) However, we have to distill correctly or we can poison ourselves. It is traditional to have a still on an abandoned isle and the first thing your rescuers are going to want to see and sample is your brewing products. They will, really! Hey, girls, it's a guy thing, OK?

Distillation is easy in principle. Aristotle was the first to observe that pure water could be made by distilling sea water. This is an example of simple distillation where ideally the liquid contains chemicals with widely divergent boiling points. As the heat is increased, the chemical with the lowest boiling point turns into vapor first. Alcohol boils off far faster than the water, so in a simple distillation, first alcohol will turn into a vapor then water will boil off, if you let it get too hot. All alcohol, unfortunately, contains diesel contaminates. The boiling point of diesel is not far above that of alcohol, making it an art form to know when to take the kettle off the stove.

In theory, your wine or toddy is in a stainless vat that has a glass cooler vent/tube on the top. The steam from the wine goes up the tube on top of the vat, is cooled down in a glass heat exchanger and then condenses on the sides of the cooling tube that turns and goes down and thence drips into the receiving container.

We don't have any of the above but that shouldn't stop castaways with plenty of time on their hands, should it? The first thing you have to develop is a vat with a sealable top. That is harder than it sounds.   (Aboard a boat it is easy,   a pressure cooker with the little

rocker weight off and a long line of bronze or plastic tubing.)   The easiest solution, I hate to say is a glass bottle found along the shore. I know you didn't make it yourself, I know. But it is easy. Otherwise a joint of bamboo with the top carefully cut off, liquid put in and then the top glued back in place with a mixture of breadfruit sap and coconut milk (Half and half). (If it leaks, carefully add the sap of a cashew tree. It can be toxic to sensitive people but it is a good substitute for gum arabic, a very good adhesive). Then carve a hole thru the top and insert a thin piece of bamboo. It would work. (Myself, I have always used a big bottle from the beach!)

The tube is more difficult. The best thing to do is to get some small sections of bamboo and open them up by burning the internal joint stops with a skinny burning piece of wood. It will take a while, but once it is formed you can use it over and over again. One piece of bamboo will not be enough, so use your breadfruit glue to seal them together. If you cut the bamboo green, you can induce a curve in its length. After an initial rise the tube has to slope down gradually. This is when the steam will condense into a liquid. With care, the first clean distillation will yield 80 proof arrack. A second distillation will produce 151 proof, (distil the distillate).   What we are trying to produce is ethyl alcohol, not methyl alcohol, which is a poison. At first as we heat up our bamboo with any vapor, the bamboo will release methyl alcohol from the wood fibers. This must be discarded, or used only for starting fires and cleaning tropical ulcers and the like. (Check out Natural Medicines section.) Usually three hours of full steam running through the bamboo will release all (hopefully; longer is safer) the methyl alcohol it has inside of it.

Methyl alcohol boils, it is released from the water, at 148°F. (212°F is when water boils) Ethyl alcohol boils at 173°F and the first of the diesel components, n-propyl alcohol boils at 200°F. What this means is the first few drops that come out of our still are almost certainly methyl. I know in the movies they are always grabbing those first few drops and exclaiming how good it is. Don't believe it. The first few drops are poison. As the liquid starts to heat up, the ethyl alcohol starts to run out of the tube, but then as the liquid starts to approach the boiling point of water n-propyl is released, which if not a nasty poison like methyl, it will still give you a hangover the next morning. Ethyl alcohol doesn't affect a human negatively, but the contaminants on either side of ethyl on the boiling point (cracking) list surely will. So, when and if the liquid on the fire starts to boil, stop collecting the distillate. Since you are probably collecting in coconut shells, you might want to delegate the first and last shell to the quick start signal fire effort.

Ok, everything is set up. The bamboo is steamed clean of methyl, the leaks are plugged, the coconut shells are ready. Here is the process. Fill your vat full of whatever wine (wine is whatever you have fermented) you have. Leave an inch of space on top. Attach and glue your cooling bamboo tube. The tube should be at least two feet above the vat before it turns to a gradual slope into the coconut shells. Slowly heat up the wine. Slowly is the key. The main difference between expensive and cheap liquors at the store is the speed at which they were distilled. Faster means more contaminates get through. If steam is coming out of the end of your cooling tube, make the tube longer, pour sea water over the outside of the tube, or better, lower the heat a touch. The first twenty drops or so that comes out of the tube is discarded into the medicine chest. Slowly collect the ethyl, slowly because we want all the ethyl we can get out before the diesel starts to come out.

Sounds easy? It is. That is why duty free alcohol is so cheap. It is cheap and easy to make. Just take care of the contaminates. And, please don't show Friday how talented you are at swinging the machete after drinking this island moonshine, this arrack. Please don't. Especially don't show her how quickly you can open a coconut with a machete. I speak from experience. But I really don't want to talk about it.

Tools

Scientists would have you believe that humans are the apes that think. It isn't true. I know half the time I act without thinking. Maybe more than half. But, we are the ape that uses tools. I mean almost every second of every day we are using a tool to do something. From alarm clocks to TVs to cars to newspapers to radios to golf clubs to stadiums to sails, masts and boats. We are always using tools. Don't think for a moment that just because you are on a deserted island that suddenly you are going to stop using tools. I just ain't going to happen!

We can separate tools into galley tools, boat building tools, fishing tools, rope making tools, harvesting tools, and navigational techniques. Select the section you are currently interested in and start doing some serious tool time!

Galley Tools

Galley tools are arguably the most important. If we aren't getting enough to eat, we aren't going to survive for long. One of the first things you have to do on your island is locate food supplies. All too often getting that food will require a tool. For example, the ability to shred coconut is crucial to fine dining on your island. In the "real world" a coconut shredder is used. This is a flat piece of metal, a circle at one end with teeth cut into the metal. Locals screw the 'handle' into wood, sit on the seat and twist a half a coconut shell with the meat still inside over the teeth and let the coconut fall into a bowl below. You don't have one of these on the island. Damn. It would have made life easier. (If you intend on a practice run, for sure buy one at any island general store. You will have to ask for it. They always keep them behind the counter.)

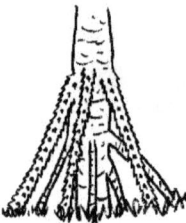

Lacking a shredder, our options are limited. If you are very good at chopping that is ok, but it is easier and faster to use one of the legs of a walking palm that is embedded with small spines perfect for shredding. Cut off a six inch section, cut the spines off three inches of the 'handle' and stick the pointy end into the half shell and wail away.

The next most important tool in the galley are platters and bowls. If you were lucky enough to end up on a high island, there is a chance to find clay. When you are exploring (Explore everyday) you are most likely to find clay along a turn in a stream, usually just in one spot.

Ok, you found some clay. Dig it up. Not having any containers to carry the clay in, it is easier to make your pot right there by the river. Remember how in first grade you made snakes out of play-doh? Guess what? That is what making pots is all about! Make a lot of snakes and build them up on top of each other until you have a general shape of a bowl. (Or platter, or cup.) Once you got it more or less finished, smooth and push the snakes into each other inside and out. A little scraping can help too. In the old days, the pot is then left out in the sun to cure. This is great for dry goods, but for liquids the pot has to be fired.

Clay fires (bakes) at very high temperatures, temperatures we cannot reach on our little island. So what we do is add silica and lime to the clay to increase the strength and to decrease the temperature it fires at. By itself clay fires at 2,900° F but with sand (in the tropics sand is primarily composed of silica and coral, read lime!) your pot will fire at 500° F. Low enough that we can fire the pot over our fire! (Not in the flames. Cover the coals with a thin layer of sand. Put the pot on the sand. It might take several fires, but what else have you to do?)

Well, you didn't find any clay. Don't despair. Bamboo joints are great pots, giant clam shells are the in thing for fine bowls, brain coral carved out with your obsidian knife (see harvesting tools) makes a passable crucible. Without clay, life will be easier, if less fancy. Clay bowls break when dropped, when fired, or when stared at meanly!

Baskets are a galley and a harvesting tool. The best ones are made out of coconut fronds. Review the building a grass shack chapter.

We made the walls by weaving together two opposing halves of a frond. To make a basket we do the same. You will need just one frond, two sides of the same frond. The longer the leaves the deeper the basket can be. Check out the grass shack for directions on making them. After
you finish, bend the woven frond in half, weave in the two ends and the bottom, much like weaving in the sides.

About two million years ago, pre-humans invented the chopper. It was mankind's first major tool and it put him on the road to a more advanced future. The chopper was a hand sized stone that had one side chipped away until it became a serrated edge. There is no reason, if beings with an IQ of about seven could make a tool, we can't, too. Choosing the rock is important. Just because you are on an atoll, doesn't mean you only have coral to play with. All coral atolls were at one time large volcanos that slowly sank into the abyss and the coral reef that surrounded them gradually continued to grow. There might still be lava rocks on your atoll. Just look. (Interestingly, our chance of finding useful rocks for choppers is actually greater on islands than on continents as when the magma erupts from the land it cools slowly, and doesn't restrict the continued flow of lava from the volcano. On islands, the magma hits the ocean floor, cools quickly, blocking the lava which then starts melting surrounding sedimentary rock trying to find a way out. The island that eventually forms has a higher percentage of the metamorphic rocks that make good tools.) What you are looking for when tool hunting is dikes. No, not like Holland! Dikes are a harder more solid type of rock in or by a lava flow. It looks like a wall. Inside and around a dike look for your chopper rocks and obsidian knives (actually obsidian doesn't occur in wet environments, what we are looking for is pitchstone which is almost the same except it contains much more water and isn't as shiny. However, I will continue to call our rock Obsidian as I was a childhood fan of Conan, Kull, Sinbad, etc, where obsidian knives were the newest fad. Besides, pitchstone knives just doesn't sound right.) Either way, good tools are caused by erosion of a dike. If you could find a dike that protruded into the ocean, your tool problems are solved.

It might be that your chopper isn't perfect when you find it. Here comes the art, the grass hats, the palm frond sweat bands, the rope making. Art is the major human accomplishment. To make a good chopper we have to put our art hats on. Sit down by the ocean waves, under the coconut trees, where the wind whistles through your hair. Listen to the wind in the trees, the pounding drum of the surf, and when you are feeling very at one with the world, look at your chopper rock and try to see a better tool inside of it. You are going to hit the rock with the back, I said BACK, side of your machete, to chip just a little piece of rock off, to make it sharper, more blade like. Don't do it till you have prepared yourself to feel what is inside the rock. Obsidian knives are made the same way, if more carefully. Pitchstone is harder to find and is harder to chip. Stone chipping was a caveman specialty. They were really good at it. You can be too.

No, I am not getting all weird here, no, I haven't been abducted by aliens. People can sense far more than they teach us in school. Really! It is much easier to take away to make a sculpture than add on to make a painting. We can sense somehow, where to hit the rock to make it sharper. But, go ahead, don't believe me! But you get stuck on a deserted island, you might want to try it. You might surprise yourself.

Chopsticks are wonderful tools. Two different sticks that can be used by one hand. You can hold a platter with one hand and pluck food out of the coals with the other with a couple of opposable very long fingers. However, as tools are concerned, tongs are far more useful, if more difficult to make. We can make both on our island. Tongs are just chopsticks with a hinge on the end. They are just a long flexible stick, snapped in the middle, but not all the way thru. We have all done this by accident while breaking wood over our knees. Do it for real this time. Carve the ends a bit to make picking up food in the fire easier.

Boat Building Tools

The most important boat building tool is the adze. This is a chopper tool (see galley tools) that has a handle attached to it. Sounds easy doesn't it? (It isn't!) An ax, the second most important boat tool, is actually the same as the adze except on a different plane. An ax is actually easier to make. The most traditional handle is a limb of a tree that has been split, the stone tool inserted in the split and then laced together with twine.

Make a chopper rock heavier than most. If you want to get carried away, make a blade on both sides with the handle in the middle. Split the hardest wood you can find. (If the handle is fresh cut, be sure to strip the bark and sink the wood in the ocean to remove all the sap before carving the handle.) Check out the rope making section and lash the chopper into the handle.

The adze is harder. The handle is now at a ninety degree angle to the chopper. You must find a branch of a tree that grew in a angle. Such grown knees (we are talking boats here, right?) are really very strong. As before, split, insert and lash.

Just as an aside, stone tools are just as useful as steel tools. In fact, they are often sharper than steel after being in use for a while. But they are fragile. You can not twist or yank a stone tool. They will snap right in two. During your boat making you are going to be making an ax or two and lots of adzes, and often "re-sharpening" both. A chopper in the galley will last a long time as it doesn't have the leverage of a handle to harm it. So how exactly do you form a serrated edge on a stone tool?

Find a good stone. Hit the future edge of it with a heavier stone while holding it in the air. Don't lay your stone against the ground or another rock to hit it. You are trying to chip it, not smash it. Do both sides at first, then as the edge begins to form chip only one side. When you are starting to be happy, start chipping with a softer stone or a hard piece of wood. This will produce smaller chips on the blade. Do both sides at first, then only the "serrated" side. (If you serrate both sides you will continue to eat away the mother stone till there is nothing left!) After you are happy, lay your blade in the sand and prepare an "awl" out of a sharpened stick that you hardened in the fire. Find a little fault in the edge of the stone and pry at it with your stick. This makes really small chips. (If you take too big a bite it will only break your stick.) Trust your feelings, survivor!

Rope Making Tools

It isn't that hard to make rope as long as you have nineteen arms and incredible dexterity. You don't? Are you in trouble, or what!
Don't worry. You can do it, even as handicapped as you are! The trick to making rope is to make yarns, which make string, which makes twine, which makes rope which makes hawsers. But lets start at the beginning.

You can make rope out of anything. Bark (rattan), fibers (sisal) or leaves (Ti). Tool wise they are the same. You need to make 'flyers'. They are round pieces of wood with splits in them around the edge. Into these splits you put your fibers (or strings, twines, etc.) You need three of these flyers for a simple strand of yarn. Put your fiber (whatever kind) into the splits and rotate them, say to the right or clockwise. At the same time you rotate the three flyers around each other to the left or counterclockwise. It is this double twist which keeps rope from unlaying. Ok, say you just made a bit of yarn out of fibers. Always use one fiber that is longer than the others and one that is shorter. When one length runs out, add in a new length. If the old fiber wants to uncurl, give it a touch of breadfruit sap. That'll teach it! Continue for one and a half times the desired length of the eventual rope.

Make three of them, and twine the three of them together same as above. Don't ruin your flyers by pushing too big pieces of line in the splits. Make a new set of flyers for each size of weave. That wasn't too hard was it? Told you, you could do it!

222

Harvesting Tools

Actually the main tools for harvesting are your machete and the basket you made back in galley tools. However, tied into harvesting is sowing and replanting. The main reason coconuts and breadfruit are so wide spread around the world is that for centuries, sea captains have been planting them on whatever island they find just in case someday someone gets shipwrecked there and would like something to
eat. Not only should you pay back their efforts preformed unbeknownst in your behalf, but also pay it forward for the next poor soul shipwrecked on your island. As such, every time you harvest you should also replant, replace, re-sow. Your main tool for this is a most advance one. It is called a stick. That is all that plants need most of the time. A hole to grow in. When you finish a mango, a breadfruit, a papaya, a guava, I know that you are not so self involved to not jab your stick into the ground, throw a seed into it and stomp on it with your foot to close the hole. You can do that. I know you can. Besides, think of the wonderful paradise you will be creating on your island! Think of the amazement of the next person to be shipwrecked there!

Javelins have been around for millenniums. You know javelins? Like the ones they use in the Olympic Games. The ones they used in the games came from a Greek model of 708 BC. Recently they introduced a smaller spear as the athletes were throwing the old ones out of the stadium and killing the ice cream vendors. We don't want the new one. We want the one they have been using for 3000 years. It is eight and a half feet long and weighs just under two pounds. The ancients spent forever to get it right. Who are we to argue?

Whenever you see a long straight, preferably hardwood tree, chop it down, peel the bark and sink it in the sea until the sap is gone. Then set it out to dry standing up. Don't let it dry laying down or it will take forever to dry and most likely warp. Have ten or fifteen of these babies in your armory. Armory? Yes, we are going to battle nature for food! Don't forget when your javelin is dry and light enough to use, to harden the tip in the fire after sharpening it. Islanders in the Santa Cruz Islands in the Pacific can spear a revolving coconut with a javelin from two hundred feet. Practice makes perfect!

Making Your Own Canoe

You have to make a canoe. It says so right there in the castaways handbook. It is a requirement. It seems to be OK if it sinks. In fact, in all the literature on the subject, sinking the boat that you just made is a major plot development. But not on our island. Making a canoe is just too much hard work. It is stupid to put that much effort into a boat just to end up sinking it. Our boat is not going to sink. Especially if we build it right. How can you build it right?

First you have to find a tree. (If you are shipwrecked on a really barren atoll, you are not going to find a tree appropriate for a canoe, but large logs will drift up on your island, so practice the log drifting dance to be preformed during the full moon.) You want a tall hardwood tree, at least twenty feet of trunk before the first branches and two and a half feet across the trunk. It might take a while to find such a tree, so from your first days on the island keep you eyes open for a good tree. The other thing is not a requirement, but could really be useful; it would be nice if your tree was not miles and miles from the nearest water. In fact, it would be really cool if it was like a hundred feet or less from the nearest stream or beach.

OK. You found your tree. Don't cut it down! Never cut down trees that are to be made into boats. They are full of sap and as the tree dries out the wood will check (a woodworker's term for split apart). First you have to kill your tree and dry it out. You do this by first girding it, cutting a circle of bark off the tree six inches wide all around the tree, and second, by building a controlled fire around the base of the tree to slowly kill the tree. Under threat, the tree will send all of its life force down into the roots and into the seeds if it is flowering. Either way, it takes a while to kill a tree. Don't rush it. You are not going to want a canoe that splits in half in the middle of a storm. Gradually dry it out. It might take thirty days.

Once the tree is almost dead, it dies from the outer layers first, you can start cutting. You are not going to use your machete. Machetes were never designed to cut down big canoe trees. Chances are you will just get it stuck deep in the wood and in yanking, trying to free it, you will snap your blade in half. Instead, build yourself an adze and an ax. Invented around 5000 BC in Egypt, an adze remains today just about the best all around tool for making canoes. What is an adze? It looks like a hoe but with a shorter handle and a much heavier blade. We can make our blades out of conch shells or lava rock. Form a cutting edge by hitting the soon-to-be-blade with other rocks. (Not your machete) When you are ready, lash it on to your handle. An ax is much the same but is lashed sideways onto the handle. We all know what an ax looks like. It is what Paul Bunyan carried around. Build your tools while your tree is dying and lets get started. Confused? Check out the tools section.

Where your drying fire has touched your tree the wood has turned into a charcoal like substance that smashes easily. (As good as your conch shell is, it is mostly just going to smash and slash stuff.) Cut and smash away until all the charcoal like stuff is gone, then light another fire. When that one is finished, cut and smash out the new charcoal. Continue on, every day, start a fire, and then bang away the charcoal. The smashed charcoal can help with the next day's burn. There is something poetic in there but it just won't come out! After a week, your tree is much skinnier at its base. You don't want the tree to fall. In falling it might split the trunk that is going to be

226

your canoe, so brace the tree by tying it to other trunks and continue burning and chopping. When there is about six to ten inches left in the diameter of the tree, it is time to let the big dog eat.

On the big day, eat a large bowl of Wheaties and go to work with an attitude. The core wood of a tree is actually the weakest part of the tree when it is still quasi-alive. It is not going to take much to cut through that last bit with your ax. (No, you still can't use your machete!) Spit on your hands and start wailing away. Even when the tree starts to fall, keep wailing, staying away from under the tree and away from the kick back. (The opposite side where the stump will fly as the tree falls. It says right in the canoe builder's handbook- don't get killed while making a canoe. OK?) Your tree is on the ground, well mostly. Believe it or not the tree is still kind of alive. Now we have to cut twenty feet up from the base, just below where the branches start to grow. It is a lot easier as the flames will eat into the tree faster than before when they just drifted up the trunk. As the fire is burning start cutting off the bark. If you can get a good split in the bark, you can get big pieces off at a time. Take all of it off the twenty foot or more length.

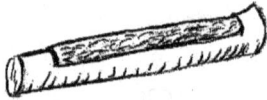

Now is the time to work fast. Never let your tree be exposed to direct sunlight as you chop the bark off. If you miss a day or two be sure to cover your tree with bushy branches, coconut fronds, whatever. As the fire still burns at the top of the twenty foot section, heat up some of your umu luau rocks that you gathered for cooking. (See Cooking Methods chapter.) When the rocks are hot, place them on top of the tree and let them burn the wood. As the wood turns to charcoal, chop it out with your adze. Don't chop along the length of the tree. It will only lead to splits in the canoe. Chop sideways. Chop a sideways channel every foot or so of your tree (don't cut the sides, right?) then chop out your 'dams' lengthwise. Heat the rocks again and again until you start to get an inside in your tree. Don't burn or chop all the way down to the center. When you are close, but the tree is still strong but lighter, it is time to get it down to the sea.

So you thought it was tough so far? You better hope your tree isn't in the middle of a forest with thorns and hills and lots and lots of other trees. Really. With all the work you have accomplished so far, you are just going to have to get the tree down to the sea, one

227

way or the other. When you are there, finally, at last, throw it in the sea and sink it by putting heavy rocks into your chopped out cavity and heavy logs to keep it steady. It sounds hard but it isn't. The tree is still full of sap, is heavy and really doesn't want to float. The salt water will slowly replace the sap in the wood and turn your tree into a canoe. Take a break. It has been a hard go of it, so far, but you did it.

After about a week underwater, pull your tree out of the water and into a 'long house'. This is a thatched low house that you built to keep your canoe in the shade. (See the house building chapter). Let it dry for two days and then sink her again. It will be a lot tougher to sink this time. The water that evaporated out carried a lot of the sap with it. After a week, pull her out and let her dry again. There will be no way you can sink her a third time so heat up your stones and start burning and chopping again. This time burn through the dead wood,
the center of the tree. Hold your hands apart from each other on inside and outside of the hull to see how much wood is left. Believe it or not your hands will know. They can tell. At the same time, start cutting the wood away for the bow and stern. (Always chop towards the ends, not from the ends towards the canoe, right?) At the end of everyday, fill your canoe with saltwater, all the way to the top and in your long house.

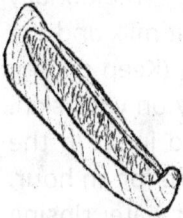

Next you have to decide what kind of canoe you want. The easiest is like an American Indian canoe or a kayak. These are symmetrical. The starboard side is the same as the port. These are fine if you want to paddle on both sides of the canoe. Often the best canoes have outriggers on them, like a Hawaiian canoe. Having a outrigger allows you to jump in the water and get out without a huge circus balancing act. But having an outrigger means that you can only row on one side or the other. In order to paddle straight, the keel of the canoe has to be offset, the canoe needs to be asymmetrical. As the outrigger will pull the canoe towards its side, the canoe has to be built to pull to the other side.

It is easy to build a symmetrical canoe. Make the inside first, dig out the "cockpit". After you are finished or nearly so, turn the canoe upside down. Make sure it is perfectly flat upside down (the keel is straight up). Then chop a little from one side or the other until the hull is thin and there is a thicker 'keel' on the bottom for grounding on reefs and the like. (No, you still can't use your machete.) The thinner the hull is (but more than an inch and a half) and the straighter the keel will determine how well the canoe sails. Don't forget, even when the canoe is upside down making the keel, you have to turn it over and fill it with water every day.

Building an asymmetrical canoe is a little harder. If the outrigger is on the starboard side and you are paddling on the port, the canoe will only turn to starboard no matter what you do. This is great if you like to go in circles or the island you are circling is really, really small. To get the canoe to go straight, the keel can not be parallel to the canoe. If you intend the outrigger to be on the left, the keel must start more to the right in the bow and end more to the left in the stern. Because of this the canoe will perform best at certain speeds. If you had three rowers, one can sit in the middle and row between the struts of the outriggers thus easing the pull to the outrigger side. This will require lots of test flights till the keel is right and the distance the outriggers go out is correct, so don't go chopping all the wood off too soon.

Your boat is finished. That is good. Checks (cracks) in a wood canoe let water in. That is bad. You have to caulk it. Traditionally you make your own caulk. Boil up a mixture of coconut milk and the sap that comes out of a breadfruit when you pick it. (Keep cutting the stem and it will continue leaking. DO NOT get any on your skin. ABSOLUTLY DO NOT get any in your eyes. If you do jump in the ocean (saline solution), open your eyes and stay in there for an hour. (It really hurts to come out so you will want to keep salt water rinsing your eyes.)

However, even though it is against this book's and my principles, in the interest of your canoe staying afloat in a voyage of discovery, you should know that you can melt plastic milk jugs (or any plastic with the recycled triangle thing on it) and caulk your boat that way. It will catch fire and liquid plastic will drip out of the flame. Don't hold the plastic in your hands. Liquid plastic gives a nasty burn. Use chopsticks, tongs or get Friday to hold it for you. (Just joking! Geez. Can't I have any fun anymore!)

OK, the thing is finished, you put it in the water and the first wave that comes along sinks the damn thing. Stop cursing. No one is paying attention, anyway. This is not at all unusual, especially if you are big (rapidly getting skinnier, thanks to being shipwrecked) Westerner. You simply have to add some side boards to the canoe, especially if you intend to go more than a few hundred yards out to sea. It is easy to do, well, considering what you have done so far, it is easy to do. The hardest part is cutting some planks.

OK, I am going back on a promise. I said we wouldn't even think of using the jetsam and flotsam found on every beach in the world in our survival efforts. But it is really, really hard to cut a thin straight plank without a saw. I really, truly know. I tried. I gave up. It is just too damn hard. So go find one, or to be a purist, stay close to shore. If you found a plank, (no plywood, come on!) shape it to fit one side of the bow of your canoe. (Paddling into waves is when you sink.) When you have it more or less right fit some fiddles to hold it in place and caulk the gap with breadfruit sap (the sap from the fruit when you pick it) mixed with coconut milk. (Not the water, milk from the meat.) It may take several applications to get it right. Do the other side. If you are intending to be out in any rough weather, cut some knees and attach them to the extension and hull with your glue and cross pieces.

The very last thing you do is put in the seats. It is very hard to tell how the boat will sit in the water till it is floating. Seats call for lots of trials. Don't glue them in place till your are sure of the right location. Paddles are easy. The fat end of a coconut frond will do for a start. Don't laugh till you try it. Those damn things never break, are easy to replace, and work half way well. (the handles are a bit rough!) Later you can carve some paddles easier to use out of wood, especially for Friday's delicate hands.

How good your canoe will turn out from now on depends on how patient and painstaking a worker you are. Either way, I bet the next time a wood canoe comes alongside of your yacht you will appreciate it more!

Non-Instrument Navigation

Presumably before you were shipwrecked, marooned, castaway-ed or sentenced to deportation, you had some idea where you were. At least which ocean, hopefully which hemisphere you were misplaced in. For the purposes of this book, however, I am assuming you left the North Pole bound for the South Pole and your plane, boat or UFO crashed enroute. You have no idea where you are. Without knowing your position there is little hope to be able to evaluate the chances of your rescue. And what if you get tired of waiting to get rescued? What if you have been on that island for years? Can you make exploratory sea voyages in a boat you made and not get lost? It would be a real bummer to leave a perfectly good island and not be able to get back. Imagine the thoughts that would run through your brain, or what is left of it, as you slowly die of thirst and starvation all because you just had to get off that damn island.

All is not lost. Polynesians made return voyages of thousands of miles without instruments of any kind. If they can do it, so can you. They did study the stars for years, but they didn't have the advantage of a college education! (If that is an advantage in facing unknown monsters, killer storms and stars that all look alike. I tend to keep asking, "Where are the help files!") But there is hope for us survivors yet.

Here is how to not get lost, Polynesian Style, as adapted by yours truly. The trick is to start out making short return trips. Say you leave in the morning, across the wind, and sail out till, you can just see your island, or noon, which ever comes first. At your farthest point out, take a good look around. See if you can see any sign of other islands. Watch for clouds that have a green bottom (indicating a lagoon) for birds that catch fish and then all head in the same direction. For clouds that always stay in the same place. (Surprisingly, when sailing towards Hawaii from California, you never see Mauna Loa and Mauna Kea, two of the highest mountains in Oceania. But you do see the clouds that shroud and envelope them.)

Chances are slim that you are going to find any island that you couldn't see from the highest point of your island. But it is good practice and slowly you will make your boat more seaworthy and you might even catch a fish! To go farther afield, (well, asea), you will have to sail at night. You will have to learn to navigate Polynesian style.

Oh, stop screaming that your head is going to explode! It isn't that hard. It is a lot easier that learning all those stupid dates in high school history. Plus you can always show off to Friday while laying on a grass mat under the stars on the beach while drinking coconuts laced with arrack, with little umbrellas in them. OK. Sorry. I got carried away. I don't know how to make those little umbrellas. Just put a leaf in the coconut and use your imagination. (That's what it is there for!) Are you ready to get started? Take a big breath and read on.

The Stars

I hope you are in the tropics, being as how that is what we are going to talk about. That you are between the Tropic of Cancer and the Tropic of Capricorn, between twenty three degrees and forty minutes north and twenty three degrees and forty minutes South. To check this, it is only within the northern tropics that you can see both the North Star (in the north, naturally!) and the Pointers (Alpha and Beta Centauri) when they are north of the Southern Cross (in the south, natch. Am I going too fast?) North of the line, you can see the North Star. (Actually, you can't see it south of 5° North because of the wind haze caused by the trades). In both tropics you can always see Orion in the winter, in fact it is most likely directly overhead when it passes your longitude. In the southern tropics, new constellations come into play. But lets start at the beginning.

In non-instrumental navigation stars are all important. The sun doesn't help determine the direction the boat is going except at or near dawn and dusk. If we could accurately measure its altitude we could find our latitude, but we can't. At night the location of the stars as they raise and set and when they pass overhead is far more important than the sun. The angle of the stars as they pass our overhead location is hard to determine but that is why they pay us castaways the big bucks. You are going to have to get good at star identification. It is easy, it is fun, your girl will love it, you will be a big hit at parties. It is really unfortunate that this book is likely to go down with the boat when it sinks. Maybe you should buy two copies!

Sorry, castaway, hate to tell you, but now is the time to learn the stars. Besides, when are you going to find the time to practice while making a grass shack, or making soap, or brewing your own arrack? (OK, maybe you will find time while drinking the arrack!) But every night, in fact, tonight, you can practice star finding. You can practice identifying stars every clear night in your backyard or on your foredeck! There are thousands of star charts for sale in every book store in the land. They must have known you were going to ask for one.

Polynesian Navigators knew thousands of stars by name and location. Stop screaming. Passengers take it as a bad sign when the Captain starts screaming while falling to his knees holding his head in his hands to keep it from exploding. I promise, you are only going to have to learn nineteen or so star names and locations. Plus we are going to use the 'normal' names, the Greek, Arabic names that we use these days. That's not so bad is it? You will have to commit to memory only a few stars, the brightest ones, the navigational stars, like the North Star, the Southern Cross and the gold star you will earn when you know these few stars by heart. We can't navigate without the knowing the stars. It isn't too hard. Ready to get started?

Everyone knows Orion, the Hunter, it rises high in the sky in October to April with its belt riding along the Equator. Orion contains two of the stars we need to know: Rigel and Betelgeuse (Beetle Juice). Look at Orion with his sword hanging down, his left shoulder as you look at him (really his right if you are going to be anal about it, cuz he is looking at you) is Betelgeuse, a Red Giant. His right knee is Rigel. Are you following along on your star chart? The center star (Mintaka) of Orion's belt, by the way, sits on the celestial equator. It rises and sets everyday on the equator, all year long (even in the summer when you can't see it.) If you follow Orion's belt to the right you will find the Pleiades, a small group of seven stars of supreme importance to the Polynesians. (Many cultures share the Polynesians fascination with the Pleiades, so many that some feel that it might be the origin of the human race. You know, where the aliens brought us from. Uh, Oh. Now I've opened a can of worms!)

Following the belt to your left points towards Sirius, the brightest star in the sky. Draw a line in the sky from Rigel to and through Betelgeuse and you will find Castor and Pollux, the twins of Gemini. (Friday Impressing Tidbit- Castor is a triple star. It consists of three stars revolving around a central point, and each of those stars is a double star!)

A line from Rigel thru the bottom of the sword leads to Procyon. From the left star in the belt thru Orion's right shoulder leads to Aldebaran. A line from Betelgeuse thru Rigel and on outward leads to the Small Magellanic Cloud. (A nearby Milky Way type Galaxy. No, don't read ahead.) A line from Orion's right shoulder thru the bottom star of the sword leads to Canopus, the second brightest star in the heavens, and then continuing on till morning will bring you to the Greater Magellanic Cloud. (Yes, another galaxy- they are everywhere out there!) There, you already know nine stars of your nineteen, if you consider Castor and Pollux as one star for navigational purposes and just use the Magellanic clouds to find the south pole. Before we leave Orion note that Sirius, Betelgeuse and Procyon, a bright star in Canis Minor just to the left of Betelgeuse and down (south) from the Twins, form a equilateral triangle with each leg twenty five degrees long. We will need rulers in the sky marked in degrees to find our approximate latitude.

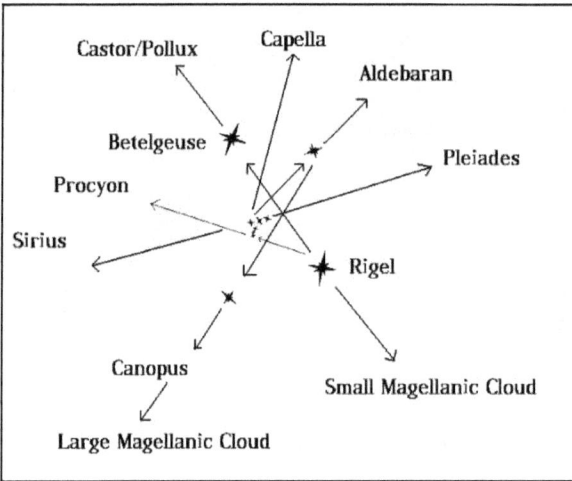

Let's try another easy one. Everyone knows the Big Dipper. The pointers, the two bright stars that form the end of the cup of the dipper point towards Polaris, the North Star. I think everyone knows that one. Are you following on your star chart? The bottom of the cup going away from the handle (sideways to the north star) points

Vega

Deneb

Polaris

Capella

Castor/Pollux

Arcturas

Spica

Regulas

The Big Dipper Star Directions   not to scale

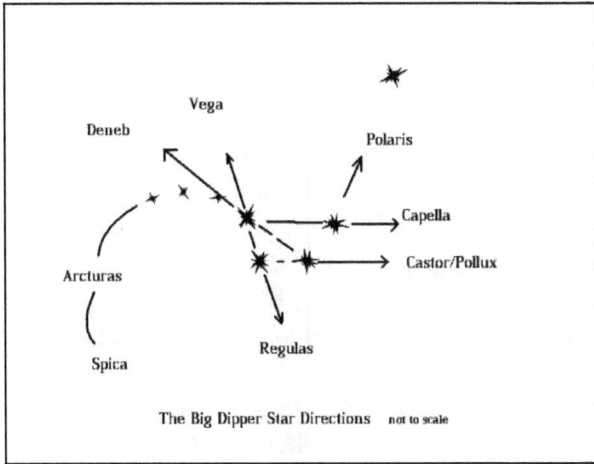

towards Castor/Pollux. The two stars that form the inside of the cup going away from the handle point towards Regulus in Leo. Going the other way, the inside stars point towards Vega. The star at the bottom right of the cup and the top left point towards Deneb in Cygnus. Are you lost yet? See if you can find them all on your chart and later tonight in the sky. The handle of the Big Dipper points, if you follow the arc of stars, towards Arcturus in Bootes and if you carry on, to Spica in Virgo. That is fifteen stars out of your nineteen and you haven't even broken a sweat yet! Wow!

How about the South Pole? The bad news is there isn't a star marking the south pole like the North Star does for the north pole. The good news is there are way more stars south of the equator than north. (What? You head is already exploding? You can't take anymore? Get a grip, Survivor. You can't go voyaging without knowledge. Really. I tried once. I covered my compass, hid my sextant and sailed from Oahu to Kauai, a mere 75 sea miles. Four days later, much humbler, I limped into Hanalei. But I definitely, don't want to talk about it.)

The south pole is found through triangles. Everyone likes triangles. Equilateral triangles (like the one they banged for chow on Bonanza) are my favorite. Achernar, Canopus (the second brightest star after Sirius) and the South Pole form a Equilateral triangle. The two Magnetic clouds and the South Pole form a equilateral triangle. Don't you just love math! You don't? Well, good. Polynesian Navigation doesn't need math! That takes a lot off you mind! Since

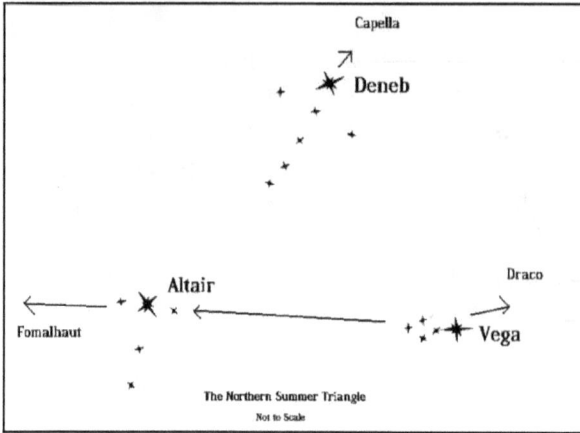

Capella

Deneb

Altair   Draco

Fomalhaut   ←————————————→   Vega

The Northern Summer Triangle
Not to Scale

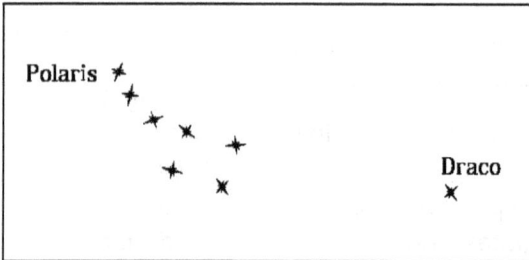

Polaris

Draco

you don't have to do math, that leaves room in your brain to learn a few new stars! Yay! Isn't this fun!

But before we do, here is another Friday Impressing Tidbit. Polaris, the North Star, wasn't always marking the pole. It seems that being responsible for world navigation is a heavy responsibility so the job is handed over to a new star every few millenniums. If fact, the star that the pharaohs used to align the pyramids wasn't Polaris! It was Draco, an even dimmer star, now days, just next to the Little Dipper. Well, Ok, maybe it is all about the Precession of the Poles. What that means, (hey, I know you don't care but maybe Friday will), is the moon is making the earth wobble ever so slightly so new stars get a chance to hog the glory! (The fact that the earth wobbles is no news to people from Southern California!)

In 26,000 years Polaris gets to be the Pole Star again. If I had to wait that long, I would definitely hog all the glory I could! 13,000 years ago Vega was the North Star. Now there was a star to point at! Ok, are you ready for some more stars? You are following along on your star

chart, aren't you? My little drawings (I did these, so don't blame Karen!) are not for navigational purposes! They are just supposed to orient you. (Towards China no doubt! Orient, get it? It's tough being a writer!)

The (Northern) Summer Triangle dominates the sky with three very bright stars: Deneb (in Cygnus), Vega (in Lyra) and Altair (in

Aquila). A line from Altair through Deneb leads to our old friend, Capella. A line from Altair through Vega leads to Draco and a line from Vega through Altair leads to the very bright Fomalhaut. The area is rich in stars and constellations but these are the only ones you are required to learn. Friday will be very impressed by extra work however!

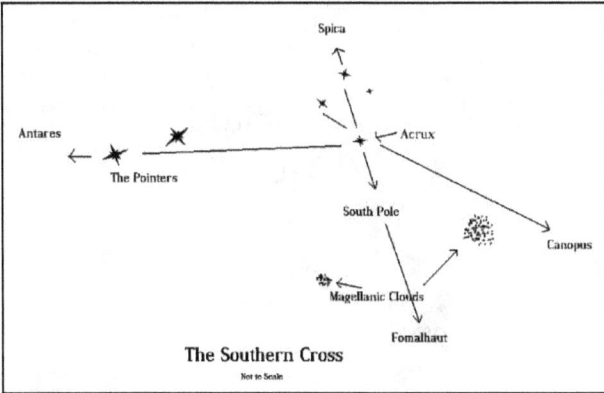

The Southern Cross
Not to Scale

And lastly, the Southern Cross area is easier than it looks. The Southern Cross, for a relatively dim constellation, dominates the skies. It helps that the two pointers, Alpha Centaurus and Hadar are both first magnitude stars. (You don't have to remember these, there is no mistaking Acrux, at the foot of the cross. From Acrux through Alpha Centaurus leads to Antares. Going through the length of the cross leads to Fomalhaut to the south and Spica to the north. From the left hand star of the cross through Acrux leads to Canopus. Well, there you are. Those are the stars you need to not get totally lost. Try to become acquainted with them and then read on about Polynesian Navigation.

Mike Riley's Perception of Polynesian Navigation

Life would be a lot easier if the world was flat. Really! All the stars would travel in straight lines. It would be easier to keep track of them. If the world was flat our nineteen stars would rise, set and their altitudes at the zenith would be the same. Here is what they would be:

Stars

Altitude (Declination)

Stars	Altitude (Declination)
Acrux	62°S
Aldebaran	17°N
Altair	9°N
Antares	28°S
Arcturus	20°S
Betelgeuse	8°N
Canopus	52°S
Capella	43°N
Castor	32°N
Pollux	29°N
Deneb	44°N
Fomalhaut	30°S
Pleiades	18°N
Polaris	90°N
Procyon	5°N
Rigel	9°S
Regulus	12°N
Sirius	17°S
Spica	10°S
Vega	39°N

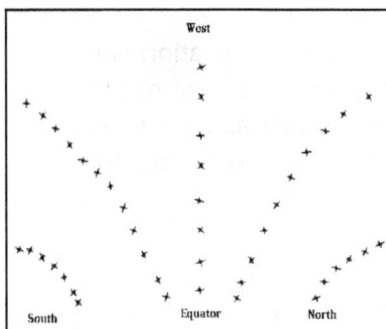

However, the world is a globe, worse the luck. (Of course we don't fall off the edge, either!) The above altitudes are still valid for the zenith position, when the star gets as high in the sky as it ever will that night. If your island was at latitude five degrees north, Procyon would cross directly above the island at its zenith. Or if your island is at latitude nine degrees south, Altair would be directly overhead at its zenith.

Mintaka, the star in Orion's belt that is closest to Rigel, not only passes directly over the Equator, but also rises due east and sets due west. But that is an exception.

Stars as seen on the Equator

The equatorial stars act as if they were on a flat earth. The stars further north or south angle off from their rising positions till they get up to their maximum altitude. That is a real shame as it makes it very hard to steer towards a star that is constantly moving its bearing.

What the Polynesians did was memorize the sequence of the stars that would be either rising in the direction they wanted to go or a direction that that was a constant at an angle from the direction they wanted to go. Say a series of stars as rising at a forty-five degree angle from the canoe's heading. It would be a simple matter as long as you had a series of very bright stars rising in a row. But, alas, that doesn't happen. Just when you thought it was safe to go to sea again, you find out this is going to be difficult. Trust me though, it isn't that difficult! So what happens if you are north or south of the Equator?

Stars as seen from 20° North

The stars around Polaris would be making a complete circle if it was night for twenty four hours. The Equatorial stars are angling

away from your latitude. The Stars on your latitude make a curve as
they rise. The only thing set in stone is if a star's declination is on your latitude then it will be directly over head at its zenith. The southern stars are starting to move out of the picture as the curve of the earth blocks them from view. Things are more confusing now, but fear not.

Stars as seen from 20° South

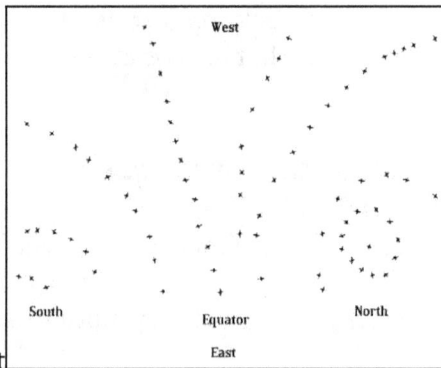

This is like the opposite of 20°N. There is no star marking the South Pole as Polaris does for the North. The Northern stars are moving out of your vision. Again things have become more confusing. Bummer. At the very least, now you know if you are north or south of the line. And by observing the star's zenith positions you can guess fairly closely your latitude. How do you tell the degrees stars are apart? I'm glad you asked! See the next page.

Say you are sitting on you beach, bored to death as Friday hasn't shown up yet, and you want to get off this stupid island and you want

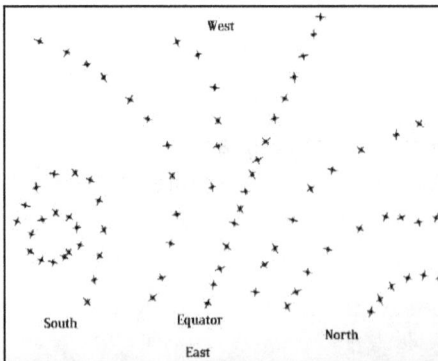

to get off it now. You made your canoe, you tested it, you stocked it up for the voyage. You are ready to go. OK, lets do it. you can't steer towards something that is straight up in the air. Just to be easy, let's make our first voyage to the north. You have already determined that your position is about 9° North as at zenith (when a star is as straight up in the sky as it is ever going to be), Betelgeuse (8°N) is just to your South and Regulus (12°N) is just to your North. You can't use these two stars to direct your course at zenith, however you can use them when the are on the horizon. Otherwise, there are stars that you can use to find north and south when they are up in the air as long as they are at zenith. (Both do reach zenith at the same time.)

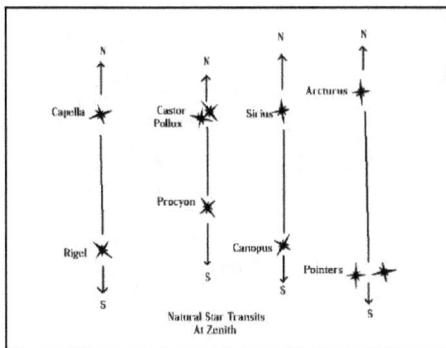

They are: Rigel and Capella, Procyon and Castor/Pollux, Sirius and Canopus, and Arcturus and the Southern Cross's Pointers. (Hadar and Alpha Centauri) This only helps us at limited times during the night, but it is great as a cross check to make sure we are on the right path. They are all very bright stars which Polaris isn't. Plus in the tropics there are almost always clouds low on the horizon, possibly blocking a view of the north star. That is the main problem with Polynesian Navigation, when the stars are at their most perfect position for utilizing them, they can't be depended on. The science of navigation then becomes an art. You know where you think the star would be if you could see it, so you aim for that spot.

I don't think that is an intelligent way to cross oceans, I really don't. I know the Polynesians made a lot of amazing passages, but you never hear about the canoes that didn't make it. Is there a better way? At least for our voyages of exploration? Yes, there is. Read on, Survivor.

Latitude from the Stars

To make a measurement of latitude (declination) tie a string to the middle of a short stick. Hold the stick between the following stars while holding the end of the string to your nose. Bring the stick closer or farther away till the stick fits between the stars, then tie a knot in the string. That knot is a measurement of angles in the sky. Use the stick and knots to measure the distance from your zenith to a star that is close to your latitude.

Sampling of Stars

Stars	Degrees apart
Lepus (little constellation south of Rigel, left of Sirius)	5° wide
Castor and Pollux	5°
Pointers of the Big Dipper	5°
Southern Cross	6° long
Constellation Lyra (Vega's)	8° long
Western Star of Orion's belt and Betelgeuse	10°
Handle of Big Dipper	15°
Rigel and Betelgeuse	18°

Deneb and Vega	20°
Betelgeuse and Aldebaran	22°
Sirius, Procyon and Betelgeuse	25° each leg
Far Pointer to Polaris	30°
Arcturus to Big Dipper	30°
Arcturus and Spica	33°

Your First Voyage

Don't make it hard on yourself. Start your first voyage of exploration in the morning. Go out on a beam reach as far as you can but don't lose track of your island. At noon or before head on back and make sure your canoe is OK. This is important as you are about to risk your life. Right now you are somewhat happy (depending on the island, Friday's existence, and your personal inner demons), it would be sad to lose the island because the canoe sank. Take a lot of fishing trips, circle the island, whatever. Become comfortable in your canoe.

Alright, get ready to leave at night, just clearing the reefs as night falls. This is a trial run. You are going to turn back at midnight and arrive back at the island at dawn. Think you can do it? Are you sure you know your stars? Did you really memorize them?

Before you go, long before you go, draw lines on the beach, or better, make a cross out of wood and align it north, south, east and west. Can you find the Cardinal directions from the night sky? Every night watch the stars come up over the horizon and set in the west. You know the main, bright stars now. You don't have to know the rest. Say Regulus comes up and then an hour later another star a little to the south of east, then an hour later another star a little to the north. You don't have to know their names, just the pattern of the sky for your latitude. This is more fun than the Simpsons any day. (Or rather night!)

Memorize the pattern, memorize it for the entire night. If we are talking about a star an hour that is only twelve stars. You can do that. Hell, you already memorized nineteen stars! This will only be good for a few days out and back. As your latitude changes so will the angle of the stars coming up over the horizon slightly change. Don't forget to memorize the star paths for returning to the island, too!

I am working on a new book which will give explicit star directions for each latitude in the tropics. In the mean time, Friday is going to love sitting under the stars with you. Isn't this much better than TV? Or at least the commercials?

Afterword

I hope you never lose your boat at sea and have to put some of my experiences into immediate use. Just the idea of my boat sinking sends shivers up my spine. But, anyway, what about the EPIRB? That will save me, won't it?

Might, then again, it might not. EPIRB's work great off the coasts of first world countries. How about in the back of beyond, where the nearest airport is a thousand miles away, they don't speak English and they don't really care about cruisers or any non-Islamic?

If you are going to be cruising for a while, if you are going to poke around off the beaten track, better get used to the idea that you are going to have to take care of yourself when the keel falls off and the mast blasts off. The biggest danger is fear. Humans don't handle fear well. They tend to panic and act irrationally, just when using their reason is most important. Fear is mostly caused by lack of the knowledge of what to do and lack of faith in ourselves that you can do what is needed. Especially true on a deserted island.

Not that it is difficult to thrive on your own on a deserted, abandoned island. You just have to know how. I hope this book has not only instructed you, but also inspired you to keep alive the skills left by our cruising forefathers, the Polynesians, the Caribs, the early Seychelles-ians.

Teach what you have learned to others. Especially at potlucks! You might help save their lives. But most of all, have fun! We are the otters of the universe. Go build yourself a grass shack! And, of course, a hammock!

Recommended reading

No book is ever written in a void. I spent much of my early years pouring over the following books. Most are out of print but they can always be found in used book stores, e-bay, and if you are anchored next to me, you can borrow my copies.

Ken Neumeyer, Sailing the Farm 1981. Ten Speed Press
This book is about supporting yourself financially by gathering
wild vegetables and selling them in first world ports.

Euell Gibbons, Beachcomber's Handbook 1967 David McKay Inc.
In this book Gibbons tells stories of beachcombing in Hawaii
in years gone by. The book is loaded with recipes and anecdotes.

Euell Gibbons, Stalking the Blue Eyed Scallop 1970 David McKay Inc.
Gibbons relates his adventures searching for marine dinner opportunities. Unfortunately, not in the tropics, but a worthy read.

Encyclopedia Britannica, Still the best over all source on everything!
The CD version loads completely on your hard drive, no more loading discs!

Index

A

B

M

N

O

P

www.ingramcontent.com/pod-product-compliance
Lightning Source LLC
Chambersburg PA
CBHW050111280326
41933CB00010B/1053